AMERICA, WHY?

JILL SHEA

ISBN: 9798218441227 (Paperback)
ISBN: 9798218442958 (Hardcover)
ISBN: 9798218442378 (E-book)

Library of Congress Control Number: 2024905767

Front cover artwork by Brandon Swofford
Book Cover Design by Jill Shea

Printed by Amazon, Inc., in the United States of America.
First printing edition 2024.

https://jillsheawriter.com/

To my adorable, kind, insightful, make you laugh
until you pee in your pants family,
with all my love:
Michael, Dylan, and Hudson

I love you to the moon and back.

And to our dogs who don't read but one day
I will actually eat your cute faces:
Leopold & Ella

"Think of how it all started: America was founded by slave owners who informed us, "All men are created equal." All "men," Remember, the founders were a small group of unelected, white, male, land-holding slave owners... who also, by the way, suggested their class be the only one allowed to vote. To my mind, that is what's known as being stunningly-- and embarrassingly-- full of shit."

- George Carlin

"The fabric of democracy is always fragile because it depends on the will of citizens to protect it, and when they become scared, when it becomes dangerous for them to defend it, it can go very quickly."

- Margaret Atwood

"I Only Believe Some of What QAnon Says About Dems Being Satanic Pedophile Cannibals, Okay?"

- Marjorie Taylor Greene, Currently in Congress

CONTENTS

Introduction: Under a Veil of Ignorance 1

PART ONE
OH, AMERICA.   11

Chapter One: A Brief History and What's Broken.................... 13

How The U.S. of A. Began (Our Constitution)............................... 13
A System of Checks and Balances in America 15
The Supreme Court Is Born.. 16
Brief Details - The Ones That Matter... 16
The Electoral College Is Killing Democracy 19
The Racist Origins of The Electoral College 20
Are We Better than England Now?... 28
Checks and Balances on The President's Power 31
The Fed and Our Economy 33
Getting Back to What Is Broken 34
Capping The Funds 35
Set Term Limits and An Age Limit of 65 36
Don't Boo. Vote! 38

Chapter Two: Partisanship/Party Loyalties Grip the Wheel.... 41

America Is in A Slow Suicide of Partisanship 41
Wait, What? Seriously Man?... 43
Unilateral Action to Override Partisanship 44
Policies With Humans in Mind Under Obama................................ 46
When Obama Chose Not to.. 48
A Game of Ping Pong: Party v. People 50

Chapter Three: TRUMP America, Why?.............................. 53

Extremism and Fascism Under Trump... 54
Freedom of The Press... 55
Fascism and Cult Status as a "Trumpian" 56
Trump's Congress and Their Extremism 58
Partisan Or Policy Loyalists 61
Donald Trump & Congress - Abuses of Power............................... 63

Abuses of Power By Trump 68

Conditional Party Governing & Trump's Impeachments 70

Trump's War Powers (Iran) 72

Constitutional Inversion (By Trump) 73

Covid Under Trump 74

Can You Imagine If Obama Did That? 76

Chapter Four: Money Rules All 83

Gun Control and The NRA 84

Interest Groups, Lobbyists & Super Pacs 86

The Special Interest Coalition 89

Scott Pruitt as Head of the EPA 89

Democracy at Its Best 91

Fox News Pulls Off The Biggest Con For Money 92

Fox News is a Cancer in Our Democracy 93

Chapter Five: Political Ideologies That Shape Us 95

Are We Really That Different From One Another? 95

Conservatism, Liberalism, Socialism 96

Socialism Helps Define Modern Liberalism 99

Are You an Owen or A Simon? 101

Should Capitalism Lean Into Socialism? 103

Conservatism 105

Positive and Negative Liberalism 110

PART TWO
LAW AND DISORDER   113

Chapter Six: What in the Actual F**K Supreme Court? 115

June 24th 2022 115

What Influences Justices? 119

Scalia v. Breyer: Opposites on the Bench to Help with the Why?. 127

The Doctrine of Absurdity 130

Should Justices Be Elected Instead of Appointed? 131

Citizens United v. FEC 133

Packing The Supreme Court: Was Roosevelt A Badass? 134

Chapter Seven: Is Justice for Sale? YES....................139

  Cash in Our Courtrooms.............................140
  Bribery Is A Reality in Our Courts 142
  Selection Process of Judges.........................144
  Purchasing The Verdict..............................145
  Power Asymmetries, Mistruths, and Money 146
  Small Town V. Behemoth Corporation..................148
  The Probability of Bias.............................151

Chapter Eight: Supreme Court Cases That Changed Us........155

  25 Year Handgun Ban Shot Down 155
  Breyer Calls It Like It Is - Yes! 159
  Background Checks are Shot Down.....................161
  Same Sex Marriage - Equal Means Everyone, Everywhere 166
  The Rights of People 169
  Porn. V. Preacher..................................170
  First Amendment & Comercial Speech.................175
  Executive Privilege................................181
  Three Fifths of A Human Being......................183
  How Can They Just Take Your House? 185
  One Man Took on The System and Won (Jury Selection)............189
  Seven Years and Tremendous Loss....................192
  The Lady Who Spilled Hot Coffee on Herself At McDonald's is Not What You Think 194

Chapter Nine: The Media in Our Courtrooms and Why We Need Them 197

  We The People Deserve Cameras in Our Supreme Court.............197
  Cameras in Court State By State 199
  "X" in The Courtroom Is a Positive 203

PART THREE
HOW WE TREAT HUMAN BEINGS 207

Chapter Ten: Caging Children Is the Trump Way.................209

  The Family Separation Crisis.......................209
  "Zero Tolerance" and Its Horrifying Mandate 210
  Way Bigger Than We Can Count.......................212

The Players and The Politics 213

The Proposals to End This and The Politicians Behind Them 215

The Impact on Our Economy 217

Interest Groups 218

The Public 218

Family Separations Continued 219

The Circus: Trump's Wall Hearings 220

Go Mark Desaulnier! 221

Go Seth! 223

**Chapter Eleven: Globalization, Abject Poverty, and
The Childcare Crisis** **225**

Core Nations Thrive off Abject Poverty 225

The Core Nations 226

Socialism and Capitalism Need Each Other 229

Welfare Policy in the United States 231

The Childcare Crisis and Biden's Plan 237

**Chapter Twelve: Humanity is All Connected and
We Must Believe This** **245**

Should America Come First? The Quagmire of
Foreign Entanglements 245

PART FOUR
WHAT MATTERS NOW   249

Chapter Thirteen: Climate Change **251**

Biden is Kicking Ass for The Planet 251

Industries and Institutions Are Behind It 254

Joe Clearly Doesn't Like Ping Pong 255

A Little Ping Pong Wouldn't Hurt 257

Tom Vilsack - The Hurdles and The Obstacles 260

The Costs of Greenhouse Emissions 262

The Monetary and Human Costs 264

Ecologism and Science -- It Is Everything 268

Chapter Fourteen: Under Vaccination and Hunger in America...273

Under Vaccination..273
Human Potential Lost to Poor Health Is Immense.........................275
Hunger in America 275
Food Deserts in America 276

PART FIVE
EXTRA TIDBITS 279

Chapter Fifteen: The Privacy of Our Information 281

Our Private Information on Social Networking Sites 281
Facebook and Instagram..282
Twitter 'X' 285
Algorithms and Money: Our Privacy 285
Snapchat Is The Worst 286
HIPPA and FERPA 287
Up For Sexting Anyone?...289

The Best For Last: Nancy Pelosi................................295

Grace and Persistence...295

Conclusion 301

The Constitution of The United States of America.....................305
Bibliography 325
About the Author..335

Under a Veil of Ignorance

WHAT HAPPENED TO CRITICAL THINKING, MORALS, COMPASSION, EMPATHY AND A UNIVERSAL GOOD?

The observers of Fox News, staunch in their allegiance without a hint of skepticism, the violent insurrectionists who forcefully breached the sanctity of our Capitol on that fateful January 6th, the politicians who unabashedly propagate audacious falsehoods, and those who ardently believe them, the proponents of AR15 and mass gun ownership as a quintessential facet of American identity, the people who fear those unlike themselves based on sexual orientation, gender identity, religion, race, ethnicity, or appearance, the people who deny climate change and basic science, and those who voted for Trump once and twice—all embody a confounding and disturbing facet of our society. The current state of our nation is deeply unsettling. Where has the essence of America gone? The irrational, inhumane, and dangerous behaviors exhibited by these groups defy logic and resonate with a lamentable and profound degree of ignorance.

Contrastingly, there are those who peacefully advocate for civil rights and gun control, the crusaders for environmental preservation who back science and progress for the sake of future generations, those who fight to safeguard our children from violence; to put an end to them getting shot while sitting in school, and the proponents

1

of universal equity irrespective of gender, race, or religion. The stark divergence in ideals among these disparate groups, all residing under a singular flag, prompts an existential question: How can such differing groups with such opposite ideals on what is right and wrong reside under one flag? America, why?

My years-long journey into researching how America got here was borne from an urgent need to comprehend the confounding depths of our nation's pervasive ignorance and darkness. My journey has proved empowering but also very humbling. In my research, I couldn't help but feel a profound awe for the chaotic and complicated war zone of American politics and moments that have shaped the (now deteriorating) building blocks of our nation's identity. Each decision, each debate, each case, and every individual who played a role in shaping our political landscape has left an indelible mark on the course of history; some are frighteningly shameful and discouraging, while others are inspiring and hopeful. The story of American history and politics is not just a collection of events and policies. It is a reflection of the people who make up our collective, from those who think it's a sound idea to storm the Capitol while wearing antlers and chanting: "Hang Mike Pence!" to those who want to empower our kids with an outstanding education and the ability to think critically.

I begin with a bit of history on our constitution, yet this book defies the constraints of chronology, offering you the freedom to engage with its contents as you see fit. You can read it from cover to cover, dive into this introduction and the conclusion alone, or seize the bolded insights scattered throughout that I isolated to make a point. Alternatively, you can peruse the table of contents and select the sections that intrigue you, or simply leave it on your coffee table for one of your iPhone-addicted teenagers to discover (Good luck with that). From our Founding Fathers' intentions when shaping crucial aspects of our Constitution to the perplexing evolution of the Supreme Court, this book scrutinizes pivotal questions.

The narrative inside these pages spans from Trump's fascism masquerading as patriotism to how we treat human beings, examining the forces steering our nation's progression— which lately feels like it's regressing at full speed. From why capitalism must start protecting and rewarding the working class to our baffling lack of gun control that makes me ask: Did I miss something? Are zombies coming? It explores Supreme Court cases that reveal the perseverance of everyday citizens and a justice system that makes you wonder: Is justice for sale?

Within these pages, you'll unearth the stark dichotomy of ideals that define our nation today, ranging from Trump's free pass to commit nefarious abuses of power to Biden's detailed policies to solve the childcare crisis and climate change. It delivers food for thought like why The Electoral College is killing our democracy and makes about as much sense as supersizing fast food meals, how America is in a slow suicide of hyper-partisanship, how Fox News pulled off the most significant American Con for money, and why our Supreme Court Justices make rulings that are downright infuriating and heartbreaking. Of course, Trump has his very own "bigly" chapter along with his unabashedly unethically loyal Congress and the fervent party loyalties that led to the inversion of our constitution by our own elected officials. One question remains, "Can You Imagine if Obama Did That?".

As many of us in America continue the struggle for civil rights and for policies that will save our planet and our kids, we must confront the disheartening power of sheer ignorance occurring in America today. Rampant disinformation campaigns and the conning of so many Americans is the biggest threat to our democracy right now——and it's all homegrown, right here in the USA. In an era driven by rapid information flow and stark, sometimes frighteningly ignorant perspectives, this book serves as a kind of compass, navigating the landscape of our history, the differing ideologies that define us, and some of the moments that have shaped today's baffling American experience. The book is an invitation to learn, empathize, and reflect on the historical narratives, policies, moments, cases, and individuals that have molded our union. It also offers a brief glimpse into the importance of American engagement abroad and the quagmire of our foreign entanglements. Some of what you are about to read will prompt you to wonder: America, why?

Before delving into this book, and to help you better understand the political and social behaviors of people in America, I've included insights from three political philosophers and their notions of human behavior relevant to today's world. John Rawls, Immanuel Kant, and John Stuart Mill encapsulate three fundamental pillars of behavior that drive politics and elucidate why American societies behave politically the way they do. Most importantly, these political philosophies reveal what is missing today in our political climate and every society in America, no matter what side of the aisle you sit on. Whether it's those who live under a veil of ignorance, those who grossly lack the ability to objectively see outside themselves to understand and accept how others live, or those influenced by the Tyranny of the Majority (Trump followers), these three brilliant men help explain the insanity.

However, what is imperative is that more people must start understanding that we are all connected. We must behave toward a universal good for all and from a place of empathy, kindness, compassion, and truth.

UNDER A VEIL OF IGNORANCE

John Rawls, an American political and ethics philosopher who passed away in 2002, (and was an incredibly brilliant badass) believed that people often choose their principles without understanding their true place in a society. Rawls espoused that most people live under a veil of ignorance and holy hell, we have seen that veil of ignorance at play in the last several years. You know; it's the guy who depends on social programs like Medicaid and food stamps, but vehemently hates those "liberal" Democrats who gave him those lifesaving programs. What makes Rawls such an influential political philosopher is incredibly simple, and when you understand the veil of ignorance that so many live under here in America it helps to digest some of the maddening things that occur here. In addition to that guy I just referred to, and all those like him, the veil of ignorance is also about our lack of empathy and compassion as a society.

What if we flip the veil of ignorance idea? What if it could in turn be the exact position by which a society should exist? Is living under a veil of ignorance the key to creating a society in which everyone prospers? If you have no idea what socio-economic group you are born into would that help everyone come from a place of equity, naturally? If only, right?

How significantly and more justly would America be structured if our lawmakers crafted policies from under a veil of ignorance? If they were unaware of their potential wealth, poverty, race, gender, disability, or health status, wouldn't they inherently develop laws and policies aimed at providing everyone with an equitable opportunity for success and equal chances to thrive? Every school district, neighborhood, and town would receive uniform funding and attention, irrespective of county lines or tax brackets. Gender-based pay disparities wouldn't exist either.

Here's an alternative way to clarify my point: Imagine if you had no knowledge of your social status or background, like being under a veil of ignorance. Would you advocate for massive tax breaks for the ultra-rich? Most likely, you'd react with disbelief, questioning why such immense tax cuts would be proposed for the wealthiest while the middle class faces higher taxes. It would seem nonsensical and unjust.

Similarly, if you suddenly found yourself on earth with no understanding of our societal norms, you'd find it deeply troubling that CEOs can earn over 200 million dollars annually while teachers struggle to make ends meet, often working multiple jobs just to survive. You would be utterly perplexed as to what we value here in America. I know I am.

Rawls believed a society should be rooted in fairness for everyone as things are not fair for so many, and so many have no idea just how unfair. Our society grossly lacks objectivity and the ability to see outside of our own circumstances. This perpetuates the very lack of fairness we see today bolstering the hate and vitriol that is increasingly becoming the modern American way.

Too many people have zero desire to objectively see how others live; nor do they possess an empathy rooted in an awareness of the inequities in our societies.

What would happen if we were all completely ignorant about our place in society? In other words, a society of people who are completely ignorant to their own circumstances, as if in the womb before birth, having no idea into what circumstances they will be born: rich, poor, hungry, sick, healthy, happy... etc.

If a person has no idea of his or her circumstances or position in a society, then wouldn't that person design a society in which every person prospers equally?

It is also only from behind this "Veil of Ignorance" that people can objectively see the details and circumstances of all parts of our societies not just their own - which is key to establishing a just society. When society is purely objective with no idea where it stands, it will always only design a society that doesn't leave anyone behind.

The capacity for people to examine the circumstances of others is crucial to achieving a just society for all.

A UNIVERSAL GOOD

Immanuel Kant, another brilliant political philosopher, believed in something universal and simple. Kant, with his "Categorical Imperative", believed that liberty and true freedom in a society exists when we act with morals, kindness, an appreciation of beauty, and with a sensible rationale and reason in everything we do. This is as simple as what is right and what is wrong - which our rational selves will always tell us. Kant believed that as individuals we must act as part of a universal being toward a universal good. This "Categorical Imperative" is essentially a universal law- that when we give over to our passions and our selfishness we must think: what if everyone did that too? What would a person's actions mean if everyone in a society also did it? We must live as a universal being with an understanding that our own behavior is not just personal to us but applies to everyone. Freedom in a society can only happen when we are our best selves. Freedom is not "do whatever you want". The insurrectionists who stormed our capitol clearly did not understand this, nor did they regard anything sound and moral. Freedom is when individuals act with a sensible rationale that promotes goodness, kindness, and ethics for everyone.

The domestic terrorists who stormed our Capitol in a violent insurrection, forcing lawmakers and assistants to hide for hours, thinking they would be killed, should take a lesson from Kant.

Kant also believed that humans are in constant conflict between the better parts of our nature and our more reasonable selves versus our passions and selfishness. When we follow compassion and morals, we then act toward the well-being of everyone universally. Kant felt that freedom is found in how the world should behave universally, which is from our best, most reasonable selves. Kant's Categorical Imperative is that morals are universal law and apply to all of us. What is right and what is wrong is what reason tells us in how to act and that is always our best selves.

THE TYRANNY OF THE MAJORITY

John Stuart Mill, a towering figure in political philosophy, articulated a theory that resonates deeply with the current state of American politics: the Tyranny of the Majority. In today's polarized political landscape, Mill's theory serves as a critical reminder of the inherent dangers posed by unchecked majority power in a democratic society. At its core, the Tyranny of the Majority warns against the potential for the majority to oppress and silence minority voices, highlighting the fragility of democracy when fundamental rights are disregarded in favor of popular sentiment. In the confounding rise of Trump, we have seen the erosion of democratic norms, the silencing of the rule of law, and the marginalization of minority groups, all under the guise of representing the will of the majority. Let's be clear: This will never be the will of the majority in America. This is tyranny.

It is crucial to recognize that Trump has never garnered majority support from American voters. His authoritarian methods paved the way for minority rule over the majority. Trump's populist rhetoric is divisive and exclusionary, exploits societal divisions and marginalizes dissenting voices. From immigration policies that violate human rights and our Constitution, to attacks on our press and the judiciary, Trump has epitomized the dangers of unchecked populism and tyranny in democratic societies. Trump's reign exemplifies how the Tyranny of the Majority can manifest in contemporary America.

There are moments when nations stand at a crossroads, unsure of which path to tread. In today's America such a critical juncture has emerged, marked by the unsettling rise of nationalist rhetoric, propelled by the dangerous currents of populism and division. This alarming trend is exacerbated by the insidious phenomenon of bullying, which seeks to silence the voices of reason and democracy. Populist leaders exploit fear and grievances, sowing division, while prioritizing personal gain over national unity. America has become a culture of bullying that stifles dissent, kills the progress we so desperately need here in America, and breeds anger and fear - and worst of all—apathy. The erosion of democratic norms and the rise of confounding ignorance and hate in today's America is deeply unsettling. Americans seem to be succumbing to the politics of fear and division and we are forgetting the ideals that define America. We are forsaking the very essence of what it means to be part of such a vital democracy. This book endeavors to close the chasm between understanding and indignation. How did America lose its way?

One thing is certain. Our Founding Fathers had
no idea what was coming.

OH, AMERICA.

CHAPTER ONE

A Brief History and What's Broken

"Before we get too depressed about the state of our politics, let's remember our history .... Many forms of Government have been tried and will be tried in this world of sin and woe. What is amazing, is that despite all the conflict, our experiment in democracy has worked better than any form of government on earth."

- Barack Obama

HOW THE U.S. of A. BEGAN (OUR CONSTITUTION)

To understand what the hell has gone so wrong here in our country, it's vital to look back at how it all began and give a bit of reference on how our nation formed its rules. The intentions of our Founding Fathers when forming our constitution was to build a new nation devoid of tyranny. They formed our new constitution through detailed and thoughtful ratifications with the humility of understanding that they had gotten it wrong to begin with. Our Founding Fathers formed our nation with true grit and a forward-thinking determination (but for slavery and the three-fifths of a human being clause that established enduring and inhumane systemic racism that is still robust today). Our Founding Fathers also formed our nation without a crystal ball or any thought that two centuries later, America would lose its mind and seemingly all respect for sound behavior.

The rules that established America were thoughtful, forward thinking (for the time), innovative (for the time), purposeful, and done with the intention of creating a strong and robust nation in which every person (unless you were black, a woman, Native American, or anything that was not white male and Christian) had a fair shot at life and liberty. Yay! USA! USA! USA! Okay, sarcasm aside, Sometimes the past gives us the most significant insight and is the most powerful tool for change. The Continental Congress ran the colonies during its struggle for independence from England yet held no formal authority, thus was eager to form a national governing body. Prior to the adoption of The Declaration of Independence, the Continental Congress selected delegates to draft a proposal for such a national charter, and the Articles of Confederation were born.

Much booze and debauchery in celebration followed until they realized that those articles were a disaster.

The Articles of Confederation created that governing apparatus they all sought, but the structure of the articles proved overly simple, flawed, and weak. Those weaknesses lead to an ardent call for a new constitution. Those inherently weak sections of the original articles illuminate the structure and purpose of the resulting constitution, and thus, are consequently more effectively executed in the new Constitution of the United States as we have it today. Freedom under a central authority was the overall purpose of the original articles. Freedom from England, freedom from oppression, and freedom for each state, each citizen, and each representative of each state in this new union. Article 5 gives clues to this purpose in "Freedom from speech and debate in Congress shall not be impeached...". This new, unfettered freedom for each state, however, created a national legislature with very weak to little authoritative powers, thus the new constitution and the "rules" of America were fine tuned. Maybe one day you might take a glance at our Constitution, **I included one at the back of this book;** Article 1 is perhaps the most powerful evidence of the true grit and thoughtful deliberations of our founding fathers to create a functioning, powerful, and flourishing independent nation.

A SYSTEM OF CHECKS AND BALANCES IN AMERICA

Under the original Articles, the federal government was essentially controlled by the sovereign states, not the reverse. The new Constitution overcame this failing by establishing a national government with three separate but equal branches of government. **It's critical to remember this as you evaluate where America is now and how far we have strayed.** The three branches were to not only keep each other in check, but they also established a balance of power, giving certain necessary powers to the national government, and reserved only some for the states. The three branches; the Legislative, the Executive, and the Judicial were constitutionally and politically separate from one another which is why...

Trump's Supreme Court nominees, Brett Kavanaugh, and Amy Coney Barrett, and the unprincipled party loyalties that voted to appoint them to our highest court, regardless of their very alarming character issues, and their very alarming beliefs, call into question the separation of powers.

Again, our founding fathers had no idea what was coming. The new Constitution dedicated specific powers to each separate branch of government to establish a system of checks on each branch's power over the other. My guess is they are rolling over in their graves.

THE SUPREME COURT IS BORN

The lack of checks and balances in the Articles of Confederation was also addressed in the New Constitution, with the establishment of the Supreme Court. Article 3, Section 1, establishes the Supreme court, and Section 2 outlines the judicial powers of the federal courts, in upholding the constitution, hearing cases, and arguments regarding federal laws. The Supreme Court was created to keep the Legislative and Executive Branches' powers in check, as a balancing of power. **Our Founding Fathers have been rolling over in their graves since 2016.** The Supreme Court of 2023 seems to defy that balance of power in which several justices seem hell bent on acting like policymakers under the guise of constitutional interpretation.

Our founding fathers would have never imagined America in 2023, and the political and personal agendas that have made their way into our highest courts and onto the bench.

The underlying principles of our constitution are the separation of powers in a checks and balances system, federalism which grants some powers to the federal government and some to the states, and the virtue of the individual rights and liberties of all citizens. The separate branches of government established in Articles 2 and 3 are a clear indication of the crucial need to create a balance of power, and the intentions and ideals behind the formation of America.

BRIEF DETAILS - THE ONES THAT MATTER

Safeguarding individual rights and liberties is reflected in the Constitution's opening words "Promote the general Welfare and Secure the Blessings of Liberty". The intended purpose of the Articles of Confederation was this same principle and is carried over to the Constitution in Article 4, Section 2.

Several Amendments stand out as clear definitions of the principle of individual rights and liberties but have been grossly abused and manipulated.

<u>Such amendments are:</u> The 2nd Amendment, giving citizens the right to bear arms, which has become horrifically abused for the benefit of the **NRA** and the politicians inside lobbyists' pockets **(Money in our political system is a bit later in this book);** The 4th amendment protecting citizens from unlawful search and seizure, and Amendment 14, Section 1 that establishes the right of due process of the law for all citizens. Most profoundly, however, is Amendment 15 Section 1 which states, "The right of citizens of the United States to vote shall not be denied or abridged by the United States or by any state on account of race, color, or previous condition of servitude". So then…

Is redistricting, the gerrymandering of districts, and voter suppression of minorities in known areas of minority populations not unconstitutional?

These are duplicitous ways to abridge the power of the vote for minorities in their very own districts and are in direct violation of Amendment 15.

The Constitution's Framers implemented a balance of powers in the United States that protected the people and the system from the kind of oppression they experienced with the English government. The Framers envisioned a balanced government where no one branch was more powerful than the other. However, the distribution of power often creates power struggles and requires compromise. The Framers most certainly could not foresee the pluralism that would flourish under the freedoms established by their Constitution. Under the system they established, the pluralistic nature is a testimony to the words "We the people" and a by-product of power distribution. The system of checks and balances facilitates a reciprocal relationship between the branches of government and is supposed to protect against reckless decisions. The majority must respect the minority, and unilateral decisions are not in the design. This is in the best interest of the nation but is not without flaws. The Constitution effectuates separate but equal powers except in some functions, such as the President's Veto power over legislation and the Senate's power in the appointment of judges and executive officers.

The Constitution and ratifications were spawned from the framers' experience under an oppressive King and the flagrant weaknesses of the Articles of Confederation. Our three branches were intended to keep each other in check and establish a balance of power, with certain powers enumerated to the national government, reserving some for the states. Specifically, the executive and the judicial branches were constitutionally separate, addressing the weak governing body under the Articles of Confederation and the oppressive tyranny experienced under King George III. The Framers aimed to protect personal liberties under a government with shared powers that can effectively address the dangers that threaten our liberties and make our union weak.

Through this balance of powers, the Framers aimed to avoid the dangers of inefficiency, weakness, corruption, rebellion, disunity, external threats, and a tyrannical executive. So, what in the hell happened?

We have a great system here in the U.S., but our forefathers would be appalled at how much we have royally (no pun intended) screwed it up. The arguments against later ratification appeared in various forms, by various authors, most of whom used a pseudonym. Collectively, these writings have become known as the Anti-Federalist Papers. They contain warnings of dangers from tyranny that weaknesses in the proposed Constitution did not adequately provide protection against. While some of those weaknesses were corrected by the adoption of the Bill of Rights, others still remain broken. <u>Very Broken.</u>

THE ELECTORAL COLLEGE IS
KILLING DEMOCRACY

In 2000 and 2016 The Electoral College critically failed Americans with destructive and profoundly detrimental consequences that will reverberate for generations.

Who really elects the President of The United States? The Electoral college, made up of 538 presidential electors, with each state's number of electors based on the number of representatives in Washington are the "Who". In most cases, Electors vote for the candidate who also won the most popular votes in their states, but should they? And do they have to? Despite popular belief, the U.S. Constitution does not provide for the popular election of the American president. It provides for popular election of presidential electors.

Each candidate who qualifies for a given state's ballot must designate certain individuals who will serve as his or her electors if that candidate wins the popular vote in that state. When each state certifies a winner of its overall popular vote, that winner is entitled to send all his or her electors to that state's capitol, where they will officially record their votes for their candidate. All the electors in all the states do it on the same day, the first Monday after the second Wednesday of December. In these proceedings in the states, the winner of the statewide popular vote generally takes all The Electoral College votes, a rule stretching back to 1824.

THE RACIST ORIGINS OF WHY THE ELECTORAL COLLEGE WAS CREATED TO BEGIN WITH

The Electoral College has a deeply disturbing and dark history tied to racism and oppression. The Electoral College was created for some horrifying reasons in the US, as it was part of a plan to keep certain states in power, especially those that had slaves. The slave owners wanted to make sure they could control things, so the creation of The Electoral College helped the smaller states and those on the side of slavery (who only counted their slave population as three-fifths of a human being) have a bigger say in elections. In addition, The Electoral College was created to stop anyone from challenging slavery. The mislead that The Electoral College was created to be about democracy while it was (in reality) created to protect those who held slaves, is unmistakable. So, instead of promoting progress and fairness, The EC was created to protect slave owners, and give more power to the states that treated an entire race as if they were not whole human beings. Let's break this down into five parts, so you can fully grasp how terrible The Electoral College was from the get-go.

Keeping Certain States in Power: (THIS IS THE BIG ONE)

The Electoral College was created to help maintain the influence of certain states, particularly those with large populations of enslaved people. By giving each state a number of electoral votes based on its representation in Congress (which was partly determined by its population, including enslaved individuals counted as three-fifths of a person), it ensured that states with more slaves had more political power. This means that states with slavery could have more say in electing the president and shaping policies, even though a significant portion of their population had no voting rights or basic human rights.

Empowering Slaveholding States:

Slaveholding states wanted to maintain their control over the federal government to protect their interests, including the institution of slavery. The Electoral College system allowed them to wield disproportionate influence in presidential elections, amplifying their political power and ensuring that their interests were prioritized, at the expense of the rights and dignity of enslaved people.

Amplifying the Voices of Slaveholding States:

The Electoral College also benefitted smaller states, many of which were aligned with the interests of slaveholders. These states were able to leverage their electoral votes to have a louder voice in national politics than their population size would suggest. This meant that states supportive of slavery could exert significant influence in presidential elections and policymaking, drowning out the voices of those advocating for abolition and equal rights.

Protecting the Institution of Slavery:

The creation of The Electoral College was partly driven by a fear among slaveholding states of losing power and control in a democratic system. They saw it as a way to safeguard their interests and maintain the status quo, particularly in the face of growing opposition to slavery. By giving disproportionate power to states with slavery, The Electoral College served as a barrier to efforts aimed at challenging or abolishing the institution of slavery, preserving the economic and social order built on the exploitation and subjugation of enslaved people.

Stifling Progress and Justice:

Ultimately, The Electoral College entrenched the power dynamics that upheld slavery and perpetuated racial injustice in America. Instead of promoting democratic ideals and fairness, it reinforced systemic inequalities and discrimination, allowing the horrors of slavery to continue unchecked.

The Electoral College became a way for slave states to keep their control and protect the status quo. The idea that each state should have its own say was twisted by the EC, with smaller states, often on the side of slaveholders, using the Electoral College to speak louder than the calls for freedom and human rights.

The Electoral College was also used as an instrument of fear to intimidate people from revolting against slavery—as those slave owning states and the smaller ones wielded considerable power due to the EC. The Electoral College stopped anyone from challenging slavery, keeping power in the hands of those who wanted to keep things as they were. The EC was about upholding a horrific status quo.

The Electoral College was not about democracy in its creation, it was a wall against progress, supporting the horrific enslavement and abuse of an entire race. The legacy of the EC is one of suffering, inhumanity, and the diminishment of a fair democracy.

BACK TO MODERN DAY
The Electoral College Is Killing Our Democracy

In the 2016 election of Donald Trump, ten electors voted for the candidate that did not win their state's popular vote. This has occurred before, but this was the most in any election in more than one hundred years, with electors being called "faithless" and The Electoral College becoming a partisan competition, and not what the framers intended. The Electoral College contradicts the principle that the president is the only official in Washington who is supposed to represent the people equally no matter where they live. In two of the past five presidential elections, The Electoral College has gone directly against the will of the people or the populous.

George W. Bush in 2000 and Donald Trump in 2016 both took the office of the presidency without winning the most votes. Our children and their children will forever endure the devastating consequences of this aberration of democracy.

The enduring ramifications we are suffering in America as a result of George W. Bush's Presidency are catastrophic.—From the Mass Shootings we have today in our schools, to the "Gulf War Syndrome" suffered by our soldiers, to our growing climate crisis.

THE HORRIFIC RAMIFICATIONS OF GEORGE W. BUSH
Who did not win the popular vote.

MASS SHOOTINGS WE HAVE DAILY

George W. Bush overturned the assault rifles ban established by President Clinton; a critical and sound law that safeguarded our children and communities from mass shootings that happen weekly now. GEORGE W. BUSH MADE ASSAULT RIFLES LEGAL.

THE IRAQ WAR

The decades long gulf war would not have happened had Al Gore been president. A mass casualty war based on a lie. The Iraq war killed thousands of U.S. soldiers, maimed tens of thousands of U.S. Soldiers, and killed over 432,000 civilians.

GULF WAR SYNDROME

Thousands who served in Iraq under George W. Bush's war are suffering ongoing debilitating and agonizing mystery illnesses from what is now known as "Gulf War Syndrome".

TRILLIONS OF DEBT

Bush's Iraq war racked up trillions of dollars of debt on our country erasing the plush surplus that President Clinton left behind. A reminder: Bush's reason for the war was a falsehood.

THE CLIMATE CRISIS

George W. Bush dismissed the proven science behind our climate crisis and refused to enact sound laws to protect our environment and invest in industries of clean energy. Twenty-three years ago, these laws could have been enacted early enough to help mitigate some of the irreversible consequences of the climate crisis we see today. But they were not.

Had Al Gore taken office, these laws and investments would have been established. America could have been the world leader of global industries in clean energy and a powerhouse of groundbreaking jobs, progress, and innovation. We were none of those under Bush. Despite not garnering the most votes Bush ascended to power. Al Gore, who was chosen by the majority of Americans, never assumed office. The repercussions of Bush's presidency will continue to harm us, our children, and our grandchildren indefinitely, for decades to come.

In the recent devastating blow to our democracy and our union in a debacle of the EC, was the election of 2016 of Donald Trump. Donald Trump empowered and championed the worst types of people in our country, giving rise to some of the most deplorable and ignorant groups in America. Hillary won the most votes by the people, but The Electoral College named the other candidate the winner. The people did not elect the president, the system did. This goes directly against what the framers intended.

The enduring ramifications we will forever suffer as a result of Donald Trump's Presidency include reshaping the Supreme Court to one that stripped women's rights (which are human rights), domestic terrorist attacks on our democracy and law makers, the safety of a free press, the sanctity of our elections, and human rights atrocities against children and toddlers.

THE HORRIFIC ACTIONS OF DONALD TRUMP

These would have never happened in our country if Hillary were president (whether you liked her or not that is fact). Hillary won the popular vote, but the EC put Donald in power.

EMPOWERING WHITE SUPREMACY.

The rise and empowerment of white supremacist groups in America, the bolstering of the KKK and Neo-Nazism, championed and encouraged by Trump.

DOMESTIC TERRORISM.

Violent Domestic Terrorism in the deadly insurrection on our Capitol on January 6th empowered, encouraged, and led by Trump.

THREATS TO OUR FREE PRESS.

Trump vowed and motivated violent threats against journalists doing their jobs in the gravest threat to the freedom of our press in history and to the founding principles of our First Amendment.

TAKING CHILDREN AND CAGING THEM.

Horrific human rights violations on children and toddlers in the name of immigration control. Immigration officers, under Trump's policy, ripped terrified children and toddlers away from their mothers and fathers. Then forced those children into large, glorified group cages without end. This is a policy championed and created by Trump himself.

RESHAPING THE SUPREME COURT TO BE FAR RIGHT.

Trump appointed far right Supreme Court Justices to the highest court in our nation. Those justices overturned the vital legal precedent of Roe V. Wade in the stripping of women's and girl's basic human rights to their own bodies.

THREATS TO OUR DEMOCRACY WITH FALSE VOTER FRAUD CLAIMS.

The dangerous threats to the foundations of our very democracy would not have been emboldened and empowered had Hillary Clinton taken office.

**America will pay for Donald Trump for
years and years to come.**

This EC's ability to obstruct the will of the people was already evident in the election of 1824. Andrew Jackson won the popular vote with 43% and John Quincy Adams won 30%, but Adams garnered more electoral votes through the House of Representatives, and so Adams became President. The Framers did not account for the great injustice this was to the mass of people who supported and voted for Jackson.

The fallibility of the EC is especially evident if you look at it state by state when in many elections the popular vote was almost

50/50 but the state goes to just one candidate in The Electoral College. i.e.: Missouri in the 2008 election, the popular vote was 49.4% to 49.3% and it went to McCain. This means that fifty percent of those people's votes are not counted toward the direct election of the President. This is a problem, and the EC is broken. <u>This begs us to question, shouldn't we abolish The Electoral College?</u>

The Electoral College is KILLING Our Democracy.
Five of our Nine Supreme Court Justices sitting on the bench were appointed by presidents who did not win the popular vote.

Let that sink in for a minute.

The defenders of The Electoral College argue that these problems are minimal. The partisan loyalties (states going to one party, not the people) are minimal since only about 10 electors in American history have been unfaithful. Another argument for the EC is that a contingency election by the house would be difficult to justify should a deadlock occur. The EC Defenders also use the election of 1824 as an argument for why it works better today citing that 1824 was before a two-party system existed. These defenders adamantly argue that without the EC, the country would be thrown into chaotic elections with single-issue candidacies and a mountain of third parties. This is possible... look at England. One argument however that remains constant is that The Electoral College system is continually failing to represent the voices of the people for which it was created.

There is no justification for a system that gives states and parties more power than the people themselves. Abraham Lincoln said, "Government of the people, by the people, for the people, shall not perish from the Earth".

Go Abe, you badass.

ARE WE BETTER THAN ENGLAND NOW?

England has soccer instead of football. They drink tea instead of coffee. They drive on the wrong side of the road (according to us).

<u>Then there is this:</u>

Gun murders in England in the last decade: <u>40</u>
Gun murders in America in the last decade:
<u>One million.</u>

In the Parliamentary System in England, the people elect the legislature (parliament) directly by voting, and then that parliament (the body of legislators) appoints/elects the Prime Minister. The people elect a body of legislators and then those legislators appoint their leader. This is as if in the US we held national elections for our Congress and then the Congress appointed/elected our president. So then, is it possible then the prime Minister in parliamentary Democracies are elected by the people more than the presidents in our presidential system? Could this be a drawback to presidential systems and a benefit to Parliamentary systems?

To wrap up a bit of history here, it's vital to compare how the US differs from its origins in England. Our founding fathers were revolutionary not just in war but in diverging from a parliamentary democracy to our presidential democracy. One of the key differences between presidential systems (ours) and parliamentary democracies (England's)—is that parliamentary democracies impart flexibility within the political system and that presidential democracies create a rigid process that leads to polarization— which is ALL we see now in the U.S. While this can be the case, it is not always the case. That very rigidity might be the largest problem in presidential democracies, but it is our fixed-term limits that create more stability (in presidential governments) than in the "flexible" parliamentary democracies.

In contrast, the flexibility in parliamentary democracies can lead to instability—as parliamentary democracies can fall at any time with a simple no confidence vote by parliament. This volatility in parliamentary regimes is advantageous and allows for better more current governing but it can be disruptive and unstable— leading to ineffective governing and fragmentation. There are a few prime ministers who only held office for days or weeks. The fact that parliament can call for a vote of no confidence on the Prime Minister even if from the same party, simply because they decide it is time for him or her to step down——is highly volatile and is certain to be used as a political tool for advantageous timing of elections for their party, not for better governing of the people.

If fixed term limits mean that the government is stable and constant, then that should enable more productive and constructive governing. Unstable and flexible parliamentary democracies (England) where elections can be called at any time——and used as an instrument of power——is not for the people by the people but for the party. A parliamentary democracy often experiences far more counterproductive volatility than what occurs in a presidential democracy.

Wait, hold on, all we see here in the U.S. are leaders putting party before the people, so is there really a difference?

There is. Fragmentation is much higher in parliamentary democracies through inherent power-sharing; with smaller coalition governments that arise in parliamentary democracies. Wait, hold on again! We have just as much counterproductive volatility as England. We have the good ol' filibuster in America! Yay! Even more apparent, (unless you've been living under a rock) party loyalties (although not formed as actual coalition governments) rule here.

Here in America, party loyalties dictate how the people are served, not public policy for the good based on a mutual understanding of what betters a society and our nation.

However, the argument that parliamentary democracies have more cohesive and disciplined parties is often completely untrue. Countries with parliamentary democracies can have many young political parties and deeply divided societies that lead to as many as <u>15 different political parties holding seats in Parliament. Fifteen</u>? <u>The United States can barely function with two.</u> In parliamentary democracies, (as opposed to presidential ones) multiple parties in legislature create a paralyzed government, and deeply fractured society, on a scale simply not possible in a presidential democracy. While less polarizing than presidential systems, this fragmentation is crippling to a government and leads to no voice holding power and paralysis of the entire system.

The key advantage to Presidential Democracies is the system of checks and balances in place to prohibit one individual or institution from holding too much power, or fifteen different parties nullifying any strong voice in a chaotic system. The Presidential System, although supposedly a winner-take all election (NOT! - THANKS, ELECTORAL COLLEGE!) is beholden to the checks and balances in a separation of powers unlike the fusion of powers in parliamentary. In parliamentary systems, the fusion of power means the executive is responsible to the legislature and chosen by the legislature. This leads to a very powerful body with an executive with one voice—that of the elected party.

A presidential democracy even with its faults, rigidity, and polarization, is more responsible to the people, for the people, and by the people who elect them. The separation of powers in presidential systems assures that no one branch, or person will ever wield too much power without being kept in check. I have no doubt the founder fathers never saw someone as dangerous as Trump happening to our democracy.

CHECKS AND BALANCES ON THE PRESIDENT'S POWER (IGNORING TRUMP)

The president is beholden to Congress. The basic rule is the president proposes and congress disposes. The president does not single-handedly approve legislation——as that is up to Congress. The president can draft and submit legislation to Congress for their approval, and depending on party lines, this can be a very arduous uphill battle. This is where the checks and balances come in for our president.

Most importantly, the president cannot declare war, only Congress can. This is essential to prevent tyranny. Presidents, however, have gone a long way toward capturing this power for themselves. This declaration of war by the president without Congressional approval first occurred in 1950. When North Korea forces invaded South Korea, President Truman sent U.S. forces into Korea without Congressional declaration, in the face of this immediate emergency. Our president does have significantly more powers in foreign affairs than in domestic because of the separation of institutional powers domestically.

The two most powerful tools the president has over Congress is the formal power of the veto, and his personal powers of persuasion. The veto is the only formal way a president can influence

Congress and is most commonly used by the president as a negotiating tool between him and Congress. This is especially useful if the president is facing a Congress controlled by the opposing party. For example, George W. Bush in his second term faced a Congress controlled by the Democrats, used the power of the veto eleven times. The limited single powers of the president, despite public opinion, is evident in how a president is essentially at the mercy of his Congress. This is also what can cause gridlock and stall progress, as we have all seen too often.

A president can use his powers of persuasion to persuade members of Congress to support and back his policy initiatives. This, of course, is dependent upon the president's current popularity. The more popular a president is among public opinion, the more powerful is his use of persuasion.

The public has always perceived the president to be more powerful than he, hopefully someday "she" is, especially regarding the economy. This also leads to what expectations the public leaves at the President's door. With an over 4 trillion dollar a year budget in our economy, many factors will shift the economy, certainly not just the president.

The public tends to give the president credit if the economy is booming, and in turn will blame the president if the economy is weak and failing. A president is handed down an already weakening or strengthening economy from the previous administration, yet that sitting president is often held responsible for the economy's current state.

If you don't read Robert Reich - Start now.

"In addition to solving the climate crisis that's become worse under Trump, passing universal health care that's become more urgent under Trump, and tackling myriad other problems that have grown larger under Trump, Democrats will once again have to clean up the economic mess left by their Republican predecessor in order to preserve and expand programs that help average Americans survive. Republicans accuse Democrats of being fiscally irresponsible. But time and again, it's the Republicans who have created economic messes that Democrats have to clean up." - Robert Reich

THE FED AND OUR ECONOMY

The Federal Reserve, "The FED" is the head bank of the US and is the gatekeeper of our economy. The FED is made up of 12 Federal Reserve banks located throughout the U.S. that regulates other member banks, uses monetary policies to regulate and control inflation and deflation, and enables and facilitates the exchange of cash credit and checks. The FED also controls interest rates and the reserve requirements every bank must have. Another power of the FED is over the Open Market Operations, in the control of the money supply in our economy.

The FED has two primary responsibilities in influencing the nation's money supply: increasing economic growth and controlling inflation. There are many factors, however, outside the FED's control, that manipulate and shift our economy such as the price of oil, an international crisis, technology, competition internationally in the markets, or as of late, a global pandemic. So, even though the FED seem all-powerful in shaping our economy and controlling our money supply, this is not the case at all.

In terms of its relationship to the federal government in regards of its policy-making capabilities and democratic input. The FED is sort of like a quasi-governmental institution, and its relationship to the federal government is somewhat insulated politically. This is due in part to the fact that Congress is the entity that crafts the rules for banking regulations. The president nominates the board of governors of the FED, and the senate confirms them, and all decisions regarding our money supply are made behind closed doors. The United States' monetary policy decisions are enacted under an often-criticized veil of secrecy.

Another easy way to explain the FED policy capabilities is to understand how it is structured. The Federal Open Market Committee FOMC is the body of the FED that creates monetary policies. The voting members of the FOMC are made up of the Board of Governors, the president of the Federal Reserve Bank of New York and presidents of other Reserve Banks around the country. The Federal Open Market Committee is structured with an interdependence on both federal and local banks. This combines the knowledge of the Board of Governors and the 12 Reserve Banks, along with local input from bank directors. All of these elements open the door for the private sector perspective and grassroots input in policy-making decisions.

GETTING BACK TO WHAT IS BROKEN

In politics, money, access, power, privilege, and familiarity are tremendous advantages the incumbents have over their challengers. This sets up a drastically unfair playing field for the potential of inspiring new representation and leadership in fresh challengers. It is the incumbent's familiarity with constituents and established donors that enables a farther reach and deeper access to campaign funds. The more you spend, the more you are known, the more votes you get. "Franking Privileges" (named after Ben Franklin) under which incumbents can send mailers and PR materials to their constituents for free using federal money, while their challengers must raise campaign funds to disseminate campaign materials, must stop.

If you look at it like this: our tax dollars pay for those federal funds. And thus, pay for an incumbent's mailers and campaign materials. Well, what if we are not behind that incumbent? Guess that doesn't matter. Franking Privileges along with hefty donors that favor the incumbent is a grossly unfair advantage given that money often wins elections.

CAPPING THE FUNDS

Setting a cap on the allotment of funds allowed per candidate would make the playing field more equal. Would the people feel less represented if they could only donate so much money to the candidate they prefer? OR would the equal amount a donor can give level the playing field between rich voters and the underserved poorer communities who can't throw money at the candidate they want or need? Wouldn't this then help new, struggling candidates get a fair shot, and the people will be equally represented?

Wouldn't a capped amount a donor can give level the playing field between rich voters and the underserved poorer communities who can't throw money at the candidate they want or desperately need?

Also, would this cap on funds help to counteract the office expenses, staff support, support from constituents, and the plethora of resources a current MC has over her or his opponent? The incumbency advantage is evident in the high rates of reelection: Over 90 percent for

JILL SHEA

House members and nearly 90 percent for members of the senate in recent years. There are several explanations to account for why incumbents have such an advantage over challengers. One school of thought is the incumbent's access to resources, perks, and funds that challengers do not get. These include the available resources to perform "casework" for already established constituents, along with franking privileges giving the incumbent access to free PR mailings for their upcoming campaign.

Another obvious factor to explain the incumbency advantage is the already well-known reputation the incumbent has the challenger simply does not have. The incumbent has established a reputation for being familiar with the needs of his or her constituents. This is a huge advantage for members of Congress seeking reelection. This established reputation also creates vastly disproportionate access to campaign donors and campaign finances for the incumbent over their challengers. It is true then in a sense, that to become a member of Congress, you have to already be a member of Congress. **This needs to change.**

SET TERM LIMITS AND AN AGE LIMIT OF 65

Leveling the playing field for Congressional elections will create a more fair and balanced democracy for all. Setting term limits, capping the age limit, and stopping gerrymandering (that's for another chapter) will create a Congress that can honestly serve the people with balanced and fair representation. Term limits and an age limit of 65 will also create a Congress that is less likely to perform just to get another term in office. There will always be logrolling—the exchanging of favors for votes, or a vote for a vote reciprocally regardless of the issue, or the patronage of legislators to constituents, but the loyalty of members of Congress must be to serve the people they represent, thus serving our entire democracy with more balance and relevancy.

Without fresh approaches to the constantly evolving issues facing our nation, how can Congress accurately and effectively represent us?

The playing-field must be leveled between incumbents and challengers for our country to continue to evolve, and for more diverse groups to be represented honestly and effectively.

If an incumbent is successful, why should she not be reelected? The reason for a successful reelection is much more complex and sometime more nefarious than that. If positive performance was the largest part of a candidate's reelection, then Congress members would always be working for the genuine well-being of the citizens in their districts. Logrolling, whips, favors, personal agendas, and gerrymandering would not exist when seeking reelection. If only... right?

The incumbent's overwhelming advantage over new challengers shapes the kind of representation the citizens receive in Washington, especially as times are changing and progressing—which seems to be happening more rapidly (which is a wonderful aspect of society right now). Our system must even the playing field for fresh new challengers in Congress and stop under representation. Our system must stop enabling the never-ending incumbent's advantage.

REDISTRICTING (GERRYMANDERING) MUST STOP

Our system's inability to have the people fairly and accurately represented by their officials is further fueled by the gerrymandering of districts. The re-clustering of Congressional districts to favor one political party is an abject abuse of the system and undermines the purpose of Congress to represent each district accurately and fairly per their concerns and needs. This is a topic that could fill a book on corruption, dirty politics, and why the system is broken and why it is failing.

DON'T BOO. VOTE!

According to PEW research **only** about two-thirds (66%) of the voting-eligible population turned out for the 2020 presidential election—and this was the highest rate for any national election since 1900. So that means that even at our highest level of voter turnout only a little more than half of eligible voters in America show up to vote. **This is shameful**.

In the 2016 presidential election, only 61% of the voting-eligible population turned out to vote. Voter turnout in America is obscenely low, especially when comparing turnout among the voting-age population in the 2020 presidential election against recent national elections in 49 other countries— the U.S. ranks 31st between Colombia (62.5%) and Greece (63.5%). Out of forty-nine other countries, America is 31st in voter turnout, and that was our highest turnout for an election in over 100 years. **This is shameful.**

The aggregate is the public, and public opinion is rarely unanimous. It is the opinion of what MOST people want, and this is where the majority rules. There are factors that affect public opinion and shape how beliefs are expressed, and preferences are made. The media, religion, personal experiences, geographical location, race, gender, and socio-economic stratifications all make up the aggregate's opinions and viewpoints. There will always be a variety of opinions and key variables to account for, but when it comes to the power of public opinion to create change; there is power in numbers. The majority rules often in how public opinion affects policies, politicians' actions, and government institutions, and this is essential to our democracy. Although…

Public opinion doesn't seem to be doing anything to enact sound gun control, or to address the climate crisis, or to protect women's rights, or for better public education.

Public opinion is expressed in every way, as seen in protest marches, blogs, social media, party organizations and most powerfully by voting. Like Obama said, "Don't Boo! Vote!"

Public opinion polls are used to assess views on public policies, on current issues, on party orientation, current circumstances such as jobs and economy, as well as social issues that affect our society. Possessing the freedom to express an opinion even if in opposition to the current political powers is a critical part of any free democracy. Public opinion is the lay persons most powerful tool to align policies with their self-interest, values, and needs as we have seen with various policies such as gay marriage, civil rights, even on the environment. Public opinion and voting are the people's most powerful tools to motivate action, and make political leaders respond to the people's needs and wants— even if they only do so to continue holding office or to be elected. Leaders often and should heed public opinion, and although policy and opinion do not always coincide; this is powerful and a critical foundation of democracy.

So, for the love of God, Always, Always VOTE.

CHAPTER TWO

<u>Partisanship</u>
Party Loyalties Grip
the Wheel

"There are always too many Democratic congressmen,
too many Republican congressmen, and never enough
U.S. congressmen."

- Anonymous

AMERICA IS IN A SLOW SUICIDE
OF PARTISANSHIP AND PARTY LOYALISTS

Our policymakers appear to revile the process of making
policies that secure our nation. They continually place the party
above the people in a brazen disregard for their oath of office to
enact their duty fairly, objectively, and constitutionally.

The policy-making process of the United States has become a flagrantly contemptuous display of destabilizing partisanship that
puts our nation's ineptitudes and vulnerabilities front and center for
the world to see. Our policy-making process is in a blazing dumpster
fire these days, as American policymakers seem to be sending America on a suicide mission. Our policy formulation is currently based on

41

vendettas against the opposing party and moves that prove to be a show of party loyalties. Our partisan driven policy-making arena in Washington is only deepening the angry divides that weaken our nation's leadership and interests worldwide.

Interest is a particularly ironic word when it comes to the policy process of the United States. The divided political arena that enacts national security policies has a vested interest in making the party the priority, tarnishing the United States' role as a world leader. Problem solving in the policy-making process is not in focus. The dysfunction of the process drowning in partisanship has led to failed international trade deals, failed arms, and gun control measures, failed comprehensive spending reforms, failure to pass a 'Fair Tax' Act, and failed climate change mitigation policies.

The partisanship on the hill that is devastating America and hurting every day Americans became especially obvious with the COVID-19 pandemic——illuminated that enacting policies that secure our nation in a time of crisis is not something our government can soundly accomplish because it requires ignoring party and politics.

The visceral partisanship in our policy-making process within the executive and legislative branches endangers the United States as much as any foreign entity bent on America's demise.

In 2019, Republican policy actors refused to convict an act of a foreign entity (Russia) meddling with our elections under President Trump's encouragement and clearly evidentiary quid pro quo. National security took the backseat with party loyalties gripping the wheel. The partisan obstruction of justice boldly on display during the Trump years is egregious and inherently unconstitutional.

Trump's allies in Congress obstructed justice for their party leader without any regard for the security of the United States or the sanctity of our democracy.

The Republican members of Congress abused their powers in an abject show of partisanship, ironically to protect Trump from an abuse of power conviction.

Their behavior is deeply disquieting.

WAIT, WHAT? SERIOUSLY MAN?

The dysfunction of the United States became alarming when Trump egregiously left both the Paris Agreement and the Iran Nuclear Deal. (Because he says they weren't deals he made.)—Wait, what? Seriously man? Protecting our world interests and national security were in the hands of partisan politics and deeply inept authoritarian-style tactics. This is the worst combo.

Remember how The Electoral College elected that guy, Donald Trump?

Yeah, Thanks, EC.

Our national security relies on nations and allies having confidence in our system and our choices. Nations who wish to strike trade deals, agree to arms-control measures, or commit their forces to fight alongside us do not know if a future president will unilaterally reverse the agreement. If there are no enduring commitments with the U.S. due to a dysfunctional national policy process, agreements appear risky to our foreign counterparts. This appearance of a corrupt national security process has given rise to fervent anti-Americanism across

Europe, and thus, awakened the call for anti-American terrorist cell recruitment.

**Can America get out of its own way and get back to
leading the world to secure and protect our
nation and the world interests it holds?**

The Framers could have never imagined the die-hard partisanship that would take hold of politics in our modern age. The president is preeminent in national security decision-making, which can lead to confrontations with Congress. In turn, in the past, Congress has asserted itself to implement national security policies, which has led to confrontations with the executive branch. This power-sharing system, where politics divide policy, can stall swift action and stymied progress.

The institutionalized confrontations that result from the decentralization of power are also interdepartmental. Conflicts between the FBI and The Justice Department are not uncommon. The nature of a system of checks and balances creates institutional power plays and can frustrate strategies and halt progress. Regardless of the frustrations and stagnation in a system of checks and balances, the system ensures that the United States citizens will never suffer reckless tyranny that is possible when one branch or individual has unfettered, unchecked powers to wield.

**Trump's FOUR criminal indictments speak to that.
Trump faces NINETY-ONE FELONY COUNTS in four
separate criminal courts in Washington, New York,
Florida and Georgia.**

UNILATERAL ACTION TO OVERRIDE PARTISANSHIP

There is the view among political scientists, that unilateral orders or prerogatives are needed and effective policy tools, but that if used by the president at his discretion in excess can give rise to the possibility that presidents will use unilateral power to avoid and diminish the separation of powers crucial to our system. More recently, as partisan divides deepen, presidents have increasingly turned to the use of unilateral measures to ensure swift action on policies. Some presidents even campaign on the issue of using unilateral means to avoid the dreaded gridlock and partisan battles that come along with most legislation. Unilateral prerogatives include executive orders, proclamations, statements of the administration's policies without the due process of Congress's touch, and in some, but not many cases, even the power of the veto can be seen as a unilateral measure. A president's success relies upon the partisanship power struggle that is aimed at tarnishing or bolstering his (someday her!) presidency. Basically, the party who rules the house ultimately determines the success of a president's agenda and actions—with one goal—the party must win regardless of what is best for the country.

Six decades ago, in 1960, Richard Neustadt, a political scientist, who served as an advisor to several presidents and specialized in the powers of the presidency, illuminated the idea of unilateral decisions and why they happen. Neustadt, through experience, noted that presidents have very few formal powers, making it very difficult to meet the tremendous expectations of a nation, and all that is assumed that can be accomplished through the presidency. Neustadt's observations and views of the unilateral approach are that it is, at times, seen as antagonistic in leadership. The fallout or benefit of a president's ability to take decisive action can affect future events and a president's desire to act swiftly.

President Obama's use of unilateral prerogatives to circumvent the Republican-led Congress determined to destroy his presidency, was continually his only option.

Obama resorted to issuing executive orders because Congress aggressively blocked his progress at every turn. Executive orders were his only opportunity as president to achieve anything for the betterment of America. An effective president must guard his power to effectively makes choices, thus enact change. This means that a president's ability to act decisively and quickly is equivalent to his ability to guard the depth and strength of his influence, thus his viewed success. President Barack Obama signed 276 executive orders ranging from domestic affairs to foreign policies, to immigration policies. Obama also made almost 1,200 proclamations or directives establishing public policy or triggering actions to uphold a law in which the circumstances of that event required such laws to be upheld and implemented. Obama's 1,186 proclamations and his 276 executive orders were the unilateral prerogatives that established his presidency as one of leadership without the shared responsibilities of a Congress that often appeared bent on slowing down the process, and his success. Obama's use of unilateral measures, and at times his unilateral presidency were his only options and were exemplary of his determined leadership.

POLICIES WITH HUMANS IN MIND UNDER OBAMA (In Stark Contrast to Trump's Policies)

In 2012, a unilateral move by Obama came domestically, when President Obama revised an immigration policy when it became very clear that Congress (because of partisanship) would not act to revise it. In Obama's unilateral move by executive order, he suspended the prosecutions of many illegal immigrants in what became known as the "mini-DREAM Act". In this executive order, the president halted the deportation of certain young undocumented immigrants, provided they meet the requirements outlined in the order. Obama's executive order made almost 800,000 young people now safe from prosecution and deportation and was a powerful unilateral move, he felt was his only option. (I go into Trump's "Zero Tolerance" policy that led to horrific family separations a bit later on.)

President Obama believed his use of unilateral powers was crucial to back the policy interests of the people, to diffuse the partisanship he faced, and a means to control a system in peril. His "Mini Dream Act" was an example of what he felt needed to be done on the critical issue of immigration reform. Obama, however, did not simply act unilaterally without prior attempts at collaboration. Obama asked the attorney general and the secretary of homeland security to look into the steps he could take within the confines of the Constitution; to repair the broken immigration system on his own. President Obama expressed that in trying to fix the broken and unjust immigration system, he was consulting all authorities to try to make progress. Obama also made it clear that every time he took a step toward using executive orders that he was working within the confines of his executive power, not in an abuse of it. Obama's frustration with the stymied and stalled progress of Congress on immigration reform initiatives, and knowing it would fall on his presidency alone, was motive for his executive order and use of unilateral power.

In 2014, Obama used unilateral measures again, when he issued an executive order to raise the minimum wage for federal contractors under federal construction contracts. President Obama's unilateral executive action to raise the workers' wages was to hope-fully lower the constant turnover and increase workers' overall mo-rale, thus leading to higher productivity. Obama's executive order di-rected the Department of Labor to set the new federal contractor min-imum wage at $10.10 per hour. This new order did not apply univer-sally across all U.S. employers, but it raised the wages of almost two million federal contract workers and reenforced Obama's commit-ment to increase the minimum wage. Again, Obama rocked the tactic of unilateral measures, and had no choice since partisanship was hell-bent on him failing.

Obama chose to do this unilaterally to signal to his supporters as well as all Americans that he is a leader who will not wait for ap-proval when it comes to ensuring that workers are compensated fairly. This goes toward Obama's campaign promise that he would fight for hard-working Americans in support of the working classes of Amer-ica, strengthening his influence and success. Obama's action is also exemplary of Neustadt's view on unilateral force when he emphasized such unilateral actions as affecting a president's ability to act on future events, especially if similar to the policy change needed at the time.

WHEN OBAMA CHOSE NOT TO...

In 2013, Obama underestimated the power of partisanship to rule even when people were suffering. Another perspective on Presidents' use of unilateral actions can be viewed through Obama's choice to not use unilateral power when doing so might have been the better option. On August 21, 2013, the Syrian military used chemical weapons in an attack that killed nearly fifteen hundred civilians, including nearly four hundred children. This horrified nations around the globe and the images of the innocent children targeted were seared into societies. President Obama wanted to order a missile strike against Syria in retaliation for President Bashar al-Assad's use of chemical weapons on children, and instead of ordering the strike unilaterally, he sought the approval of Congress. Obama's decision was the result of in-fighting on what the protocols of actions of war should be in a territory with such mitigating circumstances.

Obama and many members of Congress argued that to order missile strikes, especially in these circumstances, did not require congressional approval. It was other legislators, however, who countered that President Obama, if he did not involve Congress in this order, risked setting a precedent encouraging future presidents to act unilaterally on military strikes, thus ignoring the necessary structure of the separation of powers. Obama ultimately sought congressional approval for the strike which he could have achieved more swiftly and with a better result unilaterally. President Obama did not shy away from acting unilaterally when he felt the cause was urgent and pressing, so his seeking Congress's approval in this case was unusual. Obama felt this would be a cause that Congress could get behind and come together in agreement on, therefore acting unilaterally would not be necessary. He was wrong. Unilateral theory observes that presidents surrender their will and discretion at their own peril. Congress's reaction to President Obama's announcement for a strike reinforced that very possibility and risk. Legislators in Congress immediately put constraints on any use of force as they added their own caveats and conditions to Obama's order. The president fully expected to obtain approval for the strike, which revealed to be a confidence that was tremendously overestimated.

The use of unilateral measures allotted a president can circumvent the necessary checks and balances and the purpose of separation of powers. It is apparent, however, when Congress puts their party first— over sound policy— they are forcing the president's hand. During Obama's presidency, acting unilaterally proved to be the swiftest and often only means of enacting policies and orders a president has——especially when a Congress is hell-bent on making him fail.

A president is only as worthy and successful as his achievements, policies, and actions as a leader. Presidents have frequently ignored opportunities to use unilateral force when facing outcomes that could come with political opposition and consequences. Obama's hundreds of unilateral measures and proclamations did not come without opposition in the wings, and questions about adhering to the rules of the separation of powers. Every President has faced this predicament, and many have chosen not to pursue a unilateral strategy because they feared the political fallout would be too high. A president's use of unilateral action ensures that the outcome, the consequences, and the resulting reactions will be laid upon him solely. This is always a risk, but presidents take it and always have. When presidents contemplate unilateral action, they must, and will always try to predict how Congress and the Judiciary will respond to such action. The limits to a president's unilateral powers depend upon the capacity and willingness of Congress and the Judiciary to overturn the president.

A GAME OF PING PONG: PARTY V. PEOPLE
Party Is Winning and The People Are Losing

Would you rather a bill be pure to effectively meet the original purpose and cause for which it was introduced with the likelihood of it never being passed? Or is the compromising of parts of that bill, either in its wording or packaging (that might or might not lessen its key purpose) to at least get something achieved, better? Especially when the actual legislation an MC might tout is not as it truly appears? What is better? Nothing or something?

For example: And I am making this up and it is rudimentary, but there are similar ones like it——this is how the "packaging" of a bill can be deceiving: A bill is passed in both houses that will prohibit deforestation in a certain region where huge corporations want to over build. However, this seemingly wonderful bill only passed in both houses because it was packaged together with an ulterior agenda. The "packaging" of the deforestation bill includes language that will also lift the tight regulations of those same corporations elsewhere. This "packaging" of the bill that originally aimed to stop deforestation allows both sides to feel satisfied——and the Members of Congress can say we did it! We protected the forest, and we satisfied our constituents! Yay! Again, is something better than nothing? After all the forest is saved, but those corporations now have free rein to over manufacture elsewhere, and their stock just might go up. Double Yay!

Nope. Not a yay.

When you have a Congress and committees that are so divided; How will the House and Senate pass the same bill with the same language in text and number——or any bill that will serve the people? We all know that the language of that bill will shift over time to appease some aspect of the opposing side's desires to come to a common ground on what is acceptable to both. This Ping Ponging of a bill, it's manipulation through a back and forth—is only because of such deep internal partisan disagreements——and for the legislators need to say they have satisfied their constituents. This is the central dilemma of members of Congress: How should legislators decide to spend their time and resources? Should they appease committee leaders and party leaders to then appear to satisfy constituents?

How much compromise must take place to appease both sides before the bill is no longer what it originally set out to accomplish? Is doing this dance a signal to their constituents that they are deeply "concerned" about an issue, or is it out of self-preservation? Legislators and committee leaders must collaborate instead of acting like rivals. This partisan rivalry, unfortunately, this is the heart of congress satisfying constituents' concerns. This game of ping pong begins when the bill is first "sculpted" with its phrases or sometimes "eye-catching" title. This also includes the nefarious large bills that hide legislation- that disguise controversial measures that otherwise would not garner a broad vote of support. It is not just the wording but this iniquitous "packaging" part of a bill that can help it along. Legislators face another dilemma—vote along your convictions and for what you believe is just and sound, or ignore your foreboding doubts and cast a vote for appearances or along party lines (if those conflict)? A certain vote might help later on when said legislator wants votes in return to get his or her next bill through. **It is a game.**

It's deal making and a game and the winner must appear to be mirroring the views of their party.

CHAPTER THREE

TRUMP

America, why?

Donald Trump unearthed the worst in America, which
served as the impetus for this book.

Donald Trump emboldens the rotten and the
deplorable both in politics and people:
Those who disregard truth, dignity, human rights, and
our democracy in favor of their leader.

Donald Trump enforced the destructive power of die-hard
partisanship and unethical party loyalties. He has engineered
the catastrophic destruction of the principles of our democracy.

But first,
a word on extremism and fascism under his reign.

EXTREMISM AND FASCISM UNDER TRUMP
Authoritarianism and Totalitarianism Too

L ater in the book I dive into the ideologies that divide us in the hopes that maybe understanding why people vote along certain lines of beliefs will help lessen the divides. However, two terrifying ideologies have emerged with the rise of Trump: Extremism and Fascism. These ideologies (encouraged by Trump) gravely threaten our democracy and threaten every society's ability to thrive; and they pose the most urgent threat what our Founding Fathers fought so hard for.

Extremism and fascism have been awakened and empowered by Trump. Examining what this means is vital to quelling it.

Our nation, thanks to Donald Trump, is threatened by an extremism and passionate fascism that grossly masquerade as patriotism. These new circumstances and these extreme ideologies threaten the very foundations of our democracy and well-being. Under Trump we saw our elections tampered with by a foreign entity under his quid pro quo with our very own congress (Trump's congress) refusing to act; the freedom and integrity of the press continually threatened by Trump; the civil liberties of those human beings and children who seek asylum in our nation ignored and even abused; and the alt-right gaining a voice with support from Donald Trump.

What the hell is going on America? Did we shoot ourselves in the face on purpose?

Trump succeeds with his fascism and extremism by masking their tyrannical and dictatorial nature through appeals to traditional legitimacy. He further solidifies their hold on his followers by binding them to personal loyalties and the ideological standards of the conservative party.

Trump is quite determined to always be "winning", so when he is los- ing, he enlivens anything that enrages people, even if based on un- founded untruths that gravely threaten the fabric of our nation. Trump then makes it clear that they should only listen to only him, "their savior" as he is the only one who can fix it.

Trump is the textbook definition of a totalitarian leader.

Stopping Trump from perpetuating such destruction on societies across America and upon our democracy does not require new ideas, or new political strategies.

Remember Chapter One of this book? It requires all of us, on both sides of the aisle, to remember the traditions of the ideologies that founded our nation. Instead of going forward with a new strategy, it might be better for the nation to go backward and remember why the fundamental ideologies of conservatism, socialism, and liberalism came about and what can happen when we stray from them.

We must remember what happens to a society and a country when fascism and extremism take hold of it.

FREEDOM OF THE PRESS

If the nation could be educated on countries where a free press does not exist, it would find a blind and imprisoned society, that criminal- izes free speech and free will (Russia, China, North Korea to name a few). Illuminating the societies that exist under extreme ideologies such as communism and totalitarianism, help illustrate how danger- ous demonizing the press is. Trump ardently demonizes any media outlet which holds him accountable or questions his bold lies and mis- use of power.

Demonizing and blocking the members of our media strips the citizens of their right to a free and open press. Illuminating how extreme ideologies in other countries create oppression might be a useful tool in how to address the problems we are facing today in America—helmed and championed by Trump. We must remember what America can be without leaders like Trump and we must preserve our ideals in this new terrifying circumstance of Donald Trump.

To restate Chapter One: If Americans would revisit the founding fathers' intentions it would be starkly evident that we are straying from the ideologies that keep our democracy intact. The past often gives us the most significant insight and is the most massive tool for change.

FASCISM AND CULT STATUS AS A "TRUMPIAN"

Fascism is an anti-individual, anti-liberal, populist, ultra-nationalism that capitalizes on a crisis, and appeals to the collective masses with the promise of a better "golden" age ahead. Fascism rejects multiculturalism, preaching that some races are superior to others and should dominate over others. This element is appealing to those who clearly lack an identity and crave a sense of power and dominance. Fascism is about the collective and rejects individualism. This is appealing to many who desire to be a part of something they feel is larger than themselves, even if evil and ignorant. Trump loves to prey upon these people. Fascism is characterized by an all-powerful charismatic leader who falsely represents the will of his people, and to whom all the people are beholden.

In fascism, the people gain power and freedom through the collective, uniting in a struggle, perpetrated, and emphatically proclaimed by their all-powerful leader. This again gives people a sense of power and a sense of belonging to something larger than them-selves. This is very dangerous. Trump enlivened masses of people who yearned to feel like somebodies, to storm our very own capitol where lives were taken. Fascism gives people an identity and cause to be a part of. The most critical aspect of fascism is its view of a nation as a unit in crisis.

This is how a false "savior" can lead his people to follow him while manipulating their need to belong and appealing to their fears.

This is Trump to a T.

Fascism's ability to unite the masses in a fight against a common en-emy is at its core. The identification of enemies as scapegoats creates a unifying cause like no other, and this is the key component to fas-cism. The people in fascist regimes are rallied together into a patriotic frenzy, with the need to eliminate a common threat or enemy. Fascism is like being a part of a gang. The KKK, and the Nazis are examples of this psychology at its most powerful. Having a father figure is also why fascism appeals to people. The leader of a Fascist regime as-sumes the role of the father of the nation. In a sense, the leader acts as the father, eliciting loyalty in his people that mimics a cult status. Sounds a hell of a lot like Trump.

Extremism and fascism appeal to people who are unable to succeed, need a scapegoat to blame for their failings, desire a sense of identity, and possess a deep-rooted hate.

Extremist groups provide a refuge for individuals seeking belonging, who recognize that intellectually driven organizations or those requir-ing a certain level of intellectualism would not accept them. Such groups attract those inclined toward conflict and yearning for authoritative leadership. For individuals within society who feel marginalized or overlooked, unable to achieve their ideal life, fascism offers them an identity and power previously unattainable. Most importantly it helps give a clear enemy to blame for their struggles. In Fascism, an enemy to blame for a society's failings or low standard of life or lack of social success is appealing and empowering. Fascism appeals to fear, hate, ignorance, dominance, false empowerment, and a false promise of a better life through the fight against a common scapegoat, e.g.: the Alt Right. This is acutely the same values reflected in Trump followers.

TRUMP'S CONGRESS AND THEIR EXTREMISM (Partisanship and Party Loyalties)

How can one explain President Trump's relationship with Congress? A relationship between the executive and the legislative branches that constantly blurs the lines of the separation of powers. A Congress in which Trump's party enjoyed majorities in both chambers. Throughout Trump's relationship with Congress, the power of party alignments and partisan loyalties has never been more destructive. President Trump's defiant individual characteristics as President are the likes of which this nation had never seen. To be clear, not in a positive way.

Trump's self-serving disregard for our democracy was bolstered by the legislative branch's baffling loyalty to such obvious disregard for truth, stability, human rights, and the constitution to which they took an oath.

Trump's distortion of the constitution and his vindictive and chaotic disarray of executive leadership continuously backed by Republican members of Congress, begs the question of how this extreme support can happen. Trump's dangerous ignorance of policy and lack of desire to prepare for the job as leader of the free world, leave many perplexed—how he has Trump been able to manipulate his congress over and over, escaping penalties for his blatantly egregious and treasonous actions?

Does Trump's relationship with an inexplicably cultishly loyal congress illuminate an ongoing problem of members of congress putting party over country? Does the separation of powers work the way The Framers intended when congress will do whatever bidding the president needs, when the country is desperate for progress, answers, justice, and above all truth in its representatives?

The explanations all lead to Conditional Party Governing and Fervent Party Loyalists.

The answer in how much power a president has over Congress depends upon the cohesiveness of party ideologies and if they align with the executive branch. The president's ability to sway his Congress to do his bidding also depends upon the desire of members of Congress to satisfy ideologies with their constituencies. The polarizing ideological cleavages within our Congress, continually lead to paralysing party loyalty. This die-hard partisanship gives the executive branch considerable power (when from the same party). This is especially evident in Trump's case. Conditional party government is at the helm of Congress's undying loyalty to President Trump— A president, who at every single turn, chose to dubiously erase lines of the separation of powers in a manipulation of the constitution for his, and only his, benefit.

Party loyalty and conditional party governing continually enable Trump despite egregious constitutional betrayals, ethical breaches of conduct, and his blatant criminal behavior.

Instead of crafting a few sentences or even a lengthy paragraph to elucidate politicians' unwavering loyalty to Trump, I offer a simple equation that encapsulates it succinctly:

White Supremacists + Individuals who feel marginalized + Trump supporters who advocate for a homogeneous, white, male, Christian America + Blue-collar workers seeking their share of the American Dream but feeling left behind = Trump Wins as leader of the Republican Party = Trump gets Votes!

The unwavering allegiance of Republicans to the clearly unfit Trump as both a man and a President can be attributed to one primary factor:

VOTES. VOTES. VOTES.

With retribution thrown in too.

Retribution from the Republican Party stands as the most potent motivator behind the unwavering allegiance of Members of Congress to their formidable leader, Donald Trump.

Liz Cheney exemplified courage in defying Trump, yet subsequently forfeited her career—a stark illustration of the reprisal Members of Congress fear should they uphold principles they deem just.

Even presidents who appeared to command Congress were just mediators or architects rather than the administrators of change, as that is Congress's function. The best evidence of presidential power in the legislative process is found at the structure of Congressional decision-making when homogenous ideologies breed fervent party loyalties. With President Trump, however, there is much more at play. Past presidents understood their limitations regarding Congress and quite skillfully took advantage of whatever opportunities existed in their restricted environments, but within the confines of the powers being separate. Trump, having not faced many limitations in Congress, has skillfully taken advantage of his manipulated environment filled with hard-lined party loyalists creating an incestuous system, blurring the separation of powers.

The most powerful element of Trump's relationship with congress is the high degree of polarizing ideologies held by our representatives. The cohesiveness of the Republican party is tenacious and is bolstered by the lack of cross-cutting oppositions from constituencies represented by the Democrats. **Where are your balls Dems?** Cohesive opposition pressure from Democratic constituencies would help counter the Republicans' staunch ideologies, thus their power, but that seldom happens. The ideologically homogenous makeup of today's Republican party under Trump seems unbreakable, feeding the patterns of conditional party government. This conditional party governing is dictating decisions facing a congress that unaccountably follows their destructive and dangerous leader, Donald Trump.

PARTISAN OR POLICY LOYALISTS
(Remember Chapter Two and America's Suicide?)

There are two key groups in the legislative processes that help determine the success a president has with Congress, and the legislative successes of each branch. Legislators fall into one of two groups: Partisan Loyalists, or Policy Loyalists, and represent a dichotomy of governing. Most legislators fall somewhere between partisan and policy loyalists, with a blend of partisan loyalty and ideological dedication. However, based on the numerous fights and victories Trump had with Congress, it is hard to concede that anything other than partisan loyalists existed in the Republican-led Congress that supported all things

Trump no matter the ethical or constitutional costs. The policy loyalists do exist of course, but when the reigning party in Congress and the executive branch are staunch partisan loyalists, they are then the puppeteers as well. Trump's Presidency has never made that more apparent.

Partisan loyalists are the type of members of Congress we have seen propel Trump's victories and unabashedly support him regardless of ethical, constitutional, and moral dubiousness.

The pure partisan loyalists care very little about the issues endorsed by the party—what the party says about the issues is what matters, not the issues themselves. Partisan loyalists change positions on any issue so long as they are adopting their party's current position on it. The issues they vote on hold no meaning to these types of legislators. What matters most to partisan loyalists is what the party wants them to do. Partisan loyalists take the party line on all and every issue regardless of the consequences. It is fair to assume the partisan loyalists have a very shallow understanding or concern for the issues nor their consequences on which they are casting votes.

In contrast, to the partisan loyalist legislators are the Policy Loyalists, who legislate and vote on policies in exactly the opposite fashion as partisan loyalists. These legislators are people who exhibit high levels of consideration, with deep deliberation for the underlying principles of an issue or policy——and how a policy affects our nation and its people.

Policy loyalists remain unwaveringly faithful to the principles and ideals of an issue regardless of which party or partisan leader advocates those same views.

Under Trumps' presidency, the destruction of the separation of pow-ers between the legislative and executive branches, was at an all-time high. A president's relationship with Congress is based on the cohe-siveness of his party, and whether that party holds the majority in Congress. Commonly, presidents can expect to receive high levels of support from their party. So, whether the government is unified or divided is critical to presidential success, and thus, the presidency it-self. The president's initiatives and proposals are much less likely to pass under a divided government, but that is not news. Controlling the agenda that facilitates or obstructs the president's power in the legislative process with Congress is vital. However, with the condi-tional party government under President Trump, Congress destroyed the line between who sets the agenda and who regulates it. Trump's presidency was, and still is polarizing and uncontainable, and his re-lationship with Congress was no exception.

The balancing act that members of Congress face in satisfying their constituents often equates to satisfying the party and party ideo-logies. Members of Congress (MCs) vote along party alignments to then obtain votes needed on agendas that thus satisfy their constitu-ents, and ultimately favor their re-election chances. The basic concept behind these components in President Trump's interactions with Con-gress is that all roads lead back to the party and partisan loyalty. Trump's controversial victories with Congress's backing, are owed to such resolute Republican support. Is the Constitution the guiding force in Congress, and are the separation of powers between the ex-ecutive and legislative branches is truly separate?

DONALD TRUMP & CONGRESS - Abuses of Power

The best way to examine Trump's relationship with Congress, the conditional party government, and how partisan loyalists enable his power since he took the Oval Office in 2016 (with a then Republican

Congress) is to look at a few defining fights he had with Congress which illuminate the party divide. The many confounding fights and victories of Trump v. Congress were grounded in the conditional party government theory. Conditional party governing afforded Trump several triumphs in avoiding the scrutiny for actions that were unconstitutional, impeachable, and criminal. The impeachments of Donald Trump and the subsequent hearings starkly illuminated the party strength behind the Republicans flagrant loyalty to their leader.

Before Trump abused his power to solicit electoral intervention in the 2020 election, he committed serious acts of treason against America. I've outlined them below:

1. Trump's quid pro quo offer in a phone call to Ukrainian President Volodymyr Zelensky, wherein Trump blocked $400 million in military aid to Ukraine unless Zelensky would cooperate in providing damning false information on Biden for the 2020 election.
2. Trump pressured other countries to propagate false conspiracy theories about Biden and American politics.
3. Trump enlisted others, including Giuliani and AG William Barr, to pressure Ukraine and other foreign governments to support those conspiracy theories and dispel false stories about Joe Biden for the 2020 election.
4. Trump propagated misinformation about Russia's apparent interference in the 2016 election, which he orchestrated.

Congress voted to acquit on all charges, with divisions along party lines: Democrats voted to convict, while Republicans voted to acquit. The Republicans prioritized their party over our national security, the sanctity of our elections, the sanctity of our democracy, the sanctity of our Constitution, and the oath they took to protect it.

Don't forget Handsy McPerv.
No, not Trump this time. Another guy.

Congress pushed to confirm conservative Justice Kavanaugh to the highest court of our nation. Party loyalty to Trump's conservative pick for the Supreme Court disregarded serious and disturbing flaws in Kavanaugh's character.

The Republican majority's unapologetic, unscrupulous, and unconstitutional loyalty to all things Trump was apparent immediately after Trump first took office in 2016. Trump passionately sought to repeal Obamacare with strong Congressional support along party lines with Republican MCs overwhelmingly backing a repeal. Trump's combative and contentious relationship with Democratic Members of Congress would be called overboard if I had written it into a screenplay and I would have been told to tone it down, but it was not in a screenplay. It was dishearteningly real.

The Supreme Court upheld it, in a huge victory for Obama.

Another example of Trump's battles with Congress occurred with one of the most egregiously unconstitutional and inhumane measures ever enacted. The "Zero Tolerance" immigration policy that led to cruelly separating young migrant children from their parents at the border then detaining them without due process. The family separation crisis that began with the "Zero Tolerance" declaration by Attorney General Jeff Sessions and the Department of Justice, nefariously manipulated the executive branch's power backed by the justice department's partisan loyalty and was in blatant disregard for constitutional law.

Despite the federal court ruling against Trump's "Zero Tolerance" policy citing it to be a violation of the constitution's guarantee of due process, the aggressive anti-immigration tactic continued.

Both sides of the aisles in Congress proposed measures in a serious attempt to find a resolution that would halt the inhumane practice behind "Zero Tolerance". Each measure was unsuccessful with Democrats and Republicans unable to meet in the middle, on not just "Zero Tolerance" but underlying immigration reform issues, with partisan loyalties being masqueraded as policy loyalties. Conditional party governing, and partisan loyalties once again pulled the strings of Congress's ability to effectively legislate. At the helm, fervent party support for the uncompromising leader of the Republican party, President Trump held strong, while toddlers were snatched from their mom and dad and put into cages.

When the president cannot depend on having a compatible party majority in Congress to pass his policies and do his bidding, he must gain support from the opposition party.

Trump escaped this need through the destructive partisan divides he fostered which were then soldered in by a Republican-led Congress.

The ideologically divided congress, in turn, served as an opportunity to Trump who has made his office about loyalty to him and his party with feared retribution if abandoned.

It is this very polarization in Congress that will affect the ability of the president to reach across the aisle and obtain support from the opposition party when needed, but Trump is not the type to ever reach across the aisle anyway. Given the strong influences of ideology and constituency, it is not surprising that presidential leadership has the muscle to promote destructive cleavages within Congressional voting patterns, and Trump is still proof of that strength.

Trump made destroying bipartisanship within Congress his goal, and under his leadership, Congress has never been more divided while he ignited the support of cohesive partisan loyalists. Donald Trump's Congress has challenged the existence of the constitutional separation of powers between the executive and legislative branches. In Trump's presidency did the legislative branch neglect to truly keep the executive branch's power in check or are the Members of Congress (MC's) powers to legislate only as powerful as the party to which the MCs pledge?

If the legislative branch is only there to bulldoze the president's policies into action and protect him regardless of The Constitution, then are the powers really separate?

Republican Members of Congress' eyes wide open unwavering support allowed Trump to wield abuses of power when it came to manipulating the constitution for his own benefit and for anti-immigration policies, or in a redefinition of what our founding fathers defined as an abuse of power. Trump's relationship with Congress has undoubtedly stretched the flexibility of the power of the executive office. This has certainly expanded the limits of what America should simply accept as being within the confines of executive power. The party and Congress's incentive to make the president look good by handing him victories is nothing new. The high correlation between presidential and Congressional voting means that Republicans are strongly fastened to Trump's success and rely upon it. If Trump fails, then so do they. Republicans in all levels of office benefit if Trump is high in the polls, so partisan loyalists are exactly what Trump gets, and this affords him such immunity to punishment or scrutiny.

Republican legislators have also been defiant to discuss the president's controversial personal conduct or his chaotic management of the White House staff. Notably, the Republican MCs have routinely and unshakably defended him against charges of collusion with Russia during the 2016 campaign. **It is this unethical fervent party loyalty in Congress that has made Trump bullet-proof.** Legislative parties play a vital and consequential role in politics. It is apparent through Trump's presidency and his relationship with Congress that centralized governing is conditional. Conditional on the party, loyalty, promises, and retribution if defiant. This relationship is nothing new, but in Trump's relationship with Congress, it is undeniably more extreme than ever seen before.

Trump has impassioned an abhorrent selling of the souls in Congress for victories of the Republican Party.

When centralized governing in congress is conditional then The Constitution that separates the powers suffers.

Trump's Congress and his abuses of power force the American people to ask who or what is really in charge, and are the separate powers keeping each other in check as the founding fathers intended?

ABUSES OF POWER BY TRUMP

Trump's numerous fights with Congress and his evidentiary abuses of power include Trump suing a member of Congress in the hopes of preventing that MC from forcing him to hand over his tax records for the last decade. In addition, Trump was investigated by Congress for telling Special Counsel Donald McGahn to lie to Mueller regarding Trump's attempt to fire him. (To refresh your memory, Robert Mueller was the special counsel overseeing the Russia investigation). In another blatant and reckless abuse of power— Trump lied about overriding security clearances to give his son-in-law Jared Kushner (a civilian) an all-access pass to our nation's most perilous top secrets.

In December of 2019, The Democratic led House of Representatives impeached Donald Trump on two separate charges, leaving him to face removal from office by a Republican led senate. The first charge against President Trump was for his abuse of power when he pressured a foreign government to meddle in our presidential election. The second charge was for Trump's obstruction of Congress. When Congress sought to investigate the abuse of power charges, the president ordered his administration to ignore and block Congress's every request. Donald Trump's blatant obstruction of Congress is what the House declared to be an aggressive violation of the separation of powers, and an act by Trump to be above the law.

Despite these clear and nefarious breaches in executive authority by Trump and his alarming abuses of power, Congress never succeeded in holding him accountable.

This is very alarming.

The two chambers of Congress were at fierce odds over these charges and what they implied, creating a deeply contentious impeachment. Trump's impeachment revealed how congress and its chambers operate, especially when the parties are divided. The entire impeachment, but most obviously, the obstruction of justice charge highlights the crucial importance for the separation of powers. Both of Trump's impeachments exposed a Congress at immense odds, also bringing out the possible ambiguity of the meaning of the separation of powers—depending on who is defining them. These obstruction charges unwaveringly bring out the inner workings of congress as autonomous chambers who must share one responsibility—to the keep president's powers in check. Trump's Congress violated its responsibilities to uphold democracy because of party allegiance to a dangerous president and out of fear of political retribution if not loyal.

Nothing as of late reveals the need to protect the separation of powers, the effectiveness of checks and balances at play, and the interactions between Congress and the Presidency than both impeachments of Donald Trump. Congress keeps the president in check through the constitutional design of the separation of powers that aims (although just aims—as Trump seeks to defy this at every turn) to prevent any one person, or institution from attaining too much power. The impeachments also highlight, due to sharp divides along party lines, the separation within Congress between the two chambers, depending on which party is in the majority. Bicameralism works as an organizational frame of power. However, this contentious battle of Trump's impeachments between the two chambers proved how a republican Congress will ardently protect their prerogatives to prevent a victory by the opposing party.

Party wins and Democracy loses.

CONDITIONAL PARTY GOVERNING & TRUMP'S IMPEACHMENTS

The decision of House Speaker Nancy Pelosi when she endorsed an official inquiry to impeach President Trump quickly became known as the Impeachment Congress. Impeachments are more credible if bi-partisan, however this one was entirely partisan and with fervor. Trump's first impeachment (just a reminder there were two) was under an aggressively divided Congress holding allegiances to their party and party leaders. The ability of the Republican party to neglect what is constitutionally their responsibility when holding the office so to advance their party's brand name, is unlike anything this country has seen before, even in other impeachments. This is not something new. Members of congress, however, have always been willing to give up their individual powers to advance the party's name——so as to maximize their reelections. This is the power of the party to make or break you. The power of party, however, is grossly evident through the actions of Trump's Congress.

The theory of Conditional Party Government has never seemed so prevalent than in Congress during the impeachment of Donald Trump. The Republican party has never been more ideologically homogeneous, and the Democratic party has never been more ideologically homogeneous, and the two parties are oceans apart in their collective party ideologies. **This is war and party branding is at the forefront.** The impeachments of Trump seemed to be about just that: Members of Congress aligning with their party, to create a brand to feed to consumers. The act of even the sensible members of the Republican party to abandon constituency opinions for the Hill has never been so destructive— The power of the Hill, and the advantages of aligning with your party, even if it means abandoning the oath you took when first elected.

The impeachments of Donald Trump, although an extreme and obvious case of the inherent and critical responsibilities of Congress, illuminates the constant dilemma that Members of Congress (MCs) face. The dilemma that exists when representatives and senators must answer to Washington DC but must also act as agents for their home states and districts is a balancing act with reelection at the forefront. If reelected, MCs can better continue the agenda they started and believe in, but in order to get reelected, both the Hill and home must both feel heard and satisfied. The styles necessary to satisfy both require time, and MCs simply do not have enough of it. More daunting is that the desires of the home and the Hill can be hard to marry. The legislator has a constant dilemma: take actions that are popular with their constituents or take actions that serve his or her own best career interests.

Coalition and party alignment building is a tremendous part of Congress (not just during an impeachment) but constantly. This is accomplished not only through whips, votes, and strategies, but through the media as an innovative tactic to block or push through legislation. The use of the press, television, radio, polls, and the internet to sway voters, sway constituents, and promote the party's message has become an essential strategy to rack up votes. Trump's congress during his impeachments has never been more aggressive in using the media to propel their brand.

Fox News is at the helm of such dangerously partisan, and destructive media coverage.

TRUMP'S WAR POWERS (IRAN)

During Trump's presidency, congress, with a bipartisan measure, acted to limit Trump's power to launch military action or declare war on Iran. A U.S. drone strike killed Iran's top general back in early January which then sparked a retaliation strike on our military base, leading to the Congressional check of the president's war powers. The resolution, sponsored by Senator Tim Kaine, clarifies the Congressional power to declare war. Congress approved the bipartisan resolution that limited President Donald Trump's authority to launch military operations against Iran, declaring that Trump must win approval from Congress before engaging in further military actions against Iran. Kaine, and other supporters say this measure was not about Trump nor his presidency, but instead, it was structured as an important confirmation of Congress's power to declare war. Trump vetoed the war powers measure when it reached his desk even though the Senate had passed the resolution with strong bipartisan support despite Trump's tantrum. The Democratic controlled house passed the measure with many Republicans crossing the aisle to support it as well, in a strong show of support to check the executive branch's power to declare war. This resolution also required Donald Trump to remove troops presently in Iran, unless congress declares war or passes a new resolution allowing the use of military force.

Trump could not throw an egotistical temper tantrum like he has always done.

CONSTITUTIONAL INVERSION (BY TRUMP)

Time Kaine's bipartisan measure is a reminder of the crucial division of powers in launching military action as stated in the constitution. The constitution, although ambiguous in some of its parts, as we have seen in several opposing arguments on the grounds for impeachment or the separation of powers, is not ambiguous in how war is to be started. The constitution makes it very clear that Congress is unequivocally given the power to declare war. President Trump's threat to veto this new war measure was an act to protect his desire for unfettered power without any regard for the protection of civilians and service members.

Trump's ability to veto this war measure, unilaterally controlling the agenda and Congress's actions, counteracts the framer's intent, creating an institutional inversion. The expanding interpretation of the "commander in chief" clause, the "first-mover advantage" within that clause, and the collective action problems of congress are all causes of the institutional inversion of powers. Trump's ability to veto this measure begs question of why did the delegates give Congress power if the president can then just invalidate it?

The resolution to limit Trump's war power authority is an assertion of Congress's power to "check" the president's power especially in times of war. This measure is not just a reminder that it is

Congress who holds the power to declare war, but a reminder that if people will be forced to put their lives in peril, such a declaration should only be made with careful debate and deliberation. The institutional and constitutional inversion of the power to declare war without consulting Congress has been used by presidents throughout time, especially in Truman's war with North Korea in his reasoning behind not needing Congress's approval. Institutional (Constitutional) inversion goes as far back as Lincoln and continued to President Trump. Therefore, does Congress hold the power to keep the president's power in check during times of war? What did the convention delegates (remember Chapter One on the rules that formed this nation) intend by giving Congress the power to declare war but not make war?

Increased Presidential control over national security with the CIA reporting directly to the Executive without oversight, Congress's collective action problems, and the president's ability to act unilaterally, indicate that vital powers have been increasingly inverted into the hands of the "Commander in Chief". This is the "New Normal" no matter how hard Tim Kaine or past Members of Congress have tried to thwart this constitutional inversion of powers, that goes against the very intention of the framers, and can lead to dangerous consequences. Especially if in the hands of a president like Donald Trump.

COVID UNDER TRUMP

The horrifically tragic coronavirus pandemic certainly looked and felt like a war, only against an invisible enemy this time, with an uncertain battle toward victory. President Trump, without surprising many, had already declared himself a wartime president. (Yay, America. Nope. Not a yay.) The COVID Pandemic became an indelible war not only with unimaginable casualties and unimaginable tragedies but with declarations of emergency culminating with the calling up the of the National Guard. Some of the highlights of What America Endured with during COVID under Trump.

- **Defaming renowned infectious diseases expert Anthony Fauci which led to legitimate threats on his life.**
- **Telling the American people, they can inject cleaners or bleach into their bloodstream to thwart infection.**
- **Weaponizing science and discouraging mask wearing to stop the spread of deadly germs.**

The Coronavirus crisis, and every single frightened American desperately needed a leader to pay attention to facts and science, and to establish unity with sound behavior.
Unfortunately, none of those are Trump's strong points.

Trump proved grossly ill-equipped and divisive in an unprecedented time of tragedy when America was critically in need of soundness and unity from its highest leader. During the height of the pandemic, constitutional inversion was especially evident under Trump with Congress willing to surrender their constitutional powers over to the president. Congress urged him to declare a national emergency, yet he seemed unable to use it nor willing (at first) to implement this inversion of power being urgently handed over to him by a desperate Congress, who understood the gravity of the pandemic upon the American people. This new war that we were thrust into against Coronavirus is of course not the typical example of using "the power to declare war" we are used to discussing and seeing, but it is a war power in the hands of President Trump just the same. Once the Constitution is inverted and the president can declare war without waiting for Congress (even if on a pandemic and critically necessary) these war powers are very difficult to contain. Once used, this constitutional inversion is impossible to turn back, and with President Trump that could linger with unforeseen consequences.

Could this new power inversion highlight the constitutional danger of treating a crisis like a war, by allowing Trump or any president to have this sense of unfettered power that will likely last after the immediate crisis has passed? If Congress was worried about this possibility, why were they so willing to hand over this power to Trump? Is it so someone, anyone, would be forced to lead us in an urgent crisis, no matter the leader's ineptitude?

Holy Hell, the guy said we could inject bleach to kill the virus.

Can you imagine if Obama did that?

CAN YOU IMAGINE IF OBAMA DID THAT?

If you read nothing else in this book, please read the next Six Pages.

- Trump imitated a disabled reporter.
- Trump slept with a Porn Star while married, then used campaign finances donated by his undying supporters to keep her quiet.
- Trump openly boasted about grabbing women "by the pussy" and bragged about not waiting for consent to grab and kiss them.
- Trump praised Putin on many occasions. Many.
- Trump defrauded numerous investors in just about every single one of his companies, leaving many people bankrupt.
- Trump refuses to release his tax records (for obvious reasons). Trump has filed for bankruptcy SIX TIMES.

- Trump has been accused of rape and sexual assault by at least EIGHTEEN WOMEN.
- Trump subverted our national election: Throughout the 2020 campaign, Trump spread provably false disinformation about the voting process, then spread false claims- on rampant voter fraud **This is because he lost the election.**
- Trump incited a violent and deadly insurrection on our Capitol based on those false voter fraud and election claims.
- Trump told his chief of staff they were not leaving the Whitehouse and numerous witnesses recall Trump's belligerence when he lost.
- Trump reshaped the Supreme Court with a religious zealot and staunch conservative (who the majority of the public didn't want.)
- Those Trump appointed justices overturned and then banned women's reproductive rights and women's human rights.
- Trump appointed his own daughter and son-in-law to high level government positions giving them access to highly classified government intel and security allowances. I mean, Really?
- He took more days off and he golfed more than any other president in history. EVER IN HISTORY. He also did this at his own golf club profiting off his time there.
- Trump made extremism, hate, and disinformation in our nation the norm, and his platform.
- Trump made extremism, racism, and domestic terrorism his calling cards: championing them with fervor.
- Trump refused to Disavow former Klu Klux Klan grand wizard David Duke.

- Trump's lies endangered Americans; members of the press, poll workers, whistle blowers, everyone working at the Capitol, governors, senators, judges, and even students.
- Trump pressured Ukraine to get involved with his 2020 reelection by urging their leaders to announce a baseless investigation into Joe Biden.
- That led to one of his impeachments. He had TWO.
- Trump repeatedly threatened, fired, or bullied whistle blowers.
- Trump profited from his presidency through his numerous and numerous days off at his own Mar-a Lago Golf club—it bears stating again.
- Trump told people to inject themselves with disinfectants or bleach to stave off COVID-19.
- Trump told people that shining a UV light onto their bodies would cure them of COVID-19.

HERE IS A MORE COMPREHENSIVE ACCOUNT OF TRUMP'S ACTIONS:
CAN YOU IMAGINE IF OBAMA DID ANY OF THESE?

Before His Presidency:

1. **Business practices:**
   - Bankruptcies: Trump's businesses filed for bankruptcy six times between 1991 and 2009, including the high-profile bankruptcies of his Atlantic City casinos.
   - Trump University: Trump faced lawsuits alleging that Trump University, a real estate training program, was fraudulent and deceptive. In 2016, he settled the lawsuits for $25 million.

- Contractor disputes: Trump has been accused of not paying contractors and workers for services rendered on his projects, leading to numerous lawsuits and claims.

2. **Personal behavior: Including Rape**
   - Multiple marriages and infidelity: Trump has been married three times and has faced allegations of infidelity during his marriages.
   - He has been accused of RAPE by 18 women.
   - Access Hollywood tape: In a leaked 2005 recording, Trump was heard making lewd and sexually aggressive comments about women, including bragging about groping and kissing them without consent.

3. **Birtherism:**
   - Trump was the most prominent promoter of the "birther" conspiracy theory, falsely claiming that Barack Obama was not born in the United States and thus ineligible to be president— because Obama is black.

4. **Discrimination lawsuits:**
   - Trump and his businesses have been sued multiple times for discrimination against minorities in housing and employment, including a 1973 lawsuit by the Justice Department alleging racial discrimination in Trump-owned rental properties.
   - The 1973 lawsuit: Donald was sued by the Justice Department for racial discrimination because he would not rent apartments in one of his developments to African Americans, and he made sure that the people who worked for him understood that was the policy. His policy.

5. **Trump Foundation:**
   - The Trump Foundation faced allegations of self-dealing, mis-use of funds, and other improprieties. In 2019, Trump agreed to dissolve the foundation and distribute its remaining assets under court supervision as part of a settlement with the New York Attorney General's office.
   - He bankrupted architects and people he hired for extended periods, but never paid them.

During His Presidency:

1. **Immigration policies:**
   - Zero tolerance policy: Trump's administration implemented a "zero tolerance" policy in 2018, resulting in the separation of thousands of migrant children from their parents at the U.S.-Mexico border. Children were held in detention facilities, leading to widespread condemnation.

2. **Muslim ban:**
   - Trump issued executive orders in 2017 restricting travel from several predominantly Muslim countries, citing national security concerns. Critics argued that the orders were discriminatory and unconstitutional.

3. **Charlottesville response:**
   - After violence erupted at a white supremacist rally in Charlottesville, Virginia, in 2017, resulting in the death of a counter-protester, Trump faced criticism for his response. He initially blamed "both sides" for the violence and equated white supremacists with counter-protesters, drawing condemnation from across the political spectrum.

4. Ukraine scandal:

- Trump was impeached by the House of Representatives in 2019 on charges of abuse of power and obstruction of Congress related to his efforts to pressure Ukraine to investigate his political rival, Joe Biden, and his son Hunter Biden. A whistleblower complaint alleged that Trump withheld military aid to Ukraine as leverage for his personal political gain.

5. Handling of COVID-19 pandemic:

- Throughout the COVID-19 pandemic, Trump downplayed the severity of the virus, contradicted public health experts, promoted unproven treatments, and politicized mask-wearing and other preventive measures. His administration faced criticism for its slow and inadequate response to the pandemic, which resulted in widespread infections and deaths in the United States.

OBAMA WORE A TAN SUIT.

CHAPTER FOUR

Money Rules All

NRA money gifted to individuals in the legislature or paid toward the elections of those who would block sound Gun Control is over twenty-seven million:
$27,413,008.

"When buying and selling are controlled by legislation, the first thing to be bought and sold are the legislators."

-- P.J. O'Rourke

"It's not red or blue, it's green."

-- Rupert Murdoch
In his deposition, this was Murdoch's answer for why his Fox News hosts kept reporting the false stolen election claims and the motives behind such dangerous false news reporting.

GUN CONTROL AND THE NRA

The NRA is worth over Two Hundred and Ten Million Dollars. The NRA and Policymakers in Washington are all getting rich, so what's the big deal? Who is getting killed?

Our Children.

The 2nd Amendment sprung out of a need (before the civil war) when unorganized militias were abandoned, and the government failed to provide citizens arms with which to defend themselves. However, in modern American life, the 2nd Amendment is rendered irrelevant. We now have a national guard, military, police, and tactical forces at the ready when called. Why does anyone really need a gun? Even more perplexing: Why on earth would anyone need to own a rapid-fire mass killing machine? Why does anyone need to own a machine used to kill as many people as possible as quickly as possible? Did I miss something? Are zombies coming?

George W. Bush should be called out every time we have a mass shooting.

On September 13, 2004, George W. Bush opened a window into hell when he allowed the ban on assault rifles to expire despite openly supporting the ban himself—a Ban that Bill Clinton had established in 1994.

On September 13th, 2004, America became the most dangerous first world nation in which to reside. On that day, George W. Bush gave U.S. citizens the right to legally own Assault Rifles; shooting weapons that kill dozens and dozens of people in mere seconds. Handing over this mass murdering power to every American citizen defies all reason and logic, so follow the Money.

In a secret Deal in 2003, George W. Bush chose money and his powerful friends in the gun lobby over tiny first graders in schools, high school students, college students, people shopping in stores, people praying in synagogues, people worshipping in churches, families enjoying a festival, people attending concerts... you get it. Money won, and people are dying. **Our kids are being killed.** Bush chose his powerful friends and their money over every citizen and child in America that he promised to protect. This speaks to the power of money in politics and the absence of regulation on that money.

A Horrifying Fact:
Only three countries in the world give their people the right to privately and personally own guns: Mexico, and Guatemala, and you guessed it, The United States of America.

When our founding fathers were thinking up how the U.S. of A. would operate, this issue of money influencing our politicians was a concern. The power of money to influence policies and law makers is a no brainer. Connecting the bureaucracy and the special interest committees who are not only run by partisan rivalries but deep pockets, is a startling affront to the term "for the people by the people". **Dollars directly translate into policies**. The concerns of the citizens who rely on those committees and their elected officials to act in their interests are really at the mercy of money. At the root of the connection between the Presidency and Party to the agencies who act on behalf of Interest Groups, is much more powerful than just party rivalries and ideologies—

It's Money, and Lots of it.

INTEREST GROUPS, LOBBYISTS & SUPER PACS
(The Haves and Have Nots)

Interest groups play an integral role in politics as they both promote and hinder the democratic process. What groups hinder and what groups promote our democracy depends upon the type of group. Interest groups can manipulate the system, but they also represent an essential part of our democracy and American politics. The power of an interest group to petition the government depends upon several factors. The interest groups more influential in American politics have an upper-class bias. This is because well educated, and higher income individuals have more time and money along with the skills needed to be a part of an interest group. As a result, the majority of interest groups already serve the haves, and not the have nots. Interest groups mean private money in politics, and hindering the democratic process comes into play.

The chart on the next two pages was taken from Open Secrets a nonprofit organization that tracks data on campaign finance and lobbying.

**This chart displays the senators who have benefitted
the most from the NRA's political spending during
their entire political careers.**

**The dollar amounts listed per senator include direct donations,
independent expenditures, and other patronages
gifted toward them by the NRA.**

Senator	NRA Spending	Gun Deaths in State (per year)
Mitt Romney (UT)	$13,647,676	400
Richard Burr (NC)	$6,987,380	1,470
Roy Blunt (MO)	$4,555,722	1,288
Thom Tillis (NC)	$4,429,333*	1,470
Marco Rubio (FL)	$3,303,355	2,449
Joni Ernst (IA)	$3,129,723*	302
Rob Portman (OH)	$3,063,327	1,602
Todd C. Young (IN)	$2,897,582	1,021
Bill Cassidy (LA)	$2,870,574*	1,036
Tom Cotton (AR)	$1,971,214*	596
Pat Toomey (PA)	$1,475,448	1,628
Josh Hawley (MO)	$1,391,548	1,288
Marsha Blackburn (TN)	$1,306,130*	1,273
Mitch McConnell (KY)	$1,283,515*	770
Ronald Harold Johnson (WI)	$1,269,486*	641
Mike Braun (IN)	$1,249,967	1,021
John Thune (SD)	$638,942	112
Shelley Moore Capito (WV)	$346,688*	330
Richard Shelby (AL)	$258,514	1,090
Chuck Grassley (IA)	$226,007	302
John Neely Kennedy (LA)	$215,788	1,036
Ted Cruz (TX)	$176,274	3,647
Lisa Murkowski (AK)	$146,262	173
Steve Daines (MT)	$133,611*	214
Johnny Isakson (GA)	$131,571	1,693
Cindy Hyde-Smith (MS)	$112,047*	686
Roger Wicker (MS)	$106,680	686
Rand Paul (KY)	$104,456	770
Mike Rounds (SD)	$100,549*	112

Senator	NRA Spending	Gun Deaths in State (per year)
John Boozman (AR)	$82,352	596
John Cornyn (TX)	$78,945	3,647
Ben Sasse (NE)	$73,573*	183
Jim Inhofe (OK)	$74,708*	735
Lindsey Graham (SC)	$66,420*	964
Mike Crapo (ID)	$55,039	278
Jerry Moran (KS)	$34,718	434
John Barrasso (WY)	$26,989	125
John Hoeven (ND)	$23,050*	238
Jim Risch (ID)	$22,013*	278
Susan Collins (ME)	$19,850*	154
Deb Fischer (NE)	$19,638	183
James Lankford (OK)	$18,955	735
Tim Scott (SC)	$18,513	964
Kevin Cramer (ND)	$13,255	238
Bill Hagerty (TN)	$10,550	1,273
Roger Marshall (KS)	$5,950	434
Tommy Tubberville (AL)	$4,950	1,090
Cynthia Lummis (WY)	$2,500	125

Super PACS, (Political Action Committees), representing conglomerates and corporations with only their best interests in mind, (not the public's nor the people's), contribute the most money than any other type of interest group to influence campaigns. Super PACs destroy the process of fair, by the people, representing everyone equally, policies and elections.

Should large donations not be subjected to formal ethical scrutiny, in a non-partisan panel of forensic investigators that can trace hidden and funneled money?

THE SPECIAL INTEREST COALITION

A special interest group's power is not simply through public polling on the interest, but how much money they have. This is where members of Congress and candidates at every level, including presidential ones, can be swayed by millions contributed to their campaigns or to a cause backed by the special interest group that supports the candidate. This is literally the polar opposite of a democracy and of how elections and policies should be formed in a democracy. With more money from interest groups entering politics also comes more power to manipulate not just elections and policies but the political issues altogether. The well-organized special interests have the power and the funds to manipulate the context of politics themselves. This is known as The Special Interest Coalition, a Washington establishment. Just consider the inability of our Congress to enact sound and humane gun control.

This hindering of our democracy should be the loudest rallying cry for every American. We must eliminate lobbyists who promote special interests in Washington. We must get dirty money out of the hands of policymakers.

SCOTT PRUITT AS HEAD OF THE EPA

Pruitt was one of Trump's most egregious appointments if you don't include Jared Kushner. Party above all controls the interests of the people, but money enables what interests get attention. The massive amount of hidden money behind lobbyists and interest groups is a mighty and overpowering force in our policy-making process. Just reflect on the lack of gun control or gun regulation in our country. Secret donations backing a candidate or piece of legislation or to push the ideology behind an entire party, funneled toward enacting a veto or to block a new statute, holds such tremendous power in our policy-making system that "working for the people" is mute. A shining and very unfunny example of this was seen with Scott Pruitt, Donald Trump's appointee as the Administrator to the Environmental Protection Agency.

Scott Pruitt's duration as head of the EPA raises the crucial question of interest groups and political partisan groups using secret donations to sway political agendas without disclosure to ethics committees themselves.

Scott Pruitt resigned a year into his new appointment as head of the EPA (Appointed by Trump) while under more than FOURTEEN federal investigations by the Government Accountability Office and the EPA inspector General to name just two.

In addition to the over fourteen investigations of financial misconduct into Pruitt, Pruitt was lobbied by a Nonprofit "Pro-Pruitt" group called "Protecting America Now" who secretly accepted and then funneled money from a big oil company in Texas. In return, Pruitt successfully halted methane regulations and de-regulated big oil.

In Pruitt's case, the money came from a big oil interest group and was funnelled through a Nonprofit lobbying for Pruitt who then controlled legislation on the issue. Protecting America Now's ability to lobby for Pruitt after raising money from the same pro-oil companies he is supposed to regulate is…well… you get it by now. Trump picking Pruitt (an anti-Obama climate denier) to head the EPA, then Pruitt doing his party's bidding regarding policy (supporting the Trump base and Trump's Republican loyalists in Congress), is a prime example of the powerful money behind agendas—with the interest groups behind the EPA suffering the most, Oh and all of us here on earth.

Does money control policy change? Yes.

DEMOCRACY AT ITS BEST

It's not all negative though when it comes to public interest groups. Public interest groups (much more than private) illuminate and hold politicians accountable to issues that need attention and change, such as the environment, equal rights, and gun control. The best part and the necessary element of interest groups, whether you agree with their cause or not, is an essential part of our democracy. Interest groups are the most effective way for citizens and large groups to advocate for policies they desire. This is democracy at its best. The difference in public interest groups, however, is they work for the good of the whole society, not just one part of it. This is how they promote our democracy.

The power and ability of an interest group to see their interests reflected in government doesn't just depend upon money. It relies on the effectiveness of their leader, the support given by high-level officials as well as the level of popular support for their movement. The civil rights movement is an excellent example of how strong leadership and organization along with popular support can make a public interest group incredibly powerful and effective in Washington.

FOX NEWS PULLS OFF THE BIGGEST CON FOR MONEY

"Disinformation: False information deliberately spread to deceive people." (Wikipedia)

The American Con continues to flourish with gusto because few Americans have a deep political knowledge, nor the desire to think critically about what they hear. Public opinions and voting decisions are not always grounded in facts, truth, or let's be real basic knowledge. This low level of information and the dissemination of blatant disinformation (FOX NEWS) continually leads to danger-ously misplaced self-interests in millions and millions of people. Even more disheartening to our democracy is that because of the dis-semination of disinformation not just on FOX touted as fact and news, but also on every Social Media platform, millions of voters in every election (local and federal) vote directly against their self-interests.

Rampant disinformation campaigns and the conning of so many Americans is perhaps the biggest threat right now to our Democracy and it's homegrown, right here in the USA.

The Greatest American Con Was Made in the USA by FOX NEWS for MONEY.

Rupert Murdoch acknowledged that Fox News hosts endorsed false stolen election claims. In his deposition, in response to a question about the motives behind such dangerous false news reporting, Mur-doch replied:

"It's not red or blue, it's green."

FOX NEWS IS A CANCER IN OUR DEMOCRACY

The media and the bandwagon effect are a mighty force in our democracy, now more than any other time in history. If the idea, theory, or ideology is dangerous and reckless and spreads through a bandwagon effect, it acts like a cancer. One crazy angry cancer cell or idea slowly infects millions of others who hop on the bandwagon, and suddenly the whole group is sick. How Fox News knowingly dispels disinformation and lies for higher ratings, thus massive profits, is a cancer in our democracy and a blight upon the meaning of free speech. Fox News' agenda setting effect cues people to feel and think a certain way about the issues, and has admitted that when do this, they know they are feeding their audience false and dangerous information. Scarily, Fox News is how millions of people obtain their opinions. The bandwagon effect is a phenomenon whereby the rate of adoption of beliefs and ideas increases the more those ideas and beliefs have already been adopted and promoted by others, even if they are wholly unfounded and dangerous.

In other words, the bandwagon effect is characterized by the increased probability of an individual adopting an idea or agenda when more people have already done so. Basically, as more people come to believe in something, after watching Fox News say it's true, others also "hop on the bandwagon" regardless of the underlying evidence it's a very bad idea. Fox News does this very effectively regardless of a blatant disregard for truth and integrity. Fox News and their fraudulent, constant promotion of admitted false voter fraud claims, and dangerous false reporting of stolen election claims, motivated mobs of people to hop on the bandwagon and storm our capitol.

Oh America, really?
You must be smarter than this.

CHAPTER FIVE

Political Ideologies That Shape Us

In researching the political ideologies behind why people vote the way they do, I concluded that political ideologies, even if starkly different from one other, are all connected, just like a dysfunctional codependent, opioid-addicted, alcoholic, church going family.

I also concluded that political ideologies are just ideologies but with a lot more yelling.

ARE WE REALLY THAT DIFFERENT FROM ONE ANOTHER?

Let's all hate each other because that seems to make Americans feel alive and well.

Ideology is the imaginary relationship people have with their real-life conditions. Every political ideology, even if starkly different from one other, are all connected, just like a dysfunctional codependent, opioid-addicted, alcoholic, church going family. Understanding the ideologies of the opposing party or counter viewpoint might help build a bridge to unity, therefore progress. People on every side of politics question why those who don't think or vote like them seem hell-bent on the demise of their beloved America.

The other side is always the worst part of America and fervent divides feed more fervent divides. What fuels these impassioned divisions and ideologies which have created a brewing civil war of rage about who is right and who is wrong?

Yelling the loudest is an enticing drug to Americans but can only happen when people vehemently disagree. Ideologies aim to morph political concepts into easily discernible patterns based on beliefs and a vision of what the future should be. In return, political concepts and ideas are morphed and shaped by the very ideologies used to define them. Political ideologies are the existence, and sometimes the difference, between what "is" and what "ought" to be. Ideologies, especially political ones, are not necessarily the exploration of truth, they are society's varied perceptions of how the world should be. One political concept can have a multitude of ideologies all with different meanings, even though they stem from an identical political concept. In other words, there can be many political viewpoints, all with different meanings and intentions, with many variables, stemming from one single political concept. Ideologies are consequently the systems of thought in which specific meaning is conferred upon every political concept in their domain. Without contrasting ideologies how would we define our own? Then we can yell at each other about it!

CONSERVATISM, LIBERALISM, SOCIALISM

Liberalism, Conservatism and Socialism developed in response to historical circumstances, and sometimes in response to those circumstances that those very ideologies brought about. The relationship between politics, policy and ideologies is cyclical and a never-ending give and take. Conservatism, liberalism, and socialism intersect in their core concepts as well as their contested concepts. Each of those ideologies is a means to achieve an ideal society. If only we all understood that intention before becoming so angry at each other.

Liberalism values equal economic opportunities and respect for every human no matter socio-economic placement. Liberalism's priority is the individual's freedom to fully realize his or her potential through unfettered liberty. (But don't the other ideologies promote this exact idea too?) Yes, and I'll get to that, and well done. You clearly see where I am going with the topic of political ideologies. For now, let's dive into liberalism as individualism. Liberalism is thought of as the antithesis of socialism, which focuses on the collective whole, not the individual. Socialism's priority and its proportionately dominant theme advocate that the means of production, opportunity, and distribution of labor should be owned and controlled by the community as a whole. Socialism advocates for a classless society, and liberalism is what creates the classes in society. It is this proximity to one another, that also help define them more clearly.

Is the consequence of class divides a driving force behind socialism's priority of a society working for the common good collectively as one class? Is it in these contested concepts where liberalism and socialism intersect and shape each other? Absolutely. Socialism has helped reign in liberalism by illuminating the importance of allowing equal opportunities to the individual who is part of the greater collective. Socialism's and Liberalism's concepts of what make an ideal society may be different in their details, but at their core, these ideologies contain the same goal—a better society for everyone, equally.

Conservatism's priority is the status quo, and its proportionately dominant theme is that human beings, although imperfect, should be personally responsible with limited authority to regulate them. Isn't this like liberalism's priority of individual freedoms and unfettered liberty? No. It isn't. Unlike liberalism that promotes progress and change, conservatism primarily opposes change and innovation. Conservatism represents the antithesis of rationalist (liberalism), or utopian (socialism), ideologies. The political concepts of each of these ideologies in relation to one another, as well as their relationship with societies that live by them, help to clarify each one. Without understanding Conservatism's, Liberalism's, and Socialism's differences to one another, the understanding of each of these ideologies would be simplistic. The overly simplistic understanding of these ideologies helps feed the divides in our nation.

Understanding why certain people vote along these ideologies might help lessen the divides.

Exploring the relationship between their contested concepts of an ideal society is where the permeability of each of these political ideologies is evident. Liberalism, socialism, and conservatism all intersect at various points. Liberalism and socialism intersect in the value of socialism's influence on shaping liberalism into something that values the greater good while protecting each individual's ability to thrive. This might seem surprising, but conservatism intersects with both socialism and liberalism. Conservatism's concepts are the antithesis as well as pieces of both liberalism and socialism. Conservatives focus on both a common authority and individual freedoms in a free market—all with the idea of the whole being greater than the sum of its parts. More importantly, each of these ideologies are all permeable, as they shift and change throughout history to meet the needs of societies in modern times.

SOCIALISM HELPS DEFINE MODERN LIBERALISM
(No, Liberals are not Socialists)

The social programs of modern liberalism are a result of socialism's influence on liberalism, thus helping to redefine liberalism. Socialism has helped redefine how liberalism understands freedom. This is especially true for modern liberalism. Socialism's basic critique of liberalism also helped define liberalism. Socialism's critique is that while masquerading as freedom for all, liberalism creates a further divide of power and classes. Socialism argues that the competitiveness of liberalism creates oppression of the workforce, whereas the workers cannot actually enjoy the products for which they labor due to the oppressive economic divisions. Liberalism evolved into modern liberalism as it sought to alleviate these divides by creating social programs we know today.

"Liberals" describe the modern world as a world with a common purpose to promote opportunity, empowerment, and security for all people, especially those on the peripheries of economies and societies.

I am, and always will be a liberal.

The ability to thrive according to socialism cannot be found in liberalism as it is unstable in the competition it creates among a society. Socialism views liberalism, as not empowering a society but limiting it. It is socialism's critique of liberalism that gives rise to the contradictions within liberalism, thus defining what we know as modern liberalism: How can a society thrive if not everyone is thriving?

This critique has helped liberalism understand true freedom. Socialism argues that true liberty as a human being requires freedom from struggle which socialism allows, and liberalism creates.

Socialism represents a utopia of communal life, based on mutual responsibility and shared equality. Socialism criticizes liberalism as the destruction of community efforts that give peoples' lives a deeper meaning and that the principles of liberalism lead to isolation and oppression.

Socialism and liberalism are on opposing economic sides, despite what conservatives say.

The individual goals of liberalism that create an economic market based on enterprise and competition goes against Socialism's goal of shared economic prosperity. This is how socialism has shaped liberalism in our current economic market. Liberalism's freedom of the individual gives rise to the competition that socialism critiques as hindering equality. Socialists argue that liberalism encourages abuse of power and perpetuates deep class divides. Socialism's critique of liberalism, and the reality of how they mold together is not just theoretical though. The value of the collective in socialism has shaped our modern workforce in the creation of labor unions and labor laws. Socialism's criticisms of liberalism also influence current political debates about healthcare for all, tuition-free college, and a successful public education system in every city regardless of tax rate and economic status.

Would a deeper blending of the two ideologies be possible? If so, would there be less poverty, less stark class divides, and maybe a more secure playing field for individuals to have the freedom thrive?

Is Modern Liberalism hand in hand with Democratic Socialism? Democratic Socialism is what allows individuals to thrive without the threat of competition or immoral acts against their ability to thrive. In turn, does socialism stifle the ability of individuals to thrive by stripping away the competitiveness and freedoms of each person that modern liberalism provides? Can there be a balance between the two that would create an ideal flourishing society?

Are You an Owen Or A Simon?

In looking at how the different socialist thinkers regarded capitalism in regard to socialism and liberalism, it is interesting to compare two stand outs as differing from each other. Robert Owen and Henri Saint-Simon had notions of capitalism in relation to socialism, that highlight thought-provoking notions of capitalism; where it works and where it fails the people. When the Industrial Revolution happened, and capitalism emerged as a key component of liberalism, socialists met it with stark criticism. Robert Owen, a utopian socialist, regarded capitalism as promoting a destructive lack of social responsibility and destructive forms of competitiveness. Owen regarded capitalism or the industrial revolution as an open playing field for immoral practices causing abuse; therefore, the decline of communal efforts and equality. Owen cited the abuse of labor forces in the modern factory system as a result of capitalism, **(Look at the Auto Workers' Strike of 2023)**.

Owen furthermore regarded capitalism as promoting a "destructive lack of social responsibility and destructive forms of competitiveness" (176). Robert Owen also believed that capitalism or the manufacturing system did not promote the well-being and welfare of all classes of society. Robert Owen aimed to create a perfect society in which poverty and unemployment were eliminated. The two social experiments that Owens attempted were at the New Lanark Mill in Scotland and in New Harmony, Indiana. Owen saw these as the ideal melding together of profit and social cooperation, enabling strong social harmony. This, in Owen's view, was the antithesis of capitalism and its perils.

Henri Saint-Simon had a different view of how he regarded capitalism, although he sought the same outcome of a flourishing and prosperous society. Saint-Simon regarded the industrial class as the most relevant to the success of a society, and that this working class of people must be fulfilled and satisfied for an economy to flourish. Henri, however, believed that this labor force was not just the manual laborers, but that scientists, bankers, business managers, and inventors, were all part of the working class and should be thought of as equally important to the success of the industrialized world. Unlike others, this is, in a sense, a socialist view of a labor force. Saint-Simon's ideas, however, of how people in the workforce should be individually regarded based on individual merit is more like capitalism.

The aspect of Saint-Simon's view of capitalism differs from Owen's in that Saint-Simon believed the goal of a society, through a hierarchy of the workforce created by individual merit, would be to produce inventions and products that were useful and needed. This, in turn, promotes competitiveness to produce those goods that are more useful to life over other goods. It is this competitiveness in Saint Simon's views that are aligned with the creation of capitalism. Saint-Simon highly regarded scientists for this purpose, and in turn, felt that religion was not to be respected nor regarded in the industrialized world as having a purpose in our economy.

More importantly, and also in contrast to Owen's view of capitalism, Saint-Simon emphasized the need in a thriving economy for individuals to be recognized based on achievement, thus creating a hierarchy needed in a prosperous economy. In other words, an individual must earn, or will earn his own success based on his work, promoting a thriving economy bringing about progress. This idea of "individual" is in contrast to the core constructs at the heart of socialism and is much more naturally aligned with capitalism. Saint-Simon viewed capitalism as not being the antithesis of socialism, but rather that the state should be directed by modern science, a high achieving workforce at all levels for the creation of useful goods, thus establishing a hierarchy of workers. The ideal productive society would be organized by the most capable and most hard-working people and there must be a hierarchal system in an industrialized world for it to be productive.

Owen's and Saint-Simon's views significantly helped shape our society, our modern capitalistic society, and our economic structure. Saint-Simon's views and theories are most influential in what we see today as modern capitalism. Owen's views, however, are in fact what helps keep that very capitalism in check. Owen's view of human equality, labor abuses, and the need for the most underprivileged of the workforce to be regarded fully, otherwise capitalism will falter and self-destruct. Saint-Simon's views on the productivity of the workforce encouraged by recognition of individual successes dramatically contribute to the productivity and progress that is the positive side of capitalism, needed for a prosperous economy.

SHOULD CAPITALISM LEAN INTO SOCIALISM?

When the people thrive, capitalism flourishes from the hopeful, ambitious, and productive society behind it. A more socialistic approach to certain institutions would be beneficial to those who are abused by the enterprises of corporations, greed, or the abuse of capitalism that circumvents our democracy. Today, there is an aspect of socialism taking on strength in our healthcare system and our educational institutes. Hopefully, this consideration of equality and the ability to equally thrive will influence the top tier of people in our economy.

When the people thrive, capitalism thrives. When capitalism thrives, everyone wins; The rich stay richer, and people are employed. Don't you think each of us and our society possess bits of both Robert Owen and Henri Saint-Simon in our political ideologies, in what we fight for, and in how we vote? We all share a common intention and goal no matter the ideology that drives us.

Individualism is a key concept within liberalism, but I am not sure that it is the most prominent. I believe the liberal concept of individual freedom transgresses the border of ideas on stark individualism. Individualism is a key concept and must be incorporated in the social contract to restrain each individual from hampering the individual freedoms of another while still being able to enact their own. (yes, that was a bit of a run on but stay with me).

Under pre-liberal beliefs, before the idea of social welfare and motivations of communal benefit moved into the ideology of liberalism; it was as if individualism remained prominent but without being a priority relative to social progress.

Thus, I believe that social progress is a more prominent concept than individualism in liberalism. Social progress is something that results from and also ensures that individuals can meet their basic needs while enjoying their own freedom. This means that individualism is a necessary element of liberalism, of course, yet liberalism reaches further and envisions society as more than a tool used simply for satisfying our own needs.

I like to express liberalism in a way that also describes its vision of an ideal society: Where equal economic and gender opportunities and reverence for diverse cultures, races, religious faiths, and every human no matter socio-economic placement exists in all nations across our world.

Liberalism is the dominant ideology in the industrialized world, but it isn't always understood and followed, and the "right" deem liberals the enemy. Liberalism centers around social progress, growth, individual freedom, and equality. Liberalism is defined as allowing people to think and believe what they choose with the freedom to express those beliefs through speech, writings, and other means of exercising freedom of conscience. Liberalism describes the world as not having a natural hierarchy, and that people are entitled to equal opportunities in their pursuit of happiness and the freedoms with which to do so. I view liberalism as describing the world as one with a common purpose to promote individual opportunity, equal empowerment, and security for all people including those on the peripheries of global economies and societies.

In 2024, with such hateful political feuds, unfettered greed, zealous racism, dumbfounding ignorance, corruption, war, and abject poverty at an all-time global high, this ideal society seems very far out of reach.

CONSERVATISM

Some argue that conservatism is not an ideology because it is hard to define it in specific terms, or that conservatism is vague in what it represents. This stems from the belief that conservatism is simply being satisfied with the status quo, being afraid of change, and above all to preserve the existing political institutions and traditions. This simplified idea of conservatism is exemplary in how the ideology shifts and changes throughout history. Rooted in the 18th-century enlightenment and intellectual movement, conservatism is an ideology that has shifted and changed over time as an expression of society in relation to its institutions.

An ideology serves three main functions: To describe the world, to present a vision of the ideal society, and offer theories of change in how to achieve that ideal society. Ideologies also offer value to actions and explain why we as a society should prefer certain political institutions over others. Conservatism certainly offers all three of these functions and especially offers a vision of its ideal society. This is most evident today in the role that conservative ideology plays in politics and in society. Conservatism as an ideology is sometimes simplified into a "Fear of Progress." This can certainly be true at times and is often the case in today's world. Conservatism holds value to the idea that progressive ideals can be radical and threaten the status quo negatively.

It is this fear-based mantra that permeates the conservative ideology as it exists today; authority and order are established from fear. That Sounds a Little "Trumpian" Right?

Conservatism is an ideology rooted in using history as a tool to help the present. Conservatism uses history as an example of how past actions continually evolve and shape a society. When the people have been driven by fear and pride in our nation's history, (according to conservatives) they help shape our solutions to society's problems, solving conflict and keeping order. Under the simple assertion that conservatism as an ideology is rooted in the objection to change, then this idea of conservatism is that it is the ideology of the dominant group of people who benefit from the current political powers. This would mean that liberals can also be "conservatives" in theory, if they are the group most benefitting the existing political order, but let's not get philosophical.

This leads to the idea that conservatism as an ideology might not be committed to anything in particular, or any specific views socially, because it simply represents the suspicion of change and progress; encouraging that order is always established through fear. Conservatism is an ideology of protectionism and the status quo, and highlights how societies can greatly diverge in political values.

Conservatism is an ideology that aims to create a society that it deems ideal by rejecting other ideologies that represent change or progress.

Should the government help needy American's even if it means possibly going into deeper debt? Liberals would say yes, and conservatives would say no. Socialists believe that the government should control all, so there is no "needy" population. Liberals believe in larger government. Liberals believe it is the duty of the government to alleviate social ills and to protect individual human rights. President Roosevelt's New Deal is an example of liberals arguing for more government intervention in order to secure liberty and fairness for every citizen. Conservatives believe in limited government. Conservatives emphasize empowerment of the individual to solve problems with limited government intervention. Conservatives believe the government should only provide people the freedom necessary to pursue their own goals.

What about Universal Healthcare? The conservative ideology is to be limited in its involvement in securing social programs for individual human rights. **Healthcare should not be a privilege based on class or wealth; it is a basic human right.** This is where conservatives and liberals diverge, with socialism influencing our democracy for the better. The founding fathers wrote that every individual has the right to life, liberty and the pursuit of happiness. Socialists believe in an all-encompassing government responsible for taking care of its citizens including providing medical care, necessities, and equal wages. Socialists argue that full government control is necessary for a society to thrive and believe in turning all power over to the state. In a sense, there is less freedom under socialism, but you know you'll most likely be able to put food on the table for your family.

Do you believe in a completely classless society? Liberals and conservatives would answer no. Liberals and conservatives believe in the freedom and hierarchy of society based on individual liberties to achieve and succeed. Socialists would say yes to this question. Socialism aims to eliminate class distinctions through the even distribution of production and income. Do you believe in private property? Liberals say yes. <u>Conservatives say yes without much regulation (as we saw in the early 2000s—remember the three million foreclosures I mentioned in Chapter One?)</u> Socialists say no. The absence of private property characterizes socialism. This is akin to socialists seeing the group as the primary social order, not the individual.

Do you believe in the free markets and free enterprise? Socialists say no and argue that free markets create oppression of the lower classes. Liberals believe in the free markets, and the ability for every individual to attain success while advocating for the protection of the workforce in doing so. Conservatives also say yes and believe in Laissez Faire Capitalism with little government regulations. Do you believe in the status quo, or do you believe in change and innovation? This question is more aimed at liberals and conservatives than socialists. Conservatives believe in the status quo as it suits society and oppose change.

Liberals believe that the status quo can always be improved, advocating for progress and innovation if they contribute to the betterment of society.

These values are evident in the support of liberals for allocating more funds toward stem cell research, industries combating climate change, enhanced child education, and judicial activism aimed at refining the interpretation of the constitution to better serve our evolving society.

Socialism believes in change and innovation as a collective. Socialists believe that if you work there, or live there, you should have a say in how it is run. These questions are obviously simplified versions of how to define the three main political ideologies of our modern society. However, in asking questions, even ones that simplify complex political thoughts and ideals, maybe we can all see various perspectives behind the same intention.

Ideology is based on a subjective "truth" that we identify with and believe to be so while philosophy is the search for the truth, or the enlightenment of what is inherently true. There is a fundamental difference between philosophy and ideology, but often the two seem interchangeable and reliant upon each other. The fundamental difference between them is that ideology refers to a set of beliefs or doctrines that back a specific social institution, political institution or an organization, and philosophy is aimed at seeking the truth. <u>Ideology is aimed at changing the world and philosophy is aimed at understanding it.</u>

Exploring ideologies illustrates the flexibility and the "morphology" of those ideologies, whereas philosophy is the search for the truth behind those very ideologies. In a sense, both ideologies and philosophy are never ending in their evolvement. Ideology is a truth we believe to be so, when in fact these are subjective truths based on our perception of the world or political institution, whereas philosophy is simply the search for truth, not a definition of it. Ideologies help shape and change our world, and philosophy aims to understand it. So, is it then possible that ideologies begin with a philosophy? In other words, are philosophical pursuits the beginning of new ideologies?

POSITIVE AND NEGATIVE LIBERALISM

Positive and Negative liberalism are intricately woven and interdependent. Their differences exist not just in interpretations of what is positive liberalism and what is negative, but also in how they are implemented. The positive definition of the word liberty comes from the individual wishing to be his own master. Liberty is essentially defined as an individual's life and decisions depend on oneself, not on external forces of any kind. It is also in this positive liberalism, that the freedom for individuals to decide, not be decided for. Positive liberalism is one's freedom and right to conceive goals and policies on his or her own and fully realize them. Freedom to be one's own master, and the freedom in choosing as one feels, may seem like the same concepts, but the positive and negative notions of freedom can diverge in distinctly different directions.

"Negative" liberalism, which is the absence of obstacles and any restraint by law, creates anarchy, and often leads to social oppression and racism. Negative liberty's "absence of power" concept, can be used by individuals or groups to bully, oppress, and torture on behalf of and in the name of their 'real selves'. This abuse of freedom is masked as the liberty-to be one's own master and do what feels true to oneself. This negative liberalism, can lead to the dismantling of the overall liberalism of a society, causing deep rooted racism, oppression, and the unfettered endangerment of democracy.

Trump empowered this idea of negative liberalism that quickly becomes extremism:

The insurrection on our Capitol on January 6th, 2021, is a prime example of negative liberalism becoming extremism and how Fox News, hate, ignorance and our educational systems' decades long failings threaten the very fabric of our democracy.

To truly be out for "Oneself" without any obstacles, can get dicey, and inherently will diverge from true liberty for all if and when this "negative liberalism" is abused. Furthermore, in dissecting negative liberalism, I find that it means that every man can do as he pleases, out for his own self- interests, with no regard to restrictions or the inherent constrictions this might place on the liberties of others. Trump exemplified this behavior. Positive liberalism is also the power and liberty to do, through certain capacities and conditions, what we please. These conditions and capacities, however, do not represent restrictions on the individual freedom's inherent in liberalism. In positive liberalism, these restrictions represent the protection of that liberalism itself for all. The conditions of positive liberalism are what is necessary for people to take responsibility for their own lives, with restrictions in their power to oppress others to do so.

There is a paradox here though—if liberalism is individual freedom to do as one pleases, then does that include the freedom to express certain liberties that will also oppress others, or create racism? These conditions, in positive liberalism, is what any form of authority creates so that the people can fully live out their potential. Positive Liberalism, is liberalism without anarchy, allowing individuals to live as they choose, without being allowed to impede or oppress others.

PART TWO

LAW AND DISORDER

"Dissents speak to a future age. It's not simply to say, 'My colleagues are wrong, and I would do it this way.' But the greatest dissents do become court opinions and gradually over time their views become the dominant view. So that's the dissenter's hope: that they are writing not for today, but for tomorrow."

- Ruth Bader Ginsburg

CHAPTER SIX

What In the Actual F**K Supreme Court?

JUNE 24TH 2022
WHAT IN THE ACTUAL F**K,
SUPREME COURT?

On June 24th, 2022, I rushed to Trader Joe's in my car, with a grocery list in hand, a pit in my stomach, and a deep well of tremendous sadness. Roe v. Wade had just been overturned, leaving behind a trail of shattered historical and legal milestones. Our Supreme Court callously discarded the fundamental human rights of women and girls, relegating their dignity and equality to a dumpster. My disbelief and sadness were and still are profound.

How could the justices who sit on our highest court so callously dismantle a hard-fought and pivotal legal safeguard? A safeguard that serves as a fundamental shield against the erosion of women's rights, preventing our nation from regressing into a place where the voices of women and girls hold no sway. Our own Supreme Court shattered a vital legal and humanitarian precedent; A precedent that keeps our nation from becoming a third world country where women and girls have no rights to their own bodies and health. Overturning Roe v. Wade sends a frightening message about the value placed on the autonomy and rights of women and girls in America. It suggests that our bodily freedom and reproductive rights are completely expendable. The highest court in our nation made it clear that women's and girls' rights are not considered fundamental human rights.

In the hazy aftermath of the news, and in shock, I needed to run errands to distract myself. What I did not expect was how my visit to Trader Joe's revealed a silent camaraderie among the women navigating the aisles, each of us carrying the weight of shared shock and sorrow. Amidst this collective daze, my gaze fell upon a mother and her young daughter, and my heart fractured for her; for them both. The mom looked back at me and gave me a small smile, a heartbreaking smile, because in our unspoken connection she knew why I was looking at her daughter. My stomach hurt at the thought of the uncertainty that lay ahead for her, irrespective of her future choices regarding motherhood. The horrific truth lingered heavily—the fate of her body and life might no longer be within her own control, and The Supreme Court is the reason.

As I drove back home, I abandoned the mundane act of listening to music. I parked in the driveway, and I felt a hopelessness and sadness I don't feel often. I sat there for a moment, then finally made my way to the front door. The weight of the news permeated my every step, overshadowing the groceries I had picked up. When my husband opened the door, his understanding gaze immediately recognized the depth of my distress. No words were necessary; he simply enveloped me in his comforting embrace, gently whispering, "I am so sorry. I am so sorry." And as the tears rolled down my face, he didn't need to say anything else. His simple, "I am so sorry," spoke volumes, offering a comforting refuge.

While I don't plan on expanding my family, my husband had a vasectomy years ago, that doesn't shield me from the stark reality that the court's ruling serves as a glaring signal of societal shifts, a poignant reminder of the challenges ahead. The reverberations of the court's ruling resonated as a glaring signal, casting a shadow over the fundamental rights and agency of women in our society.

Women and girls do not count in this nation.
We simply don't, and what's worse, this was made clear
to us by the highest court in our nation.

Beyond my profound anguish and crushing sadness instigated by the Supreme Court's ruling that overturned Roe v. Wade, there have been other instances where the highest court in our nation ruled in a manner that makes one ask: What in the actual F**K Supreme Court? The Supreme Court has been a focal point for contentious and downright vexing decisions that wield direct influence over the well-being of every single American citizen. These rulings elicit a question that lingers in the minds of many: "What, precisely, in the hell, is transpiring within the esteemed chambers of the Supreme Court?"

Here are just a few of the other deeply perplexing
and distressing Supreme Court rulings.

Bush v. Gore (2000): This ruling determined the outcome of the 2000 U.S. presidential election by halting the recount of ballots in Florida, leading to concerns about the politicization of the judiciary and the integrity of the electoral process.

Citizens United v. Federal Election Commission (2010): The Court's decision in this case allowed corporations and unions to spend unlimited amounts of money on political campaigns, leading to fears of increased corporate influence in politics and the undermining of democracy.

Shelby County v. Holder (2013): The Court struck down key provisions of the Voting Rights Act of 1965, which had been crucial in preventing racial discrimination in voting practices, raising concerns about voter suppression tactics.

Hobby Lobby v. Burwell (2014): This ruling allowed corporations to deny contraceptive coverage to their employees based on religious objections. The court chose religious freedom over women's reproductive rights and access to healthcare. Wow.

Janus v. American Federation of State, County, and Municipal Employees (2018): The Court's decision in this case prohibited public-sector unions from collecting fees from non-members who benefit from collective bargaining, weakening the financial strength of unions and diminishing workers' bargaining power.

McCutcheon v. Federal Election Commission (2014): This ruling struck down limits on the total amount of money an individual could contribute to political candidates and committees. This bolstered concerns about the influence of money in politics and the potential for corruption. Remember my chapter "Money Rules All"? Well, Corporations and their endless funds rule all.

District of Columbia v. Heller (2008): This ruling affirmed an individual's right to possess firearms for self-defense within the home, striking down Washington D.C.'s handgun ban and trigger-lock requirement. It broadened the scope of the Second Amendment and made it harder for Congress to enact gun control laws.

Rapanos v. United States (2006): This case was about the interpretation of the Clean Water Act and led to a fragmented ruling that weakened federal jurisdiction over protected wetlands.

This ruling reversed protections for water quality and environmental conservation.

<u>So, what in the Actual F#@* Supreme Court?</u>

WHY DO SOME JUSTICES RULE THIS WAY?

WHAT INFLUENCES JUSTICES?
The Legal and Democratic Subcultures

On what basis and what reasons do judges in the United States rule or decide the way they do? What influences judges and their decisions? There are two influential subcultures of the decision-making environment in which Justices on the Supreme Court, trial judges, and their appellate colleagues operate. The Legal Subculture of legal tradition and the Democratic Subculture of politics. Perhaps before looking at the legal and democratic subcultures that influence judges' decisions, it is essential to understand the demographics from which judges are selected for the bench. Most federal judges in the United States come from a particular segment of the nation's middle and upper classes: the cultural and socially elite. Many are Ivy League graduates who already come from socially prominent and politically influential families, with a history of established political ideologies and party alignment.

For example, President Obama's appointees come from the most elite educational backgrounds in comparison to prior appointees, and 87.5% of them identified as fellow Democrats. Furthermore, 46% of his appointees had prior experience in partisan (liberal-aligned with Obama's ideologies) activism before their selection. President George H. W. Bush's appointees also follow the same pattern but to an even more extreme. 89.2 % of George H. W. Bush's appointees identified as fellow Republicans, and over 70% of them had past experience in Republican party activism. Judges often come from families who have a history in judicial and public service.

Almost all appointees follow the same party allegiance as their appointing official or district. The politics inside the Democratic Subculture of our American Courts is undeniable and palpable, and evidence proves these politics certainly influence how judges decide cases.

The other important factor in selecting judges, which influences their decision-making on the court, is the demographics a judge fulfills, which is often in line with the political ideology of the president making the appointment. For example, 92.3% of Ronald Reagan's appointees were Non-Latino White Males, as opposed to Obama's much less 29.2%. The number of women and racial minorities on the federal bench has always been small compared to the representation of these groups in the general population. Out of all 115 justices that have served on the Supreme court, only six have been women and only three have been black. However, what stands out the most is that presidents often make political ideology and political party affiliation the basis and guiding principle for appointing a judge.

This helps explain Brett Kavanaugh and Amy Coney Barrett who were appointees based on ultra conservative ideologies regardless of serious character flaws and high disapproval ratings among the public.

Ninety percent of federal judicial nominees are from the same political party as the president appointing them. It is as simple as understanding that if a possible appointee does not share the president's political beliefs, they need not bother to apply for an appointment to the federal bench. Judges' political alignments with the presidents who appointed them brings the Democratic Subculture in our courts and its effect on judicial decisions into focus. The political alignment of judges with the politicians who appoint them is the root of the Democratic Subculture and its effect on Judicial decision-making, but that is not the only guiding factor, nor is it the strongest, according to Robert Carp. According to Carp in POLITICS AND JUDGMENT IN FEDERAL DISTRICT COURTS (1996), the legal subculture has much more influence over decision-making in both trial and appeals courts than the democratic subculture. Carp illuminates how judicial decisions are affected by various internal and external factors, including legal, personal, ideological, and political influences.

The legal subculture consists of rules and practices that guide decision-making inside the legal profession and has withstood varying political and social shifts in our country. Within the legal subculture, judges are committed to adhering to precedent, using judicial restraint consisting of the common law, statutory law, and legal tradition. **<u>So, what happened to these values when they overturned Roe v. Wade?</u>** When there are no precedents or the judge feels the precedent lacks in any guiding stare decisis wisdom for the current, possibly more modern issue in the case, the judges turn to their democratic subculture. Judges have increasingly pulled away from rigid constraints of the legal subculture and replaced that influence with the values of the politicians that appoint them, which is more closely linked to democratic subculture.

Aligning with the politicians who appoint them is a determining and guiding force for Justices. The Justices' recent heartbreaking and maddening rulings were determined by political alignments and ideologies - Not Legal Precedent.

Sometimes, however, the judge's ruling is counter to those alignments. This is especially true in cases when the guiding principles of legal reasoning, precedent, and restraint are abstract in their application. Conflicted rulings are also seen in cases in which a legally binding precedent has established the judge's decision, or the case is of a social, political concern closely tied to the region of the court.

Evers v. Jackson Municipal Separate School District in 1964

AN EXAMPLE TO ILLUSTRATE SC SUBCULTURES

Evers v. Jackson Municipal Separate School District in 1964 highlights the effect of the Democratic Subculture vs. the Legal Subculture in influencing decisions in the American court system and how the two subcultures can sometimes aggressively collide. Instead of focusing on the case itself, what most illuminates the two subcultures at play in our court system is the presiding judge on the case, Judge Sydney Mize. Sidney Mize was a federal judge on the United States District Court for the Southern District of Mississippi. Mize was a fervent racist and an unapologetic segregationist. He represented his southern Mississippi district and the racist political ideologies that went along with it.

In 1964, several African American children and their parents sought to prohibit a district in Jackson, Mississippi from operating a segregated school system. They sought to desegregate the schools on behalf of all African American children seeking an equal education. The biracial school system violated the plaintiffs' constitutional rights under the due process clause and secured under the Fourteenth Amendment. Furthermore, the ruling ten years earlier in **Brown v. Board of Education** established that such segregation was unconstitutional and stood as a legally binding precedent for the EVERS case within the legal subculture's principles.

Without the Brown v. Board of Education precedent, would the democratic subculture have been victorious in Mississippi's Southern District fueled by racism, with a fervent racist sitting on the bench?

Despite being bound by the Brown v. The Board of Education precedent ruling such segregation to be unconstitutional, and despite being
forced to enjoin the Mississippi school district and its officials from
operating a segregated school system, Judge Mize made his contrary
ideological beliefs known. Judge Mize argued that blacks' brain capacity is not equal to whites; therefore, keeping them separate in
school is beneficial to both. Mize shockingly argued that evidence
proved the brain size and capacity of an African American to be ten
percent less than that of a Caucasian the same age. While this may be
flagrantly ignorant, it is frightening that a judge with such ideologies
is tasked with ruling on a segregation case involving young African
American children. However, the legal subculture principle of stare
decisis and precedent proved to be necessary and binding, and victorious in this case, but not without the democratic subculture making
its presence known. Judge Mize's presence in the Evers case and his
known political ideologies beg the question; had the prior ruling in
Brown not established segregation as unconstitutional, would the legal subculture still have prevailed?

The most vital takeaway from the Evers case is how our
courts' legal subculture is just as powerful and vital as the democratic
subculture. What makes this case a calling card for the democratic
and legal subcultures in our court system is how Judge Mize's political ideologies conflicted with the ruling he was bound to make
through the legal subculture's principles. Judge Mize lost to the legal
precedent set before him. What if the precedent had not yet been established? The democratic subculture so influential and present in
Evers might have been the victor.

**The influence of politics and ideologies in our courts on
how judges decide cases is unquestionable.**

In the democratic subculture of our courts, party allegiance is the most powerful influence, or at the very least, a strong indicator of how a judge might decide a case. There is most certainly strong evidence of a correlation between political party allegiance and decision-making in the courts. The high level of education required by judges creates a tendency to have strong party allegiances and judgments in terms of ideologies that align with those policy preferences. Judges have stronger perceptions of their courts' issues and their political party's position on those issues.

There is an obvious cause-and-effect relationship between judges' party affiliations and decisions.

The democratic (political) subculture, rooted in politics, not legal precedent to influence judges' decisions, suggests that Democratic judges rule more liberally than their Republican counterparts. This partisan voting pattern might be actual, but research indicates not always, as it depends on the type of case. The differences in decisions between the two parties were greatest in cases involving reverse discrimination and racism and least when ruling on cases involving governmental and union employment disputes. Democratic appointees have a clear tendency to favor liberal outcomes, and Republican appointees tend to take conservative positions on the bench. Just like Congress, the Court is more polarized along party lines and political ideologies than ever.

Localism is a critical factor in understanding the influence of the democratic subculture in judges' decisions. In trials and appeals cases, trial courts are often influenced by and undoubtedly susceptible to local democratic forces in their districts, including party affiliation, opinion polls, and influential interest groups. Understanding geographical differences helps define the differences in the legal and democratic subcultures facing each court and each judge's decisions.

Judges have close ties and connections with the state and the circuit in which their court is located. Therefore, the democratic societal forces are strong in influencing their decisions. For example, Democrats in Democratic majority held districts were more lenient with sentences of criminals and more likely to support criminals seeking a new trial. In contrast, the opposite seems to be true in Republican-held districts with more conservative ideologies. Judicial decision-making often reflects the attitudes and values of that region, and that is localism and democratic subculture at play in our courts.

Political ideologies are also reflected on the bench in high-lighting the influence of democratic subcultures on decisions. In Michigan, research reveals that Democrats on the bench were more likely to side with workers in worker's compensation cases and un-employment cases, regardless of the differences in grievances. Illinois, Pennsylvania, Iowa, Maryland, and New York, have strong patterns in partisan voting with a significant relationship between the citizen's ideologies and those on the bench. The values of voters are reflected in the patterns of state supreme court justices. Research reveals that Federal District Court Judges in over 117,000 cases usually voted along party lines. Democratic judges took the liberal position 47.1 percent of the time, while Republicans did so only 38 percent of the time. Democratic Judges voted 1.45 times more liberally than their Republican conservative counterparts on the bench.

KING V. BURWELL (OBAMACARE)

In 2015, The Supreme Court in a 6-3 decision ruled in favor of Obamacare in a HUGE WIN for the Obama administration. Without getting into the tedious details of this case, The Supreme Court's 6-3 ruling established that Obama's Affordable Care Act subsidies for health insurance were legal. Again, this was a HUGE WIN for the

Obama administration, which makes how the justices ruled surprising. In looking at the statistics of partisan voting patterns in the courts, there is a definite divide; however, partisan politics, the democratic subcultures of judges, and influences of society do not always impact decisions as expected. For example, in King v. Burwell, the politically split court upheld a key provision of Obama's Affordable Care Act, with the majority opinion including two Republicans. The idea of isolating what influences judges in their decisions is not as simple as democratic and legal subcultures. The two subcultures have a complex interplay, and voting does not always happen along party lines but certainly often. There are numerous cases where the justices have been unanimous in their rulings.

The late Justice Antonin Scalia, whom Republican Ronald Reagan appointed, and the late Justice Ruth Ginsberg, whom Democrat Bill Clinton appointed, agreed on rulings 58 percent of the time, which means they agreed more on rulings than disagreed. The judicial branch of government and forces at play influencing how judges decide cases is a continual interaction between the two subcultures. The complex interplay between the legal and democratic subcultures shapes the judicial process and its outcomes. These subcultures that influence the judicial process are rooted in politics, ideologies, party allegiance, legal tradition, who appointed the judge, and the district in which the court is located. It is evident that despite the legal subculture's tradition, the democratic subculture is a powerful force influencing judicial decision-making and shapes our court system. The influence of politics in our courts and on how judges decide cases is unquestionable.

SCALIA V. BREYER

Polar Opposites on the Bench to Help Decipher
the Why of Justices' Rulings

Justices Scalia and Breyer had very opposing views on constitutional interpretation but both Justices agreed that Constitutional interpretation is based on upholding democracy and the boundaries set forth in the text. I watched a recording of a debate at NYU that took place years ago between Justice Breyer and the late Scalia on how the justices interpret the statutes of our constitution as it applies to cases bought before their court.

The Six Tools Justices Use to Interpret the Constitution:

1. Text
2. History
3. Tradition (How the text was interpreted in the past)
4. Precedent
5. Purpose
6. Consequences

Purpose and Consequences are most critical when Justices must apply the constitution to today's modern world cases never imagined by our founding fathers.

Justice Breyer's view is that you must emphasize not just the first 4, but the last two are especially crucial: Purpose and Consequences. Justice Breyer emphasizes that the purpose of the statute and the Consequences of that statute are most important to keep judges in touch with legislature and the people the Constitution is to serve. **Justice Breyer believes that within the context of the <u>purpose</u> of a statute is how to get to the objective of its ambiguous words. YES!**

Justice Scalia, however, felt the opposite. Scalia felt that interpreting the Constitution through its purpose and consequences invites personal subjective judgment allowing non-objective interpretation. Scalia felt the way to achieve objectivity in the court is to be faithful to the text. In contrast to Breyer, Justice Scalia viewed that it is not the last two of those six tools that are essential in interpreting the constitution fairly but the first four: Text, History, Tradition, Precedent.

Scalia felt that a Justice's job is to be faithful to the text, and that the Constitution is not liquid as Breyer believes, but that it is a legal text. Scalia felt that unlike Breyer, constitutional interpretation is simple—use the text and the history. Scalia felt that the first four of those tools—text, history, tradition, and precedent are in fact how to reach that very purpose of the text—that very purpose that Breyer feels dissolves the ambiguity in the text. Justice Scalia argued that the only way to achieve objectivity is to use the words of Congress, not the Purpose of a statute. Using history, however, is perhaps the crux of their contrasting views of constitutional interpretation and where Breyer makes his most effective argument.

The basic breakdown of their differences:

Justice Scalia viewed constitutional interpretation to be what the words meant when they were adopted and to adhere to that original meaning.

Breyer asked: what do these concepts mean today; in today's drastically changed societies?
(I'm with Breyer in this)

Breyer uses a case regarding the expo facto clause on a crime committed in California over 25 years prior. Breyer explains his dive into the history and establishment of this clause lead him into events back in the 1800s, which then led to a case in the 1700's, and so on and so on. His explanation although unintentionally humorous, proved how inapplicable and futile using the history of establishment of the constitution can be in applying the root of its value to today's cases. Breyer's anecdote proved how history is not always the most important tool and can create difficult, open language in the interpretation of the constitution in this drastically different world than it was hundreds of years ago (when the constitution was written). Breyer argues that history is far removed from the roots of its value in question in today's world.

Scalia argued the opposite. Scalia posits that after 200 years of debate, we should by now have a consensus as to what the concepts mean today, and we need to stick to their original meaning. However important and essential this may be, Breyer accurately argues that the world is and has changed drastically as have the needs of the people since the constitution was adopted. Using the history and text as a base to interpret it for today's world, removes it from serving today's societies' needs of a democratic society. Breyer points out that the constitution did account for the internet 200 years ago, not to mention everything else in our modern era.

Breyer believes that we must interpret the constitution pragmatically, for the enhancement of our democracy in today's world and that finding the purpose, and the consequences of a statute are the root of that pragmatism. Breyer also argues adeptly that the "purpose" is how to get to the objective of that original meaning from the text as it applies to today's issues. The objective and purpose of the statutes are where Breyer holds value.

Justice Scalia valued originalism and strict adhesion to the founding father's intention hundreds of years ago as the most important tool in Constitutional interpretation. Even though there is still room for interpretation, the text is the text according to Scalia. Sort of like a fundamentalist with a bible.

THE DOCTRINE OF ABSURDITY

Strict Constructionism/ Conservative Justices

One of the most challenging issues of judicial procedure is applying the law when making legal decisions. While many statutes (laws) are written in very specific language, making it relatively easy in many situations to apply the law case-by-case, other laws, and the provisions of the Constitution, are rather vague. Because every legal case is unique, this poses a problem for many judges, who are left with a quandary as to interpretation. When Justices rule under strict constructionism, as do the more conservative justices, the very idea of taking such a narrow view of the nation's freedoms, obligations, and laws is seen by many to be irrational. Strict Constructionist/Conservative Justices rulings have garnered the moniker: "The Doctrine of Absurdity."

Strict constructionists (conservatives on the bench) are those Justices who believe that every law and constitutional provision should not be subject to interpretation, but applied strictly as written. This means that, under strict constructionism, there is no room for considering the context in which the law was made, or for considering the specific circumstances of any individual case.

Broad Constructionism/ Liberal Justices

Opponents to strict restrictions on interpretation of the law argue that the specific language of the Constitution cannot be directly applied to modern legal issues. Considered to be "broad constructionists," these people also believe that the broad, and often vague language, of the U.S. Constitution requires governmental or judicial interpretation using the current facts and issues. I would much rather have broad constructionists on the bench than strict constructionists.

This argument between broad constructionism, also referred to as "liberal constructionism," and strict constructionism has been commonplace since Colonial America. Throughout America's history, the nation's leaders have taken a back-and-forth stance, often relying on the then-current interpretation of the "Necessary and Proper Clause," contained in the U.S. Constitution, Article I, Section 8, Clause 18, which grants Congress the authority to:"… make all Laws which shall be necessary and proper for carrying into Execution the foregoing Powers, and all other Powers vested by this Constitution in the Government of the United States, or in any Department or Officer thereof."

SHOULD JUSTICES BE ELECTED INSTEAD OF APPOINTED FOR A LIFETIME?

The SC is failing to be an advocate for the majority of the America people more and more, so then, shouldn't justices be elected instead of appointed?

Judges are not elected and are therefore not accountable to the people whom they directly affect and serve. The partisanship, or as of late the Conservative Right appointed justices Brett Kavanaugh and Amy Coney Barrett do not echo public sentiment, nor do they represent the Populus's voices and desires. Ironically and egregiously in 2016, prior to aggressively and with deep partisanship appointing Kavanaugh and Barrett, the Republicans blocked Obama from appointing Justice

Merrick Garland. <u>The damage the Republican appointed Justices have perpetrated upon precedent, and humanitarian needs is tantamount to the dangerous ideologies that egregiously pushed them through to be appointed</u>. Sadly, this politically driven appointing of justices is not unprecedented. The Judiciary's role in our system of policy-making indicates that it is fundamentally very political.

As we have seen with the ruling that overturned Roe v. Wade and the ruling that nullified EPA regulations on corporate emissions, the far right has pushed through politically driven appointments to our highest court that critically damage our American Democracy and future well-being.

This connection of political influence on federal judges stems from how they are appointed, not elected. Presidents appoint federal judges, and his party follows in support of that appointment. Nominees are typically prominent political active members whose partisan and ideological views are similar to the leaders that appoint them. Therefore, it is within reason to assume that judges in a sense, represent the politics behind the leaders who appoint them. This is how America ends up with either a more conservative, or more liberal court. This leads to the possibility of a bias in how the laws should be interpreted in the highest court of our nation. This greatly affects our democracy, and can sway rulings based on political ideologies, instead of a pure, unfiltered review.

One thing to consider is the often-contentious politics behind the process of appointing Supreme Court Judges. Once a president nominates an individual the appointment must be considered by the Senate Judiciary Committee. This always presents a risk of a filibuster or cloture of debate, especially if the senate majority is in the opposing political party to the president and ideologically differs from the appointee's views of law and rule. Political influence or the judge's affiliation to certain political ideologies undoubtedly influences rulings on the federal court, and our fair and balanced democracy. This comes from being appointed by political leaders, not elected by the people.

The most promising indicator in this shift in power and what it means for our democracy is that they are lifetime appointees. It is this lifetime security on the bench that enables the judges to not be accountable to reelection, preventing them from being accountable to the people in all actions. The lifetime appointment can especially affect our democracy as our political climate and society progresses. Those lifetime appointees who may have been there for decades might not be "of the time" that is required for current logical assessment of the laws and how they affect our current society. If judges were elected by the people, lifetime appointments would likely be avoided, and this would not be the case.

CITIZENS UNITED V. FEC

The ruling in Citizens United certainly does not feel congruent with a fair and democratic process, for all people, equally.

An example of this political influence on judges, and how their rulings impact our democracy can especially be seen in the famous 2010 case, "Citizens United v. FEC." At the time, corporations and unions could set up separate accounts with funds for political committees to influence elections. Citizens United was a nonprofit corporation that challenged the law. The Supreme Court ruled in favor of the F.E.C., against "The Citizens", establishing that the government may not prevent corporations from spending money to support or attack candidates in political elections.

After Citizens United, corporations and unions were free to spend unlimited amounts of money to influence and change elections. In this case the Supreme Court also claimed that censoring corporations from political agendas or rhetoric takes away the most significant voices of the economy. The Citizens United ruling pretty much has more influence on our democracy than most other rulings in history.

Corporations and lobbyists have been permitted by law, with unlimited power, to financially influence elections in their favor.

What is the actual F%*$ Supreme Court?

Corporations, because of the post-Citizens ruling, can spend unlimited amounts of money (in the millions) and make unlimited contributions (in the millions) from their general treasuries to independent expenditure-only groups working in their interest. While individual voters can only contribute a maximum of $3,300 per campaign. Even more devastating is that the ruling in Citizens United vs. F.E.C. opened the door for the creation of Super PACs to support or oppose candidates to federal office with unlimited spending power on their behalf. If judges were dependent on reelections by the people instead of being appointed by political leaders, Citizens United might have had a different ruling, and our democracy just might seem fairer and more balanced. The ruling in Citizens United certainly doesn't feel congruent with a fair and democratic process, for all people, equally.

PACKING THE SUPREME COURT: WAS ROOSEVELT A BADASS?

During the height of The Great Depression when Americans were hungry and suffering, President Franklin Delano Roosevelt was beholden to several obstructionist justices on the Supreme Court who continually blocked his ability to enact his New Deal. His New Deal was a series of recovery programs targeted to help end the great depression and improve the lives of suffering Americans. As a result, Roosevelt devised a plan to get the votes he needed. He was going to pack the courts with justices on his side.

Roosevelt's proposed plan to "pack the courts" was triggered by the "Four Horsemen", all conservative justices who obstructed and continually struck down Roosevelt's legislation programs in the New Deal, thwarting Roosevelt's ability to effectively combat The Depression. These "Four Horsemen" (Justices) were the deciding factor in striking down Roosevelt's programs in his New Deal, continually garnering support from at least one other justice for the needed 5-4 rulings one after the other; on the grounds that they were concerned with Congressional and Executive actions that go beyond the constitutionality of regulating interstate commerce. The opinion that the New Deal's programs were unconstitutional was divided in the court's 5-4 rulings with the Four Horsemen at the Helm of each ruling.

Roosevelt's court-packing plan was not supported by the public, nor members of the organized Bar. Congress also did not approve, even with Democratic majorities in both houses. Despite the overwhelming support of Roosevelt's New Deal, the consensus among the public, the Justice Department, Congress, and members of the bar, was that appointing six new justices to the court would be dangerously tampering with the structure of the government, blurring the necessary separation of powers. This is why it failed in Congress but there is more to why the argument was settled in 1937. It is also evident, despite Roosevelt's justifications, that the court packing attempt was about appointing six New Deal advocates on the court to establish constitutionality of his programs. Roosevelt knew how much the nation needed the programs in his New Deal.

These arguments remained far less notable than how these programs helped to stop the hemorrhaging of the American Economy and its devastating effects on American citizens and businesses.

Roosevelt's attempt to pack the court was to combat "The Four Horsemen" in what Roosevelt viewed (as did so many) as the Court's obstructionism, over which Roosevelt could not prevail. Roosevelt, in trying to persuade the public (in his speech), relayed that it was not to pack the court, but to restore it to a fair, balanced institution. Removing the courts, (and Justice's retirement age) dependency upon the desires and prejudices of any individual justice and keeping a younger, newer flow of blood in the courts. It was, however, the success of The Four Horsemen in striking down his New Deal programs that was Roosevelt's true motivation to pack the court.

What saved the "Nine" from becoming Fifteen was an unexpected reversal in one of the Four Horsemen's voting patterns. Justice Roberts, one of the infamous Four Horsemen, "switched" sides in a key vote. Surprising the Court, Congress, and nullifying the idea of the Court's Conservative Obstructionism proposed by Roosevelt. "The Three Musketeers" was the nickname given to three liberal justices during the 1932–37 terms of the United States Supreme Court, who supported and voted in favor of New Deal programs, siding with Roosevelt. In 1937, Justice Roberts defected from the Four Horsemen and voted along with the "Three Musketeers" - in a liberal decision to approve state legislation to regulate wages and working conditions for women and children—a state—not a federal statute. Roberts' desertion from his fellow "horseman" indicated that change in the courts was on the horizon and packing it would be unnecessary.

Roosevelt's intentions with his plan and his frustrations with the Supreme provide food for thought on our Supreme Court today; especially the ideals behind his plan, including the notion of enacting a retirement age requirement. The New Deal saved and served the people in a time they needed it most and the courts (the Four Horseman) were obstructing that crucial progress. Roosevelt's frustrations were felt by the Public as well. However, Roosevelt was incorrect in trying to shape the policies made by the Supreme Court; doing so would certainly lead down a dangerous slippery slope of the executive branch building the judicial branch, literally. It is a dangerous precedent to set to tamper with the judicial system; when the Executive Branch can appoint six justices no matter how much those justices would have balanced the court in such a crisis. Roosevelt was outside of his powers in trying to restructure the Judicial System no matter how broken it seemed and how much it was failing the American people. The sanctity of the structure of the American Government cannot not be meddled with to satisfy political legislation— even if that legislation will benefit the American People in a time of crisis—as the New Deal did. This court-packing plan failing despite the overwhelming public support for Roosevelt and his New Deal, speaks to the integrity with which Congress views the structure of the government, even if disagreeing with the decisions the court may make. The fight in Congress over Roosevelt's court-packing attempt speaks to how seriously—no matter political party—the institutions were respected at the time.

The sanctity of these institutions being separate, even if perilously flawed at times, is imperative to the steady, balanced ground upon which our Democracy must stand.

Just as we experience today, divides within the Supreme Court during The Depression were sharp. The Four Horsemen, aligning in such a manner was dangerous, and deepened the political divides that already existed; and doing so while sitting on the Supreme Court blurred the necessary lines of separation between the courts and politics.

Today's Supreme Court's role in American politics is integral, but increasingly undemocratic. The politics and ideologies influencing our Supreme Court in a constitutional system is undeniable, but today's Supreme Court is an extreme example, and the majority of American people are not being heard nor served.

CHAPTER SEVEN

Is Justice for Sale?
YES.

Justice Clarence Thomas accepted luxury vacations
worth hundreds of thousands of dollars from Republican Mega-Donor Harlan Crow. He also accepted a real
estate deal and private school tuition payments for the
grandnephew he raised. The conservative groups to
which Harlan Crow was connected filed amicus briefs
in multiple matters before the Supreme Court during the
years in which his luxury and financial gifts
were made to Justice Thomas.
(Also, Thomas's wife was at the Capitol riots)

Justice Samuel Alito flew on billionaire Paul Singer's
private jet on a luxury trip to Alaska's high end King
Salmon Lodge. Singer had connections with corporate
entities who later made cases in front of the Supreme
Court and won with Alito's support.

CASH IN OUR COURTROOMS
Caperton v. Massey & "The Appeal."

The power of money in judicial campaigns to run blitz ads, blending ugly dirty politics with our Judicial system is nothing new. If you have the money behind you, you can beat your opponent. This is true with politics, but these are ads for a seat on a State Supreme Court. Something is amiss here when this is allowed. Money buys attack ads, and money can buy you a seat on the bench.

Is Justice for sale? Is Judicial independence possible when campaign financing, and multi-million-dollar funds are tangled up in our judiciary? Can justice be served in a trial when the litigant involved can essentially buy a seat on the supreme court that is hearing his case? When a judicial candidate wins election to the bench with the financial campaign help of millions of dollars from the CEO of a company, who happens to be a litigant in the case, should that judge recuse himself or herself from sitting on that case? Is this manipulation of the seats on the court unconstitutional and eroding confidence in an unbiased judiciary?

Do judges who are backed by money power machines that are stakeholders in cases in that courtroom, create a possibility of bias, thus diminishing the chances of a fair trial? <u>Yes.</u>

Justice Kennedy's opinion of the court in Caperton v. Massey, strongly and accurately addresses this problem of the probability of bias in our judiciary as being unconstitutional. In **Caperton V. Massey Coal Co.**, Massey Coal, a large Coal Corporation, wanted Caperton Coal out of business and forced Caperton into bankruptcy via nefarious actions and tactics. Caperton sued Massey and the jury awarded Caperton a 50-million-dollar verdict. Massey Coal appealed and when the case was headed to court, Massey Coal's CEO Don

Blankenship spent 3 million dollars to defeat the incumbent Justice Warren McGraw (who was predicted to uphold the 50 million verdict) to mold and elect a little know lawyer named Brent Benjamin to the court. The plaintiffs and Caperton called for Benjamin to recuse himself from sitting on the case as a clear conflict of interest and in violation of the Due Process Clause. Benjamin refused recusal and became the deciding vote to overturn the verdict in favor of Massey. This lack of judicial separation from money in the apparent purchase of Justice Benjamin by the litigant brought the case to the Supreme Court.

The influence of financial considerations for judges in the context of judicial elections, the political maneuvering surrounding sitting judges and justices, and the mounting magnitude of judicial campaign expenditures contribute to the notion that receiving a fair trial is severely compromised when the litigants perceive an inherent bias in their cases and understand that the deck is stacked against them before their cases are even heard.

In 2009, in a 5-4 ruling of Caperton v. Massey, judges were constitutionally barred from participating in cases which were connected to large financial contributions to their campaigns. Justice Kennedy's opinion of the court in Caperton v. Massey illuminates this very dire problem eroding confidence that everyone receives a fair trial in our Supreme Courts. Justice Kennedy argued just as with **Tumey v. Ohio,** under the Due Process Clause, a judge must recuse himself if he has personal and direct interests attached to the decision of a case upon which he is sitting. Actual bias is not required for recusal when evidence clearly suggests that a judge has the "probability of actual bias" in a case, and in *Caperton* that probability was certainly proven. Justice Kennedy's "probability of actual bias" refers to the imbalanced financial campaign donations to one justice over another by a litigant. This then creates a scenario of a probability of bias in a clear violation of the Due Process Clause of our Constitution as well as the Judicial Code of Conduct. Kennedy refers to the large sum of money (in the millions) toward Benjamin's campaign compared to the small amount given to the incumbent (and the sheer large dollar amount of the donations as well) in creating the probability of bias in the court.

Justice Roberts dissenting opinion, along with Scalia, Thomas, and Alito states that the majority opinion creates a precedent with an alarming domino effect more damaging on our judiciary and farther reaching than the "possibility of bias" in this case. Roberts argues that using the due process clause to overturn a judge's failure to recuse himself because of a probability of bias would only further erode public confidence in our judiciary. Increased assumptions that judges are biased will be the only end result and then where does than end?

Does that mean every justice whose campaign received contributions cannot be impartial and should recuse himself or herself? Does this then include newspapers who backed the judicial candidate, and so on and so on? Although the logic behind the dissenting opinions of Roberts and Scalia are valid, they are not justifications nor defenses for campaign money being present in the courtroom especially with a case as obvious as Caperton v. Massey.

BRIBERY IS A REALITY IN OUR COURTS

Carl Trudeau, CEO of Krane Chemical which just lost a settlement in the amount of 41 million dollars to a widowed plaintiff makes a phone call. He does not call his company's financial team to begin realigning finances to pay this settlement. He does not call his own accountant or attorney. Instead, Carl calls a retired Senator with connections to an unlisted firm that specializes in elections, with the command from Trudeau to "fix the verdict". The elections the Senator is speaking about are the upcoming Mississippi judicial elections, and that "specialization" refers to molding and buying a seat on the Mississippi state supreme court that will be hearing the appeal of Krane Chemical v. Baker. Barry Rinehart, a "fixer" from the unlisted firm, states in a later secret meeting with Trudeau, "You hire our firm, the money gets wired into the proper accounts, then I will give you a plan for restructuring the Supreme Court of Mississippi". While this is a plot and dialogue from a John Grisham's novel, the verisimilitude of this scenario is palpable, as Grisham based this on the actual events of a real-life case.

With the promise of 8 million dollars wired to accounts that cannot be connected to Krane Chemical, Rinehart, with the help Tony Zachary, plucks out a fresh-faced young man to be the new candidate for the Supreme Court of Mississippi. The team hurls campaign attack ads against the incumbent justice Sheila McCarthy, manipulates conservative Christian voters on everything from guns to gay marriage, to the incumbent's "liberal" verdict that let out a (now dead) pedophile. It is a smear campaign against the sitting justice and the grooming and manipulation of an unwitting pawn in a multi-million-dollar scheme to manipulate the courts to favor Krane Chemical. "His name is Ron Fisk, a nice gullible young man purchased (offshore) by me for chump change." John Grisham's novel is based on a true case that reveals how judicial elections are bought and paid for; and that any candidate, regardless of experience, can be elected if he or she has enough money to attract voters through nasty attack ads and publicity that destroys reputations. Earlier in this book I made an argument for why judges should be elected not appointed and this is a clear counter to that argument, and a powerful one.

When judges are elected rather than appointed, money wins, and campaign cash has entered the courtroom. Financial gains become an incestuous part of the judiciary.

SELECTION PROCESS OF JUDGES

In Merit selection system, the appointment of a judge is based on tenure and record of performance not an election campaign; supposedly keeping state justices and judges above politics and campaign cash out of the courtroom. This is the best possible system to keep money out of the judicial system but in no way, does it keep politics away. Legend has it that a long-ago Chief Justice of Texas said, "No judicial selection system is worth a damn." The merit selection system for federal judges is far from being above politics. The advocates of judicial elections base their argument on the grounds that the United States elects every official who has a role in policy and using "merit" as the selection process cancels out all classes involvement in judicial selection and creates an elitism of upper insiders within our courts.

The Merit selection is an attempt to obtain qualified judges and justices who are removed and free from political influences by a means other than nonpartisan elections. This idea is certainly close but as is evidence and research suggest, even retention elections, based on judges running on his or her tenure is not entirely free from politics. Merit-selected judges are under greater influence from attorneys than any other method of judicial selections. Furthermore, in the merit selection process the Governor appoints the judge who has been recommended by a panel of bar association attorneys and non-lawyers appointed by the Governor. This certainly leaves room for politics to be involved, as well as interest groups who have discovered that these retention elections, in reference to the prior voting patterns of judges, can be used to unseat sitting judges with great influence on judicial policy-making in regard to the group's cause. Whether the justice has hindered or helped the cause in his or her tenure which is up for scrutiny and can be weaponized by interest groups. Thus, politics have entered this merit system of selecting judges.

PURCHASING THE VERDICT

One more crucial factor calls for keeping judicial elections from being like other elections. The-no-holds-barred elective campaigns are impacting the pool of people willing to run for the bench and/or for re-election. This muddy and ugly election system of judges is working against the whole goal of fair effective judicial selections. The sometimes nasty and money influenced judicial elections system will fail to bring to the bench qualified, impartial people necessary to fulfill the responsibilities and powers of being a judge.

Money, manipulation, promises, lies, the washing of donations to a candidate's campaign through nefarious means, uncapped independent personal donations, or lobbying from interest groups, are all a part of our current Judicial elections system.

The multi-million-dollar contributions toward a justice's campaign from Don Blankenship who is the CEO of the corporation on trial, establishes an obvious probability of bias from that justice who Blankenship essentially purchased. The sheer size of the donations (in the millions) from Blankenship, acting CEO of the Corporation on trial, dwarfed the plaintiff's donations, in an obvious deliberate attempt to buy the verdict in his favor. The power with which corporations, politicians, even lawyers can wield to manipulate, sculpt, then buy a justice's seat is shocking. The amount of judicial campaign spending has increased over the years, and Grisham's novel mirrors the real-life influence that big money has on our judiciary. Many victors relish in this easily manipulated system: One in which they can essentially purchase seats on the bench in the courts that are hearing their trials. Often the justices who win their campaigns from these large contributions, are the most clueless about the underhanded operation to manipulate the courts and buy verdicts.

The role of money in judicial elections, and the millions spent on judicial campaigns often comes from political interests, and powerful entities who are stakeholders in the judicial system, not the candidates themselves. This is an acute problem that challenges every litigant's Constitutional right to a fair trial or hearing. When judges are essentially purchased, indelible financial gains become entrenched in our Judiciary. Campaign cash must stay out of our courts.

POWER ASYMMETRIES, MISTRUTHS, AND MONEY

Power asymmetries, bias, mistruths, spin, the media, money, and mounds of endless paperwork that convolute the truth, seem to make up our American Civil Justice System

The unregulated power asymmetries in many civil cases are at the helm of how the civil justice system in America has become muddied, inefficient, lengthy, and expensive, and how the people are essentially victims twice-from the tortious act and from the litigation process itself. Tort cases are common law jurisdictions based on civil wrong doings which cause someone else to suffer loss or harm, resulting in liability for the entity or person who committed the tortious (harmful) act. The victim of the harm can recover their losses or damages by filing a civil lawsuit. To win, the plaintiff in the lawsuit must prove that the actions or lack of action were the cause of that harm. This seems clear-cut enough, but is it?

Right and Wrong Equals Dollars and Cents

In a lawsuit, everybody on the other side is the enemy, and reading a trial transcript from a civil suit is a masterclass on malicious discourse. The people are victims twice—from the tortious act and from the litigation process itself.

"Lawsuits are war; when you're a small firm and they're a big one steeped in history and wealth as they always are, with their Persian carpets on the floor and their Harvard diplomas hanging on the wall, it's easy to be intimidated, don't be, that's what they want, that's what they expect, like all bullies that's how they win." - John Travolta playing real-life Jann Schlichtmann in the film, A Civil Action. Those "bullies" in civil litigation and high-value tort disputes are the power asymmetries creating an imbalance in resources in civil litigation cases that often make truth and justice the last priority.

The truth ends up buried deep down under mounds and mounds of frivolous paperwork in the familiar bottomless pit of civil litigation. Critics of our Civil Justice System equate it to the idea that Corporations can finally have their 'decade' in court. The American Civil Justice System has a long history of translating right and wrong, just, and unjust, into dollars and cents through a lengthy, costly system often bogged down by the process itself. Civil litigations often become cavernous wastelands of lengthy pre-trial discovery, erroneous pre-trial conferences, contentious negotiations, and mounds of endless paperwork while losing sight of the very people the system is supposed to serve. In our American Civil Justice System, the exorbitant costs and lengthy delays of civil litigations and high-value tort disputes vastly overtake the original monetary value of the cases themselves.

The costly and lengthy process effectively denies most litigants access to justice and undermines the civil justice system's legitimacy to deliver fair resolutions for victims.

The civil justice system is designed to correct wrongdoings, but does it?

The flaws of civil litigation can only be understood as related to the power asymmetries at play in so many civil cases, the media's spin on the narratives of civil litigation cases, the lengthy pre-trial process, and the ambiguity and complexity of the system itself. Two critical cases illuminate why the system is not only misunderstood but often disparaged by the public. How does the truth get so lost and so misunderstood in our civil litigation process? *Liebeck v. Macdonald's and Anderson v. Cryovak* are prime are examples of the problems that arise in many civil litigation cases, and why the civil justice system is so hotly criticized and misunderstood.

SMALL TOWN V. BEHEMOTH CORPORATION

Anne Anderson et al. v. Cryovak, Inc.

Small Town Victims of Woburn, Massachusetts who suffered immeasurable losses go up against a giant corporate conglomerate and are further victimized.

On May 14th, 1982, Anne Anderson, and a number of citizens of Woburn, Massachusetts filed a civil suit against Cryovac, Inc., a division of W.R. Grace Co., the John J. Riley Co., and a division of Beatrice Foods, alleging that the conglomerate had contaminated Woburn's drinking water by purposefully and recklessly dumping toxic chemicals into their ground. The people sought compensation for tremendous personal injury and wrongful deaths and asked the court to require the companies to clean up the contaminated ground water and stop dumping toxic waste into their town. The people and children of Woburn suffered tremendously as a result of Cryovak/Beatrice Foods dumping of chemicals; high incidence of cancer, childhood leukemia, liver disease, and other illnesses caused by their water being contaminated with dangerous toxic chemicals.

A young personal injury lawyer, Jan Schlichtmann, and his two partners filed the civil lawsuit against the mega-corporations Beatrice Foods Co. and W. R. Grace, alleging that they had knowingly dumped the highly toxic chemicals TCE and PCE on their factory grounds, which then leached into the soil and ended up in the Woburn, Massachusetts municipal water supply, causing illnesses and death of residents, including eight children. The uneven match between Schlichtmann and defendants W.R. Grace & Beatrice Foods, Co. are evident on every level from money, resources, to pre-trial tactics and similar in caliber to Liebeck v. McDonald's.

Anne Anderson, et al. v. a behemoth corporation that made her town sick, is about power asymmetries in civil litigation cases and how that impacts every level of cases, and certainly did with *Anderson.* The case is depicted in the film, A Civil Action (yes, I know it's dated, but it makes a great point) and before the discovery phase of the case even began, Jerome Facher, representing the Corporate Conglomerate, stands in court with a dozen dark suited lawyers behind him to file a Rule 11 motion requesting the case be dismissed. In contrast to the army of lawyers behind Facher, Schlichtmann who represents the people, (Anne) of Woburn, appears alone, without an army to fight in court. The visual is one man against a giant army, and corporations make it clear they bring money and men.

In his article "Considering a Civil Action", Jerome Facher explains that the judge's denial of the motion to dismiss was not without some doubt. Judge Skinner, the presiding judge, in a second Rule 11 decision seven years later, found that the plaintiffs' counsel (Schlicht-mann) did in fact violate Rule 11, by continuing a lawsuit against Be-atrice knowing there was not adequate evidence to justify the case. Facher discusses the first Rule 11 tactic (requesting a case be dis-missed) by the defense was not a show of the uneven match between the defense and plaintiffs but a legitimate and accurate request for the case. Facher explains that Judge Skinner's second ruling on the plain-tiff's violation of Rule 11, was rooted in the plaintiff's use of "evi-dence" which was proven to not be the deadly chemical Schlichtmann claimed to be, as well as the deliberate misconduct by the plaintiff's counsel in its dubious procurement. What is glaringly apparent is that the "lack of evidence" by the plaintiff was only because:

The plaintiff (the people) lacked the resources, access, and funds to prove how deadly and dangerous these dumped chemicals were. The people lost because they had less money to fight against the giant corporation.

The power asymmetries of this disheartening case are undeniable and are a regularity in our Civil Justice System. This power imbalance is a critical flaw in so many tort and civil cases with the victims suffer-ing even more. In a scene in the film that mirrors the real-life events, Jann Schlichtmann meets with the dozen defense lawyers in a hotel banquet room to negotiate a financial settlement. The table is set with foods and drinks indicating that Schlichtmann, who set this up, ex-pects it will take a long time. It doesn't. When the defense doesn't like the offer they leave, offering no counter, no discussion, just a clear statement that says you are not in our league.

In *Liebeck,* McDonald's refused to negotiate a settlement with the old, injured lady, even an inexpensive offer of $225,000 dollars to cover her bills. The lack of negotiating is the equivalent to saying, you are not worth it, we are not negotiating anything real here.

The reality that in tort cases and civil suits, the financial settlements are often <u>not</u> negotiated, indicates the abundant financial resources corporations have to drain the victim's resources, hope, and ultimately weaken a plaintiff who will then wish he had never taken the case. The term "bully" most certainly and aptly applies here.

The people of Woburn who suffered immeasurably, lacked the financial resources and the tactics needed to win the case. Beatrice and W.R. Grace, both Mega Corporations, were skilled in pre-trial convolution with a clear financial advantage over the simple people of Woburn and their inexpensive lawyer Schlichtmann. The pre-trial phase lasted four years, and subsequently bankrupted Schlichtmann who was then forced to settle with W.R. Grace for a measly $8 million. The victim's families ended up with less than $300,000 each, and the polluted site was not cleaned up. If Schlichtmann had equal financial resources, and the expertise of experienced corporate lawyers, the fight might have been even, and the settlement much more, while delivering justice to the victims of Woburn.

THE PROBABILITY OF BIAS

In tort cases and civil litigation, corporations often draw out cases knowingly costing plaintiffs more money, thus diminishing the plaintiffs negotiating power, while providing for themselves a stronger defense. The resources accessible to corporations to make it difficult for plaintiffs far outmatch those accessible to the plaintiffs to adequately fight back. Remember the idea of the Possibility of Bias? In addition to the uneven match of power and resources seen in so many civil litigations, **ANNE ANDERSON ET AL., V. CRYOVAC, INC**. brings the idea of the possible bias of judges presiding over cases. In civil litigation, scientific facts are often the foundations of the plaintiff's complaints, but so are the testimonies of those who suffered from the alleged tortious act. In Anderson, the presiding judge, Walter Skinner, divides the trial into three phases. The crucial, pre-trial decision (to which Schlichtmann/ objected vehemently) disallowed the victims' testimony during the first phase and resulted in the judge directing the jury to answer questions they could not possibly understand based on months of confusing science aimed to sow doubt in the plaintiffs' claims. This gets back to the resources and expertise so overwhelmingly in favor of the defense, to confuse, cast doubt, and override the human component so vital to the case as the most powerful weapon for the plaintiffs.

The victims of the defendants' actions, who will bear the verdict, were delayed then disallowed from telling their stories. Judge Skinner's trifurcation order ultimately excluded the victims from the case. Anderson was a case about people; people seeking justice. Skinner's decision to disallow the victims from telling their stories undoubtedly and most effectively weakened the plaintiff's case considerably.

"I used to believe in the idea that justice would prevail if you worked hard enough at it... I thought that if judges saw cheating right in front of them, they'd do something about it. The Woburn Case gave me a depressing dose of reality."
--(Jonathan Harr in an interview with Dan Kennedy, 1995, p. 2).

Power asymmetries, bias, mistruths, spin, the media, money, and mounds of endless paperwork that convolute the truth, seem to make up our American Civil Justice System.

Heartbreaking cases like Anderson erode confidence that truth and justice can be found inside a courtroom. The erosion of public trust in the civil justice system, regarding its independence from money, bias, and power, carries serious implications for the future of the system itself.

America, why?

CHAPTER EIGHT

Supreme Court Cases That Changed Us

Landmark Supreme Court cases that changed the trajectory of justice, dismantled gun control, changed how The Constitution is to be interpreted, and revealed the perseverance and courage of everyday people.

Two pivotal rulings on gun rights will make you ask:

America, Why?

25 YEAR HANDGUN BAN SHOT DOWN

District of Columbia v. Heller - (Goodbye Gun Control!)

On June 26, 2008, several years after George W. Bush let the ban on assault rifles expire, the Supreme Court made a ruling that forever shaped our nation on the issue of private gun control. DISTRICT OF COLUMBIA V. HELLER centered around the District's (D.C.'s) 25-year handgun ban. In a landmark ruling, the Supreme Court knocked down D.C.'s 25-year ban on handguns in homes as unconstitutional. *Heller* was the first time the Supreme Court ruled that the Second Amendment applies to individuals, providing a right to own guns for self-defense inside the home. Both Roberts and Alito ruled with the majority in a narrow 5-4 decision, that erased much hope for sound gun control.

Before its landmark decision in June 2008 in *District of Columbia v. Heller,* which scrutinized the constitutionality of a law in the District of Columbia (D.C.) that banned the possession of personally owned handguns, the U.S. Supreme Court had never directly ruled on the interpretation of the Second Amendment. Many historians agree that the primary motive behind enacting the Second Amendment was to prevent the necessity for the United States to maintain a permanent standing army. At the time of its enactment, the 2nd Amendment was not intended to grant private individuals the right to possess weapons for self-defense. So, what does the right to bear arms truly mean? Does it mean that anyone who wants to can own a gun? **Over time, the Supreme Court has interpreted the Constitution's right to bear arms as an individual's right to self-defense, making it increasingly difficult for Congress to enact gun control legislation, and sound gun control.**

District of Columbia v. Heller

The Heller ruling in 2008 completely abolished any hope for enacting critical gun control measures, prioritizing individual gun rights over public safety.

Self Defense is not a justification for allowing people to keep loaded guns easily accessible in their homes.
I mean, really Supreme Court?
Where is the logic?

The Constitutional interpretations and debate over the 2nd Amendment in the legal community were incredibly potent in the divided

Court in the case of DISTRICT OF COLUMBIA V. HELLER. Most vital to the gun control debate is understanding the consequences that come with the right to bear arms versus the individualism that grounds American freedoms and why so many support the 2nd Amendment. The case of Heller indicates American values and echoes the arguments behind the debate of individual rights and freedoms regarding guns. The history behind the meaning and intentions of the 2nd Amendment are where the arguments begin; mostly those that support that individual freedom, and where the individualists find their most valid arguments. The 2nd Amendment as irrelevant in today's world, (as I stated in chapter three) and critically dangerous given how easily guns can be purchased by just about anyone in stores, at gun shows, on the dark web.

If you want a gun, you can just go get one.

<u>America, why?</u>

Did I miss something?
Is there going to be some sort of zombie apocalypse? Why in the hell do we all need the right to own guns?

Another way to understand it is: If you own a gun then the next guy feels he needs to own a gun because you own one—now he needs a gun to feel safe because you have a gun too... You get it. However, to those who oppose a ban on handguns the logical argument that more guns only lead to more guns, doesn't seem to penetrate. What seems to matter most to those who oppose a handgun ban is the people's individual right to defend themselves in their homes, regardless of what modern protections the government can provide. The 2nd Amendment is irrelevant in modern times, but the Supreme court and pro-gun groups use it to justify giving people the right to own loaded weapons in their homes. To what degree should that right to own a gun extend? Furthermore, to what degree of restrictiveness should the courts be allowed to apply to that right when gun laws are challenged?

The District of Columbia had one of the strictest gun laws in the nations, which banned virtually all handguns. Furthermore, D.C.'s law called for guns to be kept unloaded and disassembled or trigger locked. Richard Heller believed the law made it impossible for him to defend himself in his home. He also believed that the law violated the Second Amendment. The Court agreed with Heller, in a very divided split of 5-4 and held the ban to be unconstitutional while holding that the Second Amendment protects an individual's right to keep firearms, yes, loaded as well, at home for self-defense. The Supreme Court's 5 to 4 decision striking down the D.C. handgun ban was a huge victory for the rights of American citizens who want to own guns for self-defense. The politics of gun control and the debate over gun rights is continually argued through the divided interpretations of the intent of the Second Amendment.

Walter Dillinger's opening arguments on behalf of D.C. are rooted in the language of the Second Amendment and its intent. Dillinger argues that the opening phrase of the Amendment, "A well-regulated militia, being necessary to the security of a free state," (known as the prefatory clause), limited the "right of the people" to have weapons only in connection with militia service and only organized militias. To quote Dillinger: "Every person who uses the phrase "bear arms" uses it to refer to the use of arms in connection with Militia Service. When Madison introduced the Amendment in the first Congress, he equated the phrase "bearing arms" with "rendering military service."

If I were to sum up the public policy debate over gun rights and gun control, I would use those very first sentences of Dillinger's arguments as illuminating the root of the gun rights debate. Those few statements are the basis for the divided policy debate over who should have the right to bear arms and what that means for self-defense according to our Constitution. When Justice Roberts argues Dillinger's point by asking why then would the text include "the right of the people" why wouldn't the text just say the right was for state militias? Dillinger astutely replies with the argument that when the text was written, the people were the militia. This exchange is where the divide begins on the debate of gun rights. Modern times are different from when the text of the Constitution was written. There is no doubt as to that reality. The Originalists v. those on the Court who believe the text should be fluid and conform to modern needs are also how Heller contributes to the gun control debate.

Arguing for Heller, Alan Gura's arguments were grounded in the vagueness of what the law means as far as actual literal application. What does self-defense mean in terms of lawful or unlawful, and who are we to say when that line is crossed? "The...possession of lawfully owned firearms for self-defense within the home—when self-defense would be considered lawful by other means under the district of Columbia." I take this to mean, how can we all say when self-defense is deemed lawful? And how can we say when it isn't? This vagueness is an ongoing argument in the gun control debate - and the DISTRICT OF COLUMBIA V. HELLER highlights that vagueness of what self-defense mean—the right to defend yourself in your home v. the right to freely possess a loaded handgun and the often-deadly consequences that come with that right.

BREYER CALLS IT LIKE IT IS - YES!

However, Justice Breyer's exchange with Alan Gura is the very heart of the Gun control debate. Breyer states that 80,00-100,000 people are injured or killed in gun-related accidents or crimes every year (and this was 13 years ago—that number has almost doubled since). Breyer then asks Gura does he not think the ban on handguns to be a proportional response to that statistic on behalf of the citizens of our nation and of D.C.? Gura responds that the ban on handguns does not serve to strengthen a society but weaken it. Gura argues that if the military purpose stated in the 2nd Amendment is an individual right to defend oneself—then a ban on handguns impedes that right.

To that, Breyer argues that Gura, Heller, and those who are for the freedom of personal handgun ownership should focus on the crime problem in our country as related to those guns.
(Go Breyer!!!)

In comparison, Gura and those who oppose the ban on handguns argue that the focus should be placed on a person's individual right to defend themselves against those very crimes—thus the right to bear arms. The exchange between Gura and Breyer illuminates the public policy issues at the heart of the Heller case, thus the heart of the gun control debate and what fuels the divide in the politics of gun control.

The overall and defining purpose of DISTRICT OF COLUMBIA V. HELLER is the establishment of the individual right of civilians to own guns for their own protection. HELLER'S purpose was to establish one's personal freedom to defend oneself with the right to bear arms. Scalia in his majority opinion, connects the individual's right to bear arms with his or her right to resistant tyranny. Scalia writes in the opinion of the Court: "The two sides in this case have set out very different interpretations of the Amendment." Scalia also states a bit later in the opinion, "Reading the Second Amendment as protecting only the right to "Keep and Bear Arms" in an organized militia, therefore, fits poorly with the operative clause's description of the holder of that right as "the people."

The allowance of people to personally own guns has opened the flood gates for the most dangerous type of domestic terrorist groups in our country-- fully armed ones.

In his dissent: Justice Stevens argues that the Second Amendment does not mean people have the absolute and unlimited right to possess guns for self-defense purposes (as where will that end?) Instead, Steven's dissent points out that a logical interpretation of the Second Amendment as applicable to gun control—is that it protects the right to keep and bear arms for certain military purposes- but does not impede the power of Congress to regulate personal use and ownership of weapons. Therein lies the divided views behind the gun control debate. What illuminates the heart of the gun rights policy debate is the exchange between Breyer and Gura about guns causing violent crimes and the people's right to defend themselves against those crimes using guns. The theme of individual freedoms behind the Heller case relies on interpretations of the Constitution along with self-defense principles, individual freedoms v. tyranny, and where you stand on guns.

What causes gun violence? Is it more guns? (Ummm... YES.)

BACKGROUND CHECKS ARE SHOT DOWN

Printz v. United States & The Brady Handgun Act

In 1993 President Bill Clinton signed into Law the "Brady Handgun Violence Prevention Act" which required that state and local officials perform background checks on anyone wanting to purchase a gun. These background checks (had this law stayed in place) would have likely saved countless lives, many of those children. Then in 1997, the Supreme Court shot down the "Brady Handgun Violence Prevention Act" nullifying it. Why would the Supreme Court do that?

It has everything to do with the Tenth Amendment. According to the majority on the Supreme Court, the federal government violated the Tenth Amendment when Congress required state and local officials to perform background checks on people buying guns: as this was in violation of the Tenth Amendment of Federalism (Federalism is the system of governing in this country that allocates some powers to be up to the states individually while other decisions and powers are up to the national federal government).

In 1997, County sheriffs Jay Printz and Richard Mack, separately challenged the constitutionality of The Brady Handgun Violence Preventions Act and the provision of the Brady Bill on behalf of Chief Law Enforcement Officers in Montana and Arizona respectively. The gun control issues raised in the 1993 Brady Handgun Violence Prevention Act and in the case of Printz v. the United States, are two views of federalism—which explains where we are now as a country on gun rights. Applying its principles to the constitutionality of the 1993 Brady Handgun Act, with each side clearly endorsing different models of federalism. Printz argued the Brady Handgun Act is unconstitutional, in that the federal government/Congress, cannot order local law enforcement officers to enact what is in fact a federal regulation program as this is in violation of the Tenth Amendment. Printz also argued that the Brady Handgun Act is an overreach of power as law enforcement is fundamentally a part of states' sovereignty, not under the federal government's domain.

The United States countering with the argument that this gun regulation affects commerce and therefore the Brady Act falls under the commerce clause, which falls under the Federal Government's domain of power under the Necessary and Proper Clause. The abstract principles of federalism and who is really in charge on gun control are salient in Printz v. The United States. Should gun laws be a state-by-state issue or up to the federal government for some uniformity? The models used to argue which principles are constitutional regarding gun rights have never more apparent than in Printz v. the United States.

How could this incredibly vital bill that protects citizens from gun violence be thrown away by our Supreme Court?

Understanding the opposing views of federal power in our country helps to understand how something like this can happen. At play in this case are Dual Federalism and Cooperative Federalism. Dual federalists view our nation's powers like a layer cake, where the powers of the national and state governments are clearly separated into distinct layers, and each layer operates independently from the other. Under dual federalism, there is a strict division of powers outlined in the Constitution, and each level of government operates within its own sphere without much overlap or interference from the other. Basically, the Federal Government cannot mess with the State's individual rights. In contrast, Cooperative federalists view America as a marble cake, where the powers of the national and state governments are mixed together, and they work closely together to tackle issues, often sharing responsibilities and resources. In Cooperative Federalism, there can be an overlapping of jurisdiction between the states and the federal government when it best serves the people and the country.

Justice Scalia argued for the majority that the federal government's regulation of state law officers (in what is a federal program regulating guns) was unconstitutional and in violation of the Tenth Amendment. Scalia's arguments on the constitutionality, (rather unconstitutionality of gun regulation for the states), endorse the Dual Federalism Model—Dual Federalism is when the states, not just the federal government have powers too (in this case it is about regulating their individual state's gun rights). Scalia argued that it is undeniable that the Constitution clearly established a system grounded in "dual sovereignty" and the United States is in violation of that principle here in this case. Scalia used federalist #39 to justify his position, in that #39 clearly states the separate powers of municipal authorities as distinct and separate in a necessary balance of power between the states and the Federal Government. Scalia also used Federalist #15 as proof of the Constitution establishing two political capacities—one state and one federal that must be protected from infiltration or tyranny by the other. Remember in Chapter Six the description of Scalia as a Strict Constructionist on the bench? Remember how those types of judges (usually conservative ones) apply the constitution strictly as it is written, adhering to the original text without considering the social context of every individual case?

Scalia, an originalist (strict constructionist) in his interpretation of the Constitution, views the Constitution's text as binding, and evidentiary that the principles of Federalism in accordance with the constitution were violated by The Brady Handgun Act. Justice Stevens in his dissenting opinion offers an alternate definition of what the Tenth Amendment and Federalism means, clearly endorsing the cooperative federalism model. Stevens argues not what the Constitution says, but rather what it does not say. He argues that The Brady Act does not violate the Tenth Amendment, because the Tenth Amendment does not address or impose any restrictions on the exercise of delegated powers—but simply confirms those powers to be what is granted in the constitution, not a limiting of the powers of Congress. Stevens also argues Article 1, and the Necessary and Proper Clause support the Federal government's enlistment of local law enforcement in the regulation of handguns.

Stevens argued that the Brady Act is not out of the scope of the constitution and falls within the Federal government's power.

Steven's view of federalism is a cooperative one—where the Tenth Amendment does not give states more power, (the states must cooperate with the federal government's laws). The Necessary and Proper Clause can be applied in this case, and the states are in cooperation with the federal government under the Supremacy Clause that empowers the federal government to regulate states' functions when necessary and proper to do so. This is clearly in stark contrast to Scalia's view of a "dual sovereignty" with a dual federalism between the states and the federal government.

The concept of federalism is never specifically mentioned in the constitution, so applying the principles of federalism (what powers our federal government has over individual state's powers) to political controversies is difficult, with arguments that could go on forever and likely end with a very a divided outcome—as with Printz v. United States in a 5-4 decision. Federalism means the government is not a unitary power but not a confederation either, so depending on where one believes those lines of powers between the federal government and the states should be drawn—and how one interprets the principles of federalism to be structured within the constitution—applying critical laws to solve salient issues will always be more complicated than it may initially appear—as seen in Printz v. The United States.

Gun Control is one issue however, that should bridge the gap between those who value states' rights over federal powers, and what the Government is required to do to safeguard our communities and our children.

SAME SEX MARRIAGE
EQUAL MEANS EVERYONE, EVERYWHERE

Obergefell v. Hodges (2015), Reed v. Reed (1971)

In 2015, a married same sex couple, James Obergefell and John Arthur who lived in Ohio, filed a lawsuit challenging the state's refusal to recognize same-sex marriage on death certificates. Rick Hodges was the director of the Ohio Department of Health at the time. James and John were legally married in Maryland in 2013, but their marriage was not recognized in their current state of residency, Ohio. John suffered from a terminal illness and sadly died shortly after litigation began in the suit, and never got to see the landmark ruling that guaranteed equal rights for same sex couples that he helped establish. The issue of whether James would be recognized as John's spouse on his death certificate sparked the suit against Hodges and the Ohio Department of Health, and the Supreme Court took it on. Under Ohio law at the time, established in the Ohio Constitution and the Ohio Revised Code, James and John believed Ohio would refuse to indicate Mr. Arthur was married at the time of his death and that Mr. Obergefell was his spouse.

The Supreme Court, in their Landmark Obergefell ruling struck down same-sex marriage bans for violating both the Due Process Clause and the Equal Rights Clause. The 5-4 victory for equal rights ruled that the fundamental right to marry, regardless of sex or gender must be guaranteed to same sex couples in All Fifty States, not just some. The ruling established equality and dignity not just for same sex couples but their families and their children. The landmark ruling required that every state perform and recognize marriages of same sex couples in the same legal terms as opposite sex couples. The

Court also held that every state must recognize same-sex marriages legally performed in other states.

In our democracy, policy-making is presumably supposed to be up to the elected representatives of the people, not judicial appointees who are unelected and carry life terms.

However, when concerns arise regarding the constitutional rights of the American people-under the law-especially if seen as being threatened or diminished, The Court has certainly stepped in and acted as policymaker.

Although unelected, the role of the Supreme Court to act as policymaker when civil liberties, equal rights, civil rights, are being hindered, is necessary—as the states may very well not adhere to cohesive definitions of what those rights mean, and who should have them. Leaving it up to the states simply means some state will have equal rights and some will not. **When I last checked, the Constitution is titled "The United States Constitution"- not the Constitution to some states, and to others, well...act as you see fit per person based on how you view gender and race.** The 14th Amendment States "equal protection of the law". Equal means everyone, in every state, in every color, for every gender. Equal means everyone is treated the same everywhere. It's really that simple. The bigger question is whether or not this equality mandate means the Supreme Court is overstepping is judicial boundaries, using powers that should be reserved to the states' powers.

For four decades, The U.S. Supreme Court, with strong majorities, has made it very clear that the 14th Amendment, which guarantees "equal protection of the laws," includes protection against sex discrimination on all fronts-which includes the right to marry regardless of your sex, as seen with the 5-4 ruling of Obergefell v. Hodges.

The Supreme Court's role as policymaker when upholding the 14th amendment regarding discrimination based on sex was first seen in the 1971 landmark ruling, **Reed v. Reed.** The ruling on Reed v. Reed overturned an Idaho law that gave fathers (men) automatic precedence and authority over mothers (women) when administering a deceased child's estate (The Women's Legal Defense and Education Fund, 2020). Although Reed v. Reed is not about same sex marriage, it is an example of the Supreme Court's history acting as policymaker in matters regarding sex and gender as being protected equally under the 14th Amendment.

Obergefell v. Hodges illuminates the Supreme Court's role in acting as a policymaker, and how divided the court itself is on that power—but as precedent has revealed this was not the first time the Court acted as a policymaker when it comes to the 14th Amendment and the Constitution, i.e.: Brown v. The Board of Education, and all the way back to Marbury v. Madison. In Obergefell, Justice Kennedy delivered the majority opinion that the fundamental right of same-sex couples to marry on the same terms and conditions as opposite-sex couples, with all the accompanying rights and responsibilities, is guaranteed by both the Due Process Clause and the Equal Protection Clause of the Fourteenth Amendment States Constitution. The ruling established that the Supreme Court, a group of unelected officials, should be the final word on the right to same sex marriage in the United States as fundamentally an equal right under our Constitution.

Justice Scalia's dissent is a counter to the majority's interpretation of the 14th Amendment, in which he feels the majority opinion created a new right not explicitly stated in the Constitution: same sex marriage. Scalia in his dissent felt such political activism and political change should never happen by unelected officials but by the people through elected representatives. Scalia felt the states are free to adopt whatever laws they want, and to strip that power from the states is not a democracy and is furthermore not Constitutional.

Equal Rights and the freedom to enjoy those "Equal" Rights should be shared by everyone, nationally, and EQUALLY.

Scalia argued that the majority in Obergefell overstepped its boundaries by exercising legislative power that should be up to each state, by each state, as reserved to the states' powers. Scalia's dissent was that legislating from the bench in Obergefell, the judiciary expanded its power beyond what the Constitution allows. Scalia felt that recognizing same sex marriage as legal is up to each state, not nine non-elected officials. **I disagree with Scalia's opinion completely.**

Not just because of my strong support of gay marriage, but because leaving civil rights up to the people, the states, thus those people in those states who elect their officials is perilous-as we have seen in the outcome of Plessy v. Ferguson and other civil rights cases. Many states continued clear constitutional violations of equal and civil rights because the Supreme Court felt it was not in their power to stop them. According to Scalia same sex marriage is not in the 14th Amendment, but "equal protection" is. Well, if every state is not on the same page—then what does "equal" mean?

THE RIGHTS OF PEOPLE

Should the rights of the people and the freedoms under which people live be protected by a uniform unelected group? A group of people with life tenure who have zero career aspirations tied to satisfying biased constituencies or tethered to reelection goals. It is only with that important untethered group to safeguard people's freedoms (even if those freedoms are offensive to some), that the Constitution's words are truly respected; for everyone, alike, equally, everywhere. So, yes,

Scalia is correct, that the Judiciary is not meant to nor supposed to legislate. However, **when it comes to protecting civil liberties, equal rights, and ensuring the equal freedoms of the American people, The Supreme Court must serve out the Constitution of the United States.** Justice Kennedy stated for the majority opinion:

The fundamental right to marry is guaranteed to same-sex couples by both the Due Process Clause and the Equal Protection Clause of the Fourteenth Amendment to the United States Constitution.

The role of the Supreme Court to act as policymaker when civil liberties, equal rights, and civil rights are being hindered, is critical, as the states may very well not adhere to cohesive definitions of what those rights mean, and who should have them.

PORN. V. PREACHER

Hustler v. Falwell

In 1983, the November issue of Hustler Magazine published an advertisement or rather a "parody" which portrayed Falwell as having a drunken incestuous sexual encounter with his mother in an outhouse.

On December 2, 1987, Hustler Magazine and Larry Flynt versus Jerry Falwell appeared before the Supreme Court for oral argument. Jerry Falwell, a nationally recognized Conservative Christian minister and commentator on politics and public affairs, filed a lawsuit in Federal District Court against Hustler, and its publisher, Larry Flynt in response to an advertisement published in the nationally circulated magazine in 1983.

Falwell brought suit against Flynt to recover damages citing the parody was an invasion of his privacy and intentionally inflicted emotional distress as well as citing the ad's falsity. The district court found for Falwell on the defamation and invasion of privacy claims, and The United States Court of Appeals for the Fourth Circuit affirmed the ruling in favor of Falwell, rejecting Hustler and Flynt's argument that the standard of actual malice set in the precedent of **New York Times Co. v. Sullivan** must be met before a respondent can recover damages for emotional distress.

The Court of Appeals rejected the argument by Hustler that the parody could not be perceived as an actual fact—the argument that people didn't actually believe that Falwell had sex with his mom in an outhouse, therefore the ad is just an opinion which is protected under the First Amendment—and The Supreme Court of the United States granted certiorari and agreed to hear the case. Alan Isaacman, the attorney representing Hustler Magazine and Larry Flynt argued before The Supreme Court that the First Amendment protects satirical and critical commentary or parodies of public figures.

Alan Isaacman's overall argument contends that when an advertisement is clearly parodying a public figure that depicts actions or makes statements which no reasonably intelligent person could take as true, that public figure cannot prevail or recover damages under the claim of emotional distress. Isaacman's opening remarks argument is grounded in the contention that no reasonable person would consider the parody of Falwell committing incest with his mother in an outhouse as true or factual, and is therefore rhetorical hyperbole, or satire, and should be protected under the First Amendment of the Constitution. Isaacman opens his oral argument asking whether or not the court should expand the First Amendment to areas left unprotected as illuminated by this case.

Isaacman asserts that this includes the new area of satirical or critical commentary of Public Figures that do not contain any assertions of truth or facts. Isaacman later on in his arguments, points out how perilous it would be to our nation to keep this type of speech unprotected, and cites the First Circuit **LL. Bean v. Drake** ruling that ruled parody to be protected speech. When Justice O'Connor asks Isaacman if the case would be different had the jury found the statements in the ad to be factual, Isaacman asserts that "It certainly would be a different case." Isaacman's argument that such hyperbole is not taken literally contends that if no average person would assume it's a serious fact, then the level of actual malice cannot reach the magnitude to which defamation is present.

Isaacman asserts that Falwell, a nationally recognized minister and the leader of The Moral Majority, a prominent Christian Conservative political organization is a public figure with as much political influence as those who legitimately hold political office. Isaacman argues that Falwell's status as a powerful public figure puts him in the less protected group with all other public figures. Isaacman argues that Falwell, a nationally recognized figure with influence should not be permitted to elude first amendment protections that were established as precedent in New York Times v. Sullivan.

Isaacman also cites **Garrison v. Louisiana**, in reference to whether or not the intention of Flynt toward Falwell, a public figure who was depicted in a ridiculous cartoon, is enough to claim emotional distress. Justice Scalia asks Isaacman if such intent is enough to make an exception to the **New York Times** Precedent. Isaacman responds that it's not intent, nor spite, nor hatred that the First Amendment is directed at, but rather actual reckless falsehoods stated as fact and those that are presented and perceived as factual and perceived to be true. Isaacman also argues that there is not one person of reasonable intelligence that would read the speeches in the cases of New York Times and Garrison, that would deny that the speaker intended to cause harm, as that is not the First Amendment issue at stake in this case. Intent, Isaacman argues, in perhaps one of is his most illuminating arguments, is not the question here, the critical issue at play here is when someone intends to say something critical, or something that may cause distress in the form of opinions, satire, parody, or rhetorical hyperbole that is speech that is protected under our Constitution.

Satire and parody, especially when aimed at political figures, are crucial expressions of free speech protected by the First Amendment.

Can you imagine how bland SNL would be without it? Even worse, The Daily Show wouldn't exist.

Personal expression, even if distasteful, is protected under the First amendment, and Isaacman argues that this case is not a case about defamatory statements, it is merely a case about taste and decorum. Isaacman argues that causing harm through falsehoods or reckless falsehoods as with Garrison, can only occur when the statement is considered to be fact and true, and that certainly does not occur in this case, as the jury found with Flynt's absurd parody.

Isaacman argued that the case leaves out the vital component that Falwell is a public figure who is less protected under this category than would be a private citizen regarding emotional distress. When one Justice asks Isaacman about the argument that parody or opinion about a public figure is not actionable even if the intent is to cause emotional distress, Isaac finishes the question with his answer that it also "this (parody) contains nothing that can be understood as a false statement of fact." The justice then continues asking that "if a public figure was not involved could we sustain the judgment?" Isaacman cleverly responds that fortunately that doesn't matter here, as that is not the case here. Isaacman clarifies that even if it's regarding a private citizen, if the statement is not perceived to be a fact, then yes, it is protected speech. The absurd parody of Falwell suggesting he had sexual intercourse with his mother, although in bad taste to many, does not rise to the requirements necessary to call it defamatory, and is therefore, protected by our constitution. In response to Justice O'Connor's questions regarding the establishment of Falwell as a public figure, Isaacman stresses the need to keep Falwell's status in mind, citing the precedent set by New York Times. Isaacman makes the point that Falwell and Flynt are opposite sides of the Political Spectrum, and Hustler's ad parodying Falwell is similar to the robust unpleasant, harsh and "caustic" language that was exchanged in the debate in the case of New York Times.

Isaacman makes another vital point early in his oral argument that the First Amendment is intended to ultimately protect the speaker. Even if that speaker made statements of facts that are knowingly false it is incumbent upon the court to review that statement with the priority of protecting the speaker first and foremost. The First Amendment protects speech and freedom of expression not the feelings they create. Tying together Falwell's status as a public figure and the ultimate intention of the first amendment, Isaacman makes one of his more substantial contentions to the Appellate Court's ruling. Isaacman requires the court to consider that when public figures who are commonly victims of this this type of parody or critical satire (even if tasteless and offensive) are awarded damages for the infliction of emotional distress as a result of such satire or criticisms, it creates a perilous path that limits the areas of speech that are protected under the First Amendment.

Isaacman's entire oral argument continually restates that if a jury had found the allegation of Falwell having sex with his mother presented in a cartoon ad to be perceived in any way as true and factual, then this case would not be here in front of the Supreme Court. What is perhaps the overarching theme in Isaacman's oral argument is that the parody of Falwell, just as with all parodies, cartoons, opinion pieces, etc., cannot be taken literally, and are not perceived as statement of truth or factual; therefore, malice cannot rise to the level that would reward Falwell for emotional distress.

The parody, while admittedly in bad taste, is protected speech under the First Amendment. Throughout his argument Isaacman argues that to award damages for intentional infliction of emotional distress to a public figure who is the victim of a parody or satire, that in no way is perceived as true or factual, is simply not consistent with the First Amendment, nor its intended purpose. Alan Isaacman, representing Hustler Magazine, prevailed.

FIRST AMENDMENT & COMMERCIAL SPEECH
The Central Hudson Test Is Born

In 1980, a case not only illuminated critical areas of First Amendment conflicts when restricting commercial speech, but it established a current legal framework for determining such restrictions. In Central Hudson Electric Corp. v. Public Service Commission of New York, The Supreme Court established the current legal framework for determining and the constitutionality of commercial speech restrictions and "The Central Hudson Test" was born. The Central Hudson Test became the framework and guiding post to serve as precedent in deciding future cases regarding the constitutionality of commercial speech restrictions and regulations. It has been over fifteen years since the third circuit ruled in the case of Pitt News v. Pappert, holding, that under the Central Hudson Test, a state ban on alcohol advertisements in a college newspaper violated the First Amendment right to free speech. In 2010, the Fourth Circuit, in Educational Media Co. at Virginia Tech v. Swecker, utilized the Hudson Central Test in same manner, yet the court came to an entirely different ruling. The Court's decision in Educational Media Co. at Virginia Tech v. Swecker was completely the opposite to that of Pitt, ruling that a similar state ban was not in violation of the First Amendment. To understand how the courts came to such opposing decisions in similar cases, while both applied the Central Hudson Test, it is critical to understand the requirements of the Hudson Test. What is the test cases must go through to determine if the commercial speech in question is protected under the First Amendment?

The Central Hudson Test has a threshold of four pronged questions that must be answered to determine if the uses of commercial speech in question are protected by the First Amendment. Does the speech concern a lawful activity or product and is it non-misleading or false? If the commercial speech in question meets these requirements, then there are three other prongs to the Hudson Test, but above all, the government must have a substantial interest in regulating the speech. The three other questions that determine if the restriction is constitutional are: Does the government have a substantial interest in restricting the speech? Does that restriction directly advance the government's interest? And is the restriction narrowly drawn—so as to not set a precedent that sweeps into it other cases of commercial speech even if similar? What stands out in the Central Hudson Test as applied to these two cases, is that the government must prove that the regulation or restriction directly advances the government's substantial interest.

What is fascinating about the cases of Pitt, and Educational Media is that these opposing rulings, and the resulting circuits' differing interpretations of the Hudson Test, illuminates the fragile, vague, and continual uncertainty in decisions on the constitutionality of commercial speech. While the Central Hudson Test seems straightforward, it can deliver conflicting outcomes.

In Pitt v. Pappert, after the court applied the four question Central Hudson Test, a Pennsylvania law that banned advertisements for alcoholic beverages in student newspapers was declared unconstitutional in third Circuit of Appeals in 2004. The Pitt News, the student newspaper at the University of Pittsburgh filed suit in April 1999 against the Pennsylvania officials who were responsible for enforcing the unconstitutional ban. Pitt News challenged the law as violating its rights to freedom of expression, freedom of the press and was deserving of equal protection just as all other forms of media. In Pitt, the court acknowledged that there is a substantial governmental interest in prohibiting advertisers from promoting alcohol use to young people in college. However, if preventing or suppressing any speech (even if not favored) by preventing the speaker (in this case the paper) from being paid through selling ads is allowable, then we are gutting the First Amendment.

The court observed that the first two questions of the Central Hudson Test were met. Alcohol is a legal product and there is substantial government interest in preventing our youth, and underage people from drinking and abusing alcohol. Advertising the sale of alcohol or alcoholic beverages in a college paper seems to be a dangerously irresponsible usage of commercial speech. Therefore, there is no denying the government's interest is clear. The third and fourth prongs of the test are where the state failed in the eyes of the court. The ban in no way truly advanced the government's interest to prevent underage drinking and underage alcohol abuse, therefore the ban on ads did not serve to advance the substantial interest at stake. Furthermore, the court concluded that when an act impacts any type of media, (even if it seems narrowly drawn) it ultimately sets the boundaries or restrictions for all media. The Court determined that the ban was not narrowly drawn, and that any ban upon any type of media is simply unconstitutional, thus, the fourth question was also not met in the eyes of the Court and Pitt News prevailed.

In the case of Educational Media Co. at Virginia Tech v. Swecker, the Central Hudson Test served to result in an opposing ruling. Although the two cases are strikingly similar and revolve around the same constitutional questions, the rulings were not congruent even when both courts applied the Hudson Test. In Educational Media Co., Virginia's Alcohol Beverage Control Board "The Board" was charged with restricting and governing the possession, transportation, distribution, and the sale of alcohol in the Commonwealth of Virginia. The Collegiate Times, a student run newspaper at Virginia Tech, and the Cavalier Daily, a student run newspaper at the University of Virginia challenged the Board's restrictions, and the ban on advertisements of alcohol.

Both Newspapers, just as with the case of Pitt News, relied upon the sale of ads to generate revenue. Each newspaper estimated a loss of thirty thousand dollars each year in advertising revenue due to the Board's prohibition of alcohol advertisements. The two Virginia college newspapers filed suit in the Eastern District of Virginia challenging the Board's regulations as clearly violating the First Amendment. The district court ruled in favor of the college newspapers, finding that the regulation was an invalid ban on commercial speech and was, thus, unconstitutional. The Board appealed and this is when the ruling of the court diverges from the precedent set in Pitt.

Under the Central Hudson Test, if the regulated or banned commercial speech is truthful, involves a lawful product or legal activity, the government must demonstrate that it has a substantial interest in restricting that speech and that the restriction advances that interest while being narrowly drawn.

The last two questions in the Hudson Test are critical to focus on when dissecting how the two cases of *Pitt* and E*ducational Media* resulted in diverging outcomes. Like Pitt, regarding the 2nd question of the test, the court did not dispute Virginia Board's argument that there is a substantial governmental interest in combating underage and excessive drinking on college campuses.

However, when the court reached the third and fourth questions of the Hudson Test in Educational Media Co. at Virginia Tech v. Swecker, it came to a different decision. Unlike in Pitt News v. Pappert, the court concluded in the case of Educational Media Co. that the Board's regulations clearly advanced the government's interest in controlling dangerous alcohol abuse and consumption by college students. The court concluded that "history, consensus, and simple common sense (8)" supported the connection between bans and restrictions of alcohol-related advertisements in college newspapers to a decrease in college students' demand for alcohol. The Court, in response to question three of the Hudson Test, argued that alcohol sellers would not spend money on ads in college papers, if they didn't think that these ads would generate business from college students. This argument supports the assertion that the Board's restriction was serving to advance the government's substantial interest.

But doesn't this seem to permit a possible unconstitutional restriction on speech?

The fourth question of the Central Hudson Test is also where the court diverges from that case of *Pitt*. The Fourth Circuit supported the Virginia Board's argument that the ban was narrowly drawn, and therefore not infringing upon the First Amendment. The Fourth Circuit ruled in *Educational Media Co*. that the Board's regulation on advertisements was not a whole sweeping ban on all types of alcohol advertisements in all print media, because it applied only to publications and papers for underage students.

The colleges and their publications responded adamantly that there were many more effective ways to serve the government's interest in addressing and curbing college alcohol abuse and underage drinking. The court still held in favor of "The Board" arguing that in fact the ban was very narrow in a large and growing problem of underage drinking on college campuses. Unlike the ruling in Pitt, the regulations and bans of alcohol advertisements in college papers in Virginia were deemed constitutional, even after applying the four-pronged Central Hudson Test.

These two similar cases and how their rulings diverge when put to the same test, and examined under the same questions, illuminates the gray area of commercial speech restrictions. The Central Hudson Test is very clear, or is it? Is more required to determine if commercial speech is protected by the First Amendment? What is missing then in the Central Hudson Test that when applied the same way in two cases that are essentially fighting for the same constitutional protection, the outcomes differ? Should there be more challenging, or more evidentiary based questions than those in the Hudson Test?

These two cases and their split rulings shine a light upon the courts' varying interpretations of the constitutionality of regulating commercial speech. The flaw of The Central Hudson Test is that it can be broadened or simplified to fit into the arguments of either side. These two cases argued for the same constitutional protections of the same commercial speech and were put to the same test, yet their outcomes were starkly different.

But come on, really?
Banning ads for alcohol in college papers will NOT slow sales of alcohol. Do any of you really think that is where college students got the idea to get alcohol?

EXECUTIVE PRIVILEGE

United States v. Nixon - (Now with Trump!)

The idea of executive privilege came into focus never more clearly and with more debate than during the case of United States v. Nixon. In not one single place in the Constitution is there any explicit mention of executive privilege, but then again nor is there any mention of any oversight of the powers of Congress. So, this idea of executive privilege, and the reach of the power held with "executive privilege" is solely based on the interpretation of the Constitution, ultimately coming down to the idea of the separation of powers, and what that means as intended by the constitution (or how you interpret it). Does the separation of powers mean that Nixon and the executive branch are entitled to confidentiality in his communications? Yes, to a degree if it serves and protects the people's interests. However, in Nixon's case, doesn't that separation of powers then also set forth the Judicial Branch's responsibility to keep the executive branch in check when grossly abusing that "executive privilege" that Nixon so claimed was his right.

Yes. It does.

With United States v. Nixon, withholding relevant evidence from a criminal case using the power of "executive confidentiality or privilege", directly goes against due process of the law as set forth in the Fifth Amendment. In United States v. Nixon, the judicial branch did its job in keeping the executive branch power in check, no matter what independence Nixon claimed was rightfully part of the executive Branch—Due Process of Law is not only tantamount to that executive privilege/executive confidentiality, but in Nixon's case, it prevailed, and justly. **The competing interests brought out by this misuse of executive privilege on the part of Nixon underscore the gray areas of presidential power—what does presidential power truly mean and how far can that go?**

We are seeing this again with Trump. Presidents and ex-presidents are not entitled to absolute privilege to pursue abuses of executive powers. Absolute power, if held to no standard of checks and balances, directly contradicts the executive branch's duties to serve the people in the best interest of our national security.

In United States v. Nixon, the competing interests of preserving the confidentiality of the communications of high government officials v. due process of the law are evident, with both sides using the constitution's separation of powers as its defense. In Nixon's case, there is a clear distinction between the importance of protecting the confidentiality of the executive branch and using it in an obstructive overreach against the duties of the court and public interest. Due Process is a necessary function of the courts. Nixon's abuse of executive privilege cannot override evidence that is necessary to administer criminal justice. The courts used this as the justification for its ruling.

United States v. Nixon could aptly be called the Supreme Court v. Nixon, or the Judicial Branch v. the Executive Branch. Nixon clearly mutated and manipulated the idea of executive power to commit obstruction of justice to withhold evidence. (TRUMP COMMITTED THESE EXACT CRIMES ON AN EVEN LARGER SCALE) The Supreme Court in Nixon justified its ruling through the 6th Amendment—in that the production of relevant evidence is necessary in the criminal process—and through the 5th Amendment regarding Due Process of the law. The court's ruling made it clear that a fair adjunction of a criminal case with the administration of justice in the courts supersedes executive privilege. The Court rejected Nixon's use of executive privilege as a constitutional justification to escape due process of law.

Unlike Nixon, Trump escaped conviction for his crimes through a partisan Congress who refused to act and do their job.

THREE-FIFTHS OF A HUMAN BEING
Scott v. Sanford

Congressional Representatives for each state counted each slave as only three-fifths of a human being.

SERIOUSLY AMERICA?

In 1833, a U.S. Army surgeon, Dr. John Emerson, bought a slave named Dred Scott in St. Louis, Missouri. Dr. Emerson took Scott with him when he moved to an Army base in the Wisconsin Territory, where the Missouri Compromise had banned slavery. Scott lived in the area for four years, remaining and seeking employment during the stretches that Dr. Emerson was away. During this time, Scott married and had children. In 1840, Scott and his family moved with Dr. Emerson to St. Louis, where the doctor died, bequeathing the entire Scott family to his wife. In 1846, Dred Scott, who had worked diligently to save money, sought to buy his family's freedom from the doctor's wife.

She refused.

Scott sued the woman in state court, arguing that he and his family were free, as they had lived in a territory where slavery was outlawed. After four grueling years, the court finally declared the Scotts to be free. There was further arguing in court, as Scott had been denied his pay the entire time the matter was before the court, and Mrs. Emerson refused to pay, instead taking the matter to the Missouri Supreme Court, which overturned the state court's ruling.

When the matter made its way to the U.S. Supreme Court in 1856, the Court issued what is quite possibly the nation's most infamous ruling based on strict constructionism. In the Court's ruling, Chief Justice Roger Taney expressed the opinion that certain clauses of the Constitution "point directly and specifically to the negro race as a separate class of persons and show clearly that they were not regarded as a portion of the people or citizens of the Government then formed." NO! WHAT? Seriously America?!!

Justice Taney, in explaining why the Constitution tied the Court's hands in the Scott matter, stated that no change in opinion, or any one person, or the nation, should prompt the court to interpret provisions of the Constitution with "a more liberal construction in their favor than they were intended to bear when the instrument was framed and adopted" and if the people found any provisions of the Constitution to be unjust, there is an approved method for amending it. The Dred Scott case is certainly representative of the issue of strict interpretation of the text of the law, and whether personal or public opinion should have a place in the U.S. legal system.

Scott v. Sanford is a reminder of the inhumane crimes of our nation's origins. America, why?

HOW CAN THEY JUST TAKE YOUR HOUSE?

America, why?

<u>Kelo v. City of New London,</u>
<u>Lucas v. South Carolina,</u>
<u>Penn Central v. City of New York</u>

What is a taking? In many cases it is evident that a taking has occurred, and that the property owner has been stripped of ownership rights and is entitled to adequate compensation. What happens when a government actively "takes" the property owned privately by an individual deeming it necessary for public benefit and use? How broadly interpreted can the Fifth Amendment takings clause be stretched? How does the eminent domain provision of the Fifth Amendment defend property rights? The provision establishes when a governmental body, or a private body exercising delegated power, takes private property it must provide due compensation and take the property only for a public purpose.

In reading over the case of Kelo v. City of New London and the subsequent ruling; The urban redevelopment in New London, Connecticut through the private corporation Pfizer for the purpose of revitalization and economic growth benefitting the public falls within the Fifth Amendment's public usage language. The interests of the private homeowners, with the specific interests of Susette Kelo, were considered and properly balanced with the public interests of the citizens of New London in the court's decision. The development of the Pfizer research facility as well as the offspring of surrounding businesses would greatly serve a public purpose for New London under the public use provision in the constitution, but do they really get to take someone's home?

The questions at the root of most taking cases as with Kelo are what defines a public purpose and what government actions constitute a taking within the definition of the Constitution? In Kelo the petitioners argue that economic development seizures are not for a public purpose but for private business, violating the Fifth Amendment. The issues in the divided ruling of Kelo are twofold; concerning whether a taking has occurred and what defines "public purpose"?

The Constitution's Fifth Amendment states: "nor be deprived of life liberty or property without due process of the law; nor shall private property be taken for public use, without just compensation". In Kelo, this division between the language in the constitution describing a "public use" requirement and how public use has been interpreted to encompass a "public purpose" is evident in how divided the court was in this ruling. It is essential to relegate any sentimentality regarding Susette Kelo and her home, as well as the other eight homeowners to not salient arguments for this case and focus solely on what the constitution allows as "eminent domain" and proper takings.

The Constitution has been used to defend takings, and although this can be broad, Kelo falls under such jurisprudence as seen in the ruling of the case. Justice Stevens delivers the opinion of the court, with an understanding that the provisions of the Constitution do not permit the City, nor any Governmental body to take the petitioner's land for the purpose of private benefit for a private party or business as Susette Kelo argues, nor would the city be allowed to take the homes under a false pretext of public purpose.

In Kelo, however, the public purpose and public use was adequately defined by Pfizer. Although the business is a privately run one (Pfizer) the purpose and benefit of such a business was established as clearly for the public purpose and usage for the ailing city of New London and its citizens. The public purpose for these takings has been deemed for the economic stimulation and revitalization of a dying and desperately declining city. What makes this case so heated, and complex is that the argument from the petitioners is not without serious merit, but the public purpose use for these takings is also evident.

The use of eminent domain in Kelo through the private business development seems to have been applied broadly as the Petitioner argues, but it still aptly applies within the Constitution's provision as being for public purpose and use with just compensation offered to Susette. Justice Stevens, in delivering the opinion of the court, substantiates the city's statute which authorizes the use of eminent domain to promote economic development for a public purpose. The Court in Kelo ruled that the New London City Plan with Pfizer Corp. as its vehicle for economic growth, serves a public purpose, and amply satisfies the public use requirements set forth in the Fifth Amendment.

While this made sense at the time, The *Kelo* ruling opened up a free-for-all allowance for corporations to buy up neighborhoods, and homes of people who spent generations in them.

What in the actual F$@! Supreme Court?

Promoting economic growth and development for the purpose of public prosperity and dignity is not outside of public use or purpose as the petitioners argue in Kelo. It is quite vividly and acutely the opposite regardless of the merits of the petitioner's arguments.

**Broadening the concept of public purposes to encompass any
and all economically beneficial goals leaves poor communities
ripe for takings, leaving the poverty-stricken towns more
susceptible to such losses while also being the least
politically powerful to fight them.**

The Kelo case certainly justifies a judicial review of these broader interpretations of the "takings' and "public use" provisions in our Constitution as necessary to protect the less powerful individuals and groups the public purpose clause is in fact supposed to protect.

The precedent in **Lucas v. South Carolina** expanded the "takings clause" with the majority ruling the Fifth Amendment is violated only when the "taking" of such land does not largely advance the legitimate city's or state's economic interests, but that a taking did in fact occur upon Lucas. This is succinctly in line with the court's ruling in Kelo. The court, in a 6-2 ruling held that Lucas had suffered a taking and that he was owed compensation, as was also applied to Kelo. The Lucas precedent expanded the definition of the "takings clause" and defined the compensation requirement when a taking has occurred, regardless of public interests, which was echoed in Kelo who was offered just compensation.

The 6-3 ruling of **Penn Central v. City of New York** which dismissed the "takings" challenge by Penn Central further defined a "taking" like the reasoning used in Kelo. The majority ruled the restrictions placed upon Penn Central to construct a building over Grand Central Terminal was for the promotion of the general welfare of the public. This is mirrored in the argument by the court in its dismissal of Kelo's takings challenge as well, rooted in the interpretation of the public usage language of the Fifth Amendment. It is in the ruling on Penn that further established the precedent that an "unconstitutional taking" is one that must be in clear defiance of the Fifth

Amendment and must violate due process of the law under the Fourteenth Amendment.

The decision in Kelo v. City of New London broadened the government's power to invoke eminent domain and this is scary. The court must protect the people's property rights, while ensuring public welfare at the same time, but what defines "public use"?

Should the taxpayers be left to carry the burden when compensation for the taking occurs or should the property owners be burdened by legislation restricting their right to their private property?

ONE MAN TOOK ON THE SYSTEM AND WON (JURY SELECTION)

Edmonson v. Leesville & Batson v. Kentucky

There are Landmark Supreme Court cases that have changed the trajectory of justice, changed how the constitution is to be interpreted, and have impacted all the nations' citizens today but most of those landmark cases did not start out as a simple civil suit, but were initially about a violation of the rights of citizens as stated in the constitution.

Edmonson v. Leesville illustrates how the people need to believe in a fair and just system and the equal rights of every citizen in that system.

This case is about the inspiring perseverance and courage of every people who take on the system and not only win but change the system for the better.

In 1984, Thaddeus Edmonson, employed by Leesville Concrete Co., was working on a construction site in Louisiana when he was badly injured on the job. Leesville Concrete agreed to cover his expenses for a time but in the end, Thaddeus Edmonson was left with piles and piles of debt and a mound of bills he could not pay. Leesville's compensation to Edmonson was far from fair, and Thaddeus was suffering, So, he sued the corporation. This was a simple personal injury suit about money, right? Then how did this case end up in the Supreme Court?

During jury selection, Leesville Concrete dismissed two potential black jurors without any explanation under their right of peremptory challenges. (Peremptory challenge is the lawyers' or a defendant's right to dismiss or object to a juror without needing to give a reason as to why). It was obvious to Thaddeus Edmonson and his lawyer, James Doyle, that Leesville Co. was targeting only the black jurors (Edmonson was a black man himself). Edmonson and James Doyle fought back, requesting a new trial based on Leesville's apparent racial discriminations that violated the 14th Amendment and the equal rights clause that would ensure fair trials in our courts no matter race or gender. The case wound up in the Supreme Court.

Edmonson v. Leesville, a straightforward civil lawsuit between private parties in a district court, transformed into a violation of the constitution's 14th Amendment, and a violation of the Equal Protections Clause.

In 1991, years after Thaddeus Edmonson filed his simple civil suit in a small district in Louisiana, The Supreme Court made a landmark ruling that shaped our courts forever. Thaddeus Edmonson, a construction worker from Louisiana, battled for what he believed was right, and because of his fight, no potential juror in any American court, in any type of case, can ever be excluded from a jury because of race. It's highly unusual for issues in cases to transform as dramat-ically as the issues in Edmonson v. Leesville Concrete transformed and tells a story of how one man's fight against an injustice became a fight to protect every single person's constitutional rights. The issues in Edmonson vs Leesville were no longer about money or an injury but about the right to a fair trial by a jury of citizens chosen by their quality of character not by the color of skin or gender. The Supreme Court's ruling in favor of Edmonson protects every citizen's right to a representative jury in a fair trial, and every qualified citizen's equal right to be a part of that jury regardless of race or gender.

What prompted the transformation were two key elements: The Prosecution's use of Peremptory Challenges used in the jury se-lection to dismiss two black jurors, and the precedent (although a criminal case, not a civil one like Edmonson's) set forth in **Batson v. Kentucky** on the unconstitutionality of the abuse of per-emptory challenges, that create an unfair racial bias in juries.

THE CASE CHANGED A CONSTITUTIONAL ISSUE

That every court, not just criminal, should be protected under the 14th Amendment and the Constitution. Edmonson became about solidify-ing the jury system as a voice of the people to be a fair check on the government, and how peremptory challenges prevents that, but most importantly it violates the right to a fair trial as stated in the 6th and 7th amendments. The case of Edmonson also sets the foundation that every court case, both criminal and civil, is acting in government con-text; and therefore, must adhere to the same rules as set forth in the Constitution no matter what type of case is being heard. What was most dramatic about the transformation of the issues in this case that lead to a 6-3 victory changing the arbitrary abuses of peremptory challenges based on race and gender: Attorney for Thaddeus Edmon-son, James Doyle's arguments. This case evolved into a principle. In front of the Supreme Court, years after Edmonson's first civil suit, James Doyle argued not about how the ruling affected his client, but how, just like in Batson v. Kentucky, peremptory challenges affect every citizen's equal right to a fair trial and every citizen's right to be a part of a jury granted to them by the Constitution. Jury selections using peremptory challenges based on race or gender is unconstitutional no matter what type of case of being heard and is a clear violation of the Equal Rights Protection Clause. Leesville was no longer just about a man who needed to eat.

> **A case is a case—criminal or civil—and denying a fair trial is unconstitutional on every front no matter what type of case or in what courtroom.**

SEVEN YEARS AND TREMENDOUS LOSS

The precedent set in Batson v. Kentucky, (although criminal, not civil like Leesville), and the intent of the 14th amendment Article 3 of our Constitution, makes the amount of time Edmonson had to wait to receive a fair trial because of the peremptory challenges used in his case all the more egregious. Those long seven years throughout which as a result of the abuse of peremptory challenges, granted Thaddeus very little compensation. He lost his house and he hit rock bottom—which of course is not the argument in front of the Supreme Court—but it lends to the fact that a case is a case, criminal or civil, and denying a fair trial is simply unconstitutional no matter what type of case or in what courtroom. The case was no longer about Edmonson needing money to eat and pay bills but about the interpretation of the Constitution in how the abuse of peremptory challenges violates the rights set forth in the Constitution. The Courts operate within the context that was created by the government no matter the case or courtroom.

Batson v. Kentucky is applicable to every abuse of Peremptory Challenges no matter how small the case or the type of case.

Edmonson v. Leesville illustrates how the people need to believe in a fair and just system and the equal rights of every citizen in that system. There are cases brought before the Supreme Courts that clearly have transformed our judiciary and end up in the highest court—Edmonson vs. Leesville is unique in how it went from a small civil suit to a larger issue on equal rights and constitutionality. Doyle fought not just for Edmonson but for a judicial system with a fair trial process, for every citizen alike equally, regardless of race or gender.

A man seeking compensation called into question and underscored the abuses within the justice system that violate the Constitution and the Equal Rights Protection Clause.

The initial ruling in Edmonson v. Leesville certainly did not glaringly in any way appear to be a violation of the constitution—just wholly unjust for Edmonson as the Big Corp once again won out. So, what is so fascinating about this case is that is not directly about that ruling; it is about the people that shaped the courtroom within Edmonson v. Leesville as the case was heard: the jury, and the selection of that jury. Doyle's resolve to fight against a system that was enabling an abuse of a power, and violating the 14th Amendment, is not only crucial, but certainly not what he thought he was going to end up arguing when Edmonson came to him. The case began as Edmonson v. Leesville but became Edmonson v. the Peremptory Challenge, Edmonson vs. The Justice System.

The people and our Constitution won.

THE LADY WHO SPILLED HOT COFFEE ON HERSELF AT MCDONALD'S IS NOT WHAT YOU THINK

Liebeck V. McDonald's Restaurants

A little old lady who just wanted to be reimbursed for her medical bills and for McDonald's to cool down their coffee so others will not suffer her same injuries, took on the giant.

In 1992 in Albuquerque, New Mexico, 79-year-old Stella Liebeck bought a cup of coffee from McDonald's. While seated in the passenger seat, with her son at the wheel, the two parked the car, and as Stella tried to put creamer in her coffee, it spilled into her lap, causing agonizing third-degree burns and two weeks stay in a hospital. Her injuries were severe, and her pain and suffering were uncontested. The coffee was scalding hot, with scientists proving its high temperature would cause third degree burns in less than three seconds. It was clear the hot coffee caused her injuries, yet McDonald's denied Liebeck a refund for her medical bills, so the case went to trial.

Liebeck's injuries were not frivolous nor exaggerated, and the cause of her harm was the dangerously hot coffee served by McDonald's. The case was clear with photographic evidence of the plaintiff's suffering and permanent disfigurement, yet the case became an argument about individual responsibility v. corporate liability. Liebeck did, after all, spill the coffee on herself, so why should McDonald's bear the blame? This case, seemingly straightforward, failed to be solved through negotiations, and mediations were fruitless.

Liebeck v. McDonald's vividly illustrates the glaring power disparity inherent in civil litigation. It pits ordinary working-class individuals, often constrained by financial limitations and

limited legal support, against corporate giants armed with
seemingly endless resources and unfettered access
to top-notch legal representation.

The unmistakable power asymmetry evident in this case under-
scores a fundamental imbalance within the legal system.

In the end, the jury **awarded Liebeck** $200,000 in compensatory
damages, which was then reduced to $160,000 because the jury found
her to be 20% at fault (she did spill the coffee on herself) and $2.7
million in punitive damages against McDonald's callous conduct
(McDonald's revenue from **coffee** sales alone exceeds $1.3 million a
day). So, this case is not what most people think it is. Some old lady
was not greedy and working the system. Stella Liebeck was treated
callously by a huge corporation who thought they could get away with
it.

The court made it clear in this case that a working-class
victim can beat a huge team of corporate lawyers and make
the world a better place because of it.

The mass media played upon mistruths in this rapidly infamous case,
resulting in Liebeck v. McDonald's becoming a rallying cry for frivolous lawsuits and a cultural icon for what is wrong with our American Civil Justice System (McCann, et al., 2001). How does this happen? Liebeck v. McDonald became a rallying cry for tort reform because the truth got lost in the chaos of a large corporation's ability to
manipulate the information campaign behind it. Thus, the media often
ignored the facts. Inaccurate and inflammatory headlines read everything from "Old woman wins 2.9 million because she spilled coffee
on herself while driving" to "Woman spills coffee on herself and wins
2.9 million" to "We should all spill coffee on ourselves and get rich!"

The "Hot Coffee" case gave rise to legislative actions and campaigns against frivolous lawsuits. The media bolstered the attacks on Liebeck led by mistruths, in a clear display of a power asymmetry between an elderly woman just seeking minor compensation and one of the most well-known powerful corporations in our country. According to the article "Java Jive: Genealogy of a Juridical Icon," the media's role in fanning the flames of criticisms of the civil justice system is profound. With Liebeck v. McDonalds, popular and conservative news outlets focused on individual responsibility and personal negligence. The media emphasized greedy plaintiffs rather than large corporations' responsibilities to ensure citizens' welfare and safety. Although the media's place is outside the justice system, this toxic spin results from the power asymmetries in civil litigations, warping the public's perceptions of the law, and plaintiffs often, as with Liebeck, unjustly become victims twofold.

CHAPTER NINE

The Media in Our Courtrooms and Why We Need Them

Recent Supreme Court Decisions have been heartbreaking and infuriating and have turned back the clock on Women's Rights, Environmental Protections and Gun Control.

Don't you think we as the people deserve the right to view these proceedings that directly affect us and our children?

WE THE PEOPLE DESERVE CAMERAS IN OUR SUPREME COURT

That gut-wrenching day in 2022 when Roe v. Wade was overturned (and I came home from Trader Joe's and cried in my husband's arms) is not the only appalling Supreme Court ruling recently that served as a blow to humanity. There was the day when the Supreme Court lifted the personal handgun ban, and the day when The

Supreme Court ruled against student debt relief, and the day when the Supreme Court made a ruling that overturned five decades of wetlands protections. These rulings baffle us, leaving us disheartened and angry. As we grapple with these destructive and disheartening rulings that directly affect the well-being of U.S. citizens and will continue to negatively affect us and our children for generations, we might ask: Why can't we watch these proceedings on camera, live? Do we not, as a people, have the right to see and hear the justices when they make rulings that affect us, the American people, directly? These rulings will forever affect our children and their children.

In Chapter Two of this book, "What in the Actual F**k Supreme Court?" I dive into the ideologies behind why justices rule the way they do to digest some of the maddening decisions of our highest court. Decisions that are heartbreaking and infuriating and turn back the clock on Women's rights, Environmental protections and the EPA, and Gun Control. These rulings, might be less baffling if we, as the people, could view them as they happen live,? Don't you think we as the people deserve that right?

When the trial, (and there will most likely be more trials) of Donald Trump gets underway, cameras in the courtroom will be critical.

Unless you've taken a vow of silence in the mountains with Jared Leto, or you are only watching Fox News, Donald Trump and his people unabashedly dispel lies, and play Donald like a victim, bolstering the dangerous false rhetoric that our very own justice departments and AGs are corrupt.

Donald Trump is a criminal and cameras in the courtroom are the only sure-fire way to exterminate the lies that will come from his side throughout his trial. Cameras in the court are the only way to deliver the trial without spin and without the dangerous mistruths that Donald dispels to his ardent anti-intellectualist followers (not that they will be watching the trial—but we can hope). There is not a uniform federal rule on cameras in our courts as it is up to each state to decide, but it is evident that we need them, everywhere.

Here is how the states differ…

CAMERAS IN COURT STATE BY STATE
How Some States Differ

For decades, the allowance of cameras in courtrooms has stirred up much debate. Those opposed and those who are for cameras in courtrooms all invoke the constitution to justify their positions. Proponents argue First Amendment rights that guarantee public access to judicial information, the Sixth Amendment that guarantees a public trial, and the Fourteenth Amendment that protects due process rights. Opponents say that those very same rights under our constitution are disrupted and violated by the presence of cameras in the courtroom, specifically the fair trial aspect. Opponents say that the presence of a camera distracts and deters participants from being wholly organic and accurate when in a trial. All fifty states have their own rules regulating cameras inside their courtrooms, but filming and photographing criminal proceedings in Federal Courts is prohibited under the Federal Rule of Criminal Procedure. Some federal district courts and circuit courts will allow recordings under very specific and limited circumstances. Overall, cameras are rarely allowed in federal courts but are generally allowed in state courts.

Comparing California, Florida, and Pennsylvania illuminates the differing rules and hurdles broadcasters must go through to film inside courtrooms. However, what seems a uniform rule across most states, is that any coverage of jury selections, spectators, proceedings held inside chambers, between attorneys, or between counsel and the judges is strictly prohibited. In California, the LA Superior has banned all types of photography inside its courtrooms. In Los Angeles, a person must be in a designated media coverage area when filming outside the courtroom. The San Francisco Superior Court prohibits filming in hallways and on certain floors. California allows only one camera at a time inside after the request for coverage has been submitted 5 days prior and by a written order of approval by the judge. Under California rules, the media is responsible for managing their own pooling arrangements for that single camera. Furthermore, any person in a California courtroom must obtain written permission to use an iPhone, laptop, or any type of sound or video recording device inside the court. In summation, California allows one camera with an audio and or video webcast and a media guide. All of these must be approved by the judge's written order, 5 days in advance, and is at the individual judge's discretion, case by case.

Similar to California but more relaxed is Florida. Florida allows at least one camera and no more than two still cameras in both trial and appellate courts. The court, however, decides the placement of cameras, and the equipment must not be distracting in court. The media members must prove to the judge, prior to proceedings (although no time frame is given on how prior), that their equipment is not going to disrupt or distract the participants. In Florida, the media is prohibited from covering private conferences between attorneys and clients and attorneys and the judge. Florida's loose language leaves much room for flexibility. Florida rule states that the exclusion of media coverage is only allowed where it is proven that such coverage will disrupt or adversely affect the proceedings of the court and when media coverage proves to be less quality than other forms of coverage. There is also no mention of disallowing coverage in areas outside the courtroom. Florida's rules seem loose and vague, with much wiggle room.

Pennsylvania is on the opposite side of the spectrum of California and Florida regarding cameras in their courts. Under Pennsylvania rule, judges must prohibit all cameras unless approved by the Supreme Court of Pennsylvania. Therefore, in Pennsylvania, any broadcasting, televising, recording, or taking photographs in the courtroom is not allowed. This ban on cameras includes all areas, not just those directly involved in the proceedings in the courtroom, but areas immediately nearby sessions of court as well as the recesses between sessions. There are only a few exceptions to any type of camera (film or photography) equipment being allowed in any area. These exceptions are if the photographic or filming device is necessary to present evidence, if the equipment is used to record judicial management duties, and for the broadcasting, recording, or photographing of a ceremonial or naturalization proceeding. These exceptions are also only allowable if the media proves that their means of recording will not distract participants or compromise the decorum of the proceedings. Furthermore, these allowances can only occur when all the parties have consented to the filming or the photography.

So, as the polar opposite to California and Florida's rules on cameras in court, Pennsylvania does not allow cameras, only partially allows cameras under stringent protocols and specific exceptions, and only in certain areas. Audio and webcasts are not allowed, and media guides are not allowed. However, what is interesting is that the rules of personal devices in the courtroom vary from court to court. Also, The Supreme Court of Pennsylvania does allow the Pennsylvania Cable Network to record and broadcast its proceedings, but only those that are not sealed and after approval.

Wisconsin is the winner for broadcast journalists.

In researching the states' varying regulations, the state that gives me the most flexibility to bring my video camera into court in Wisconsin. In Wisconsin, up to 3 television cameras and 2 still cameras are allowed in any courtroom proceeding. The forgiving language states that" 'If possible', the trial judge shall be given notice, at least 3 days in advance of the intention of the media to bring cameras or recording equipment into the courtroom. Just like in California and Florida, this is up to the discretion of the judge. Also, this 3-day advance notice rule may be waived if a cause for the waiver is demonstrated.

The only minor hurdle in Wisconsin, if you want your camera to have the best coverage, is that priority consideration is given to one of the 3 cameras to televise an entire proceeding from beginning to end. In addition, there is no mention of disallowing cameras in other areas. There are only two restrictions under which a judge can prohibit the photographing of a participant with a video or still camera. If a participant requests the ban and the judge approves that request. The other restriction is that individual jurors cannot be photographed, except in cases when a juror or jurors give consent. This restriction is somewhat mute. In courtrooms, the jury is part of the background, and thus it is impossible to photograph or film the proceedings without including the jury. A judge must consider the importance of maintaining the public's right to an open court, the preservation of the privacy rights of the participants in the proceedings, the effect of camera coverage on the counsel's ability to select an unbiased jury, and the rights of the accused to an open and fair trial.

In 1965, in *Estes v. Texas*, The Supreme Court overturned the conviction of the accused (Estes) on the grounds that the camera in the courtroom distracted the participants so much that it hindered the participants' abilities to give Estes a fair trial. Cameras in court are a balancing act, which is why there is no uniform national policy.

Judges often use discretion on a case-by-case evaluation, regardless of if the court is in Pennsylvania, Florida, or California.

"X" IN THE COURTROOM IS A POSITIVE

Twitter "X" is a powerful media platform instantaneously disseminating information and opinions to millions of people worldwide. Journalists, pundits, and news outlets across America use "X" to disseminate the daily events of trials as they happen from inside the courtroom. "X" provides the public with real-time information concerning our judicial system through the live communication of events during a trial. The debate over whether this technology should be allowed inside courtrooms stems from constitutional violations, fears about privacy, due process, prejudicial reporting, and the defendant's right to an untainted jury.

"X", however, is in real time, while reporters take notes or record the court's proceedings to report on later that day. X's real time speed is why the debate exists. Witnesses and members of a jury in a trial being tweeted about can instantly attain real-time information that may sway their roles and behaviors in the trial and, subsequently, the defendant's fate. The concern is valid, and there is no doubt that trial lawyers in a courtroom with "X" coverage are facing new challenges. However, there is no difference between providing news via traditional coverage and electronic methods such as "X". When any press or form of reporting is banned from the courtroom, it violates First Amendment rights of free speech, a defendant's Sixth Amendment right to a public trial, and the accused's Due Process Rights guaranteed by the Fifth and Fourteenth Amendments, as well as the presumptive right of public access to the proceedings.

The debate over allowing reporters to tweet (or now "X") from inside courtrooms has been ongoing for years. The opposition argues that Twitter and all reporting technology inside the courtroom distracts from the court's business and thus interferes with a fair trial. Well....

Given that the term "media circus" exists for a reason, the opposition make a valid point, but freedom of the press is essential in a democracy. Freedom of the press is what keeps the system of powers in check. Closing off courtroom trials from public access because you do not like the means by which the reporters report information, runs the gamut of being unconstitutional.

Several years ago, Judge Mark Bennet of the United States District Court for the Northern District of Iowa allowed Trish Mehaffey, a reporter for the Cedar Rapids Gazette, to tweet live courtroom updates during a high-profile insurance fraud trial. Judge Bennet stated his position on tweeting in an interview with the ABA Journal, "I thought the public's right to know what goes on in federal court and the transparency that would be given the proceedings by live blogging, outweighed any potential prejudice to the defendant. I allowed it because of my belief that we are the most mysterious branch of the federal government, and we need to find ways to be more transparent (8)".

Following suit, Judge Thomas Marten of the United States District Court for the District of Kansas allowed Wichita Eagle reporter Ron Sylvester to cover the trial of six accused gang members using Twitter. Thomas told the Associated Press, "The more we can do to open the process to the public, the greater the public understanding— the more legitimacy the public system will have in the eyes of the public (4)".

Amid growing mistrust of our judicial, legal, and penal systems, "X" in the courtroom provides immediate access to courts of law. "X" enhances transparency between the judicial system and the public it serves.

Allowing reporters to tweet gives the public citizens instant access to the judiciary and criminal trials that often affect their very own communities. Allowing reporters to tweet during a trial increases transparency so critical between the public and our legal system, thereby strengthening the public trust in the system itself. Isn't this precisely what the First, Sixth, Fifth, and Fourteenth Amendments envisioned?

We need the media in our Courts.

PART THREE

HOW WE TREAT
HUMAN BEINGS

ESPECIALLY CHILDREN
HERE AND AROUND
THE WORLD

CHAPTER TEN

Caging Children
Is the Trump Way

"When you prosecute the parents for coming in ille-
gally, which should happen, you have to take
their children away."

- Donald Trump on June 19, 2018

THE FAMILY SEPARATION CRISIS

Donald Trump's successful 2016 presidential campaign owes much credit to his extreme and controversial standpoints on immigration. The influx of migrant families crossing our southern borders seeking asylum has become a monumental crisis and became a calling card issue for Donald Trump. Trump's fiery rhetoric on illegal immigrants led to extreme action and turned the human beings seeking a better life in America into the image of a group determined to destroy America's way of life. The most egregious part of his hard-lined view of immigration is Trump's policy of forcibly, without due process, separating children from their parents when they cross our southern border seeking asylum.

Images and reports of children being ripped from their parents' arms at our southern border dominated news and social media.

Heartbreaking photos and leaked audio recordings of traumatized little children wailing in fear when taken from their parents catapulted Trump's separation of families to the forefront of controversial policies and set off an international outcry. Illegal immigration has continually been a hot button issue for both sides of the aisle, and addressing this crisis has been no easy feat, nor has there been a clear-cut way to deal with it, but was separating families and caging small children the answer? The complicated, yet simple inhumane facets of this humanitarian crisis range from how we got here to begin with, the grave statistics, the players and the politics involved, the proposals aimed toward ending the merciless policy, how this still impacts our economy and how the public views this crisis.

"ZERO TOLERANCE" AND ITS HORRIFYING MANDATE

On April 6, 2018, Attorney General Jeff Sessions announced to all U.S. Attorney's offices along the southwest border of a new "Zero Tolerance" policy. Under this Zero Tolerance policy, the Department of Justice would criminally prosecute every person who crosses the border with a child without authorization or who enters unlawfully instead of at an official port of entry. Under this new "Zero Tolerance" policy, if a mother or father is with their child or children when illegally entering, their child or children are to be forcibly and physically taken from their parents, while the anguished parents are to be hauled off to detention centers to await trial. The traumatized and terrified children watch their parents go, and are then placed in government custody group cages, often hundreds, sometimes thousands of miles from their mom and dad. After this horrific ordeal the parents are to be interviewed by federal agents to determine if their pleas for asylum are legitimate.

Aside from the brazen cruelty of this policy, one problem (among many problems) is the timing of the interview of the parents. The parents were typically screened shortly after their children were ripped away from them, (as a mother I cannot imagine this torture). The parents were not in any psychological state to be clear and present in the interview. These interviews, however, needed to meet the requirements of asylum for the parents to be treated like human beings. The government failed to consider the psychological state that the mother or father was in at the time of the first interview. Under current U.S. and international laws, people arriving at our border seeking asylum are entitled to basic constitutional protections, including due process. Upon arriving at our border, families were forcibly separated by customs and border protection or turned away without any opportunity to make their case. Even if you don't care about the unbelievable inhumanity of this process, this treatment of migrants goes against due process and is wholly unconstitutional.

Nearly 3,900 children were taken from their families, including hundreds of children under the age of four.

Family separations without due process at the border was a horrifying and inhumane Trump strategy. Our nation has seen an influx of asylum seekers grow each year, so addressing this problem has become daunting. Trump sought to address this crisis aggressively but ignored the basic principles of our courts, our constitution, and human rights. There is no official law mandating family separation. The Trump administration used this approach as a deterrent to scare families who want to cross our borders for asylum. The separation of families was the outcome or rather the result of "Zero Tolerance" and then became the norm. [Ripping kids away from their parents then hauling them off became the Norm.]

WAY BIGGER THAN WE CAN COUNT

Under the "Zero Tolerance" policy, nearly 3,900 Children were forcibly separated from their parents. The exact number of families that have been separated could be greater than that by the thousands and is still unknown. The reason the exact number (in the thousands) is unclear is due to the lack of a coordinated tracking system, and the lack of clear communication between the Departments of Homeland Security that separates the children from their families, the arm of Health and Human Services that takes the children in, and the Office of Refugee Resettlement. This lack of organization and communication between departments indicates that the nightmare for these small children and these parents is far from over. Reuniting these children with their parents will be challenging at best.

This huge number (again, in the thousands) does not even represent the full scope of family separations. The Federal Court did not issue an order to account for these families until 2018, so there was no accounting of them during their first influx in 2017. This lack of accounting means there is most likely many more children without their parents and many more parents in anguish over losing their kids. This discrepancy suggests the Trump administration separated hundreds more families than we can count. Lee Gelernt, representing the ACLU in challenging this policy in court said:

"This cruel family separation practice is way bigger than the administration let on."

In June 2018, a Federal judge in San Diego, in response to the ACLU's lawsuit, ordered the Federal Government to halt the practice of separating families at the border, and to reunite the already separated families within 30 days. The Federal court ruled that the policy of aggressively wrenching families apart who are seeking asylum in the U.S. violates the Constitution's guarantee of due process. Trump in response, rescinded the "Zero Tolerance" policy and all seemed on the right track toward ending this nightmare for thousands, as well as for the citizens of America who watched this heartbreaking situation for many months.

When immigration agents forcibly ripped children and toddlers away from their moms and dads, the records that would have been used to reunite these families were deleted because the computer systems in place had not been updated to handle or account for separated children.

The disturbing truth, however, is Federal investigators found that despite the court ordering a reverse of the order, the separations have continued to occur. Furthermore, when immigration agents forcibly separated children from their moms and dads at the border, the records that would be used to reunite these families were deleted because the computer systems in place had not been updated to handle or account for separated families. Addressing the perilous immigration crisis at our southern border has been handled negligently and incompetently, with an inhumane approach that seems neither to solve the problem nor address the real crisis of migrants seeking asylum in the United States.

THE PLAYERS AND THE POLITICS

There is no question that there was political fallout from the Trump administration's policy to separate children from their families, and this did not bode well for Republicans in Congress. The immediate need to work out a bipartisan bill that Democrats and Republicans agreed upon to end this crisis seemed an impossibility. Why is this? On one side, was the Trump administration and his loyalists, in the middle were the Republicans, and on the other side stood the Democrats. Each side held firm onto what they believed was the best solution for their party, and what each side believed to be the best solution to the immigration crisis.

The Democrats had one clear message, and that is that Trump created the family separation crisis at the borders, and he is the only one who could and should rescind it. Chuck Schumer, the Democratic Senate Majority Leader, representing the Democrats stated: "the president alone can fix it with the flick of his pen." While on the other side, the Trump administration argued that Congress needs to fix this, with former Homeland Security Secretary Nielsen stating that Congress created this problem so Congress should fix it. In an even more partisan move, Trump vowed that he is not willing to consider family separation fixes offered by his own, (Republican) party. The divides were deep and robust, with finger-pointing and blame going back and forth, based on party lines, and political loyalties, without much compromise from the top.

Meanwhile, terrified children were still being taken and their anguished parents could do nothing.

Congress, despite months and months of negotiations, failed to produce a solution, which was mostly attributed to Trump's unwillingness to compromise and step away from his hard-lined approach to immigration. Both Democrats and Republicans have pointed out that Trump could and should have called upon his administration to reverse its "zero tolerance" policy. There are several proposals in the Senate that aimed to permanently stop family separations that are from both Democrats and Republicans, signaling that the lines dividing the opposing sides on this issue blurred in the urgent need to stop this humanitarian crisis.

THE PROPOSALS TO END THIS AND
THE POLITICIANS BEHIND THEM

Democrats backed the "Keep Families Together Act" introduced in the Senate by Democratic Senator Dianne Feinstein of California and introduced in the house by New York Democrat Rep. Jerrold Nadler. The "Keep Families Together Act" which had support from every single Democrat would outlaw family separations except for extreme cases, such as evidence of child trafficking or child abuse, and only if that separation is in the best interest of the child. Republicans on the other side had an issue with Feinstein's proposal deeming it a return to a "catch and release" system, with hard right Republicans such as Senator Tom Cotton calling it extremely radical.

Republicans instead were in favor of Texas Republican Senator Ted Cruz's "Protect Kids and Parents Act" which would have expedited the process for asylum seekers to fourteen days and double the number of immigration judges on the border to 750. Cruz's proposal would have also created new shelters that could accommodate families, keeping them together as long as there is no criminal conduct involved. Cruz's idea, although costly, appeased the Republicans yet Trump outwardly rejected the proposal, mischaracterizing it as a ploy to hire more judges. North Carolina Republican Senator Thom Hill, introduced a mixed proposal, calling it the "Keep Families Together Act and Enforce the Law Act" that echoes some of what is in Ted Cruz's proposal, to approve more judges and larger detention spaces, but also echoes some of Feinstein's proposal. The interesting aspect about Hill's proposal that blurred the lines between Democrats and Republicans is that, although a Republican, Thom pulled elements from Diane Feinstein's proposal regarding the protection of children from trafficking and abuse. Another notion of blending the proposals came from Republican Senator Jeff Flake to use ankle bracelets to abate worries about the catch and release aspect of Feinstein's proposal.

Majority Whip Republican John Cornyn of Texas also aligned a group of Republican Senators to draft comprehensive legislation that would address the family separation crisis. The details of it were not precise. However, Cornyn and other Republicans in his group sought to revive HUMANE (Helping Unaccompanied Minors and Alleviating National Emergency). HUMANE requires that a migrant child is not held longer than 72 hours and requires judges to act swiftly in deciding their cases.

The most promising bill focused on protecting the children first and foremost and was introduced in the Senate by Democrat Tina Smith of Minnesota, and in the House by Democrat Rep. Lucille Roybal-Allard of California. Tina Smith is the lead author of the Humane Enforcement and Legal Protections (HELP) for Separated Children. The bill is called the "HELP Separated Children Act". HELP would implement a humane approach to separating families by allowing parents to make calls to arrange for the care of their children and would make sure children can visit their parents when detained. At the Judicial level, in addition to finding the separation of families unconstitutional for its lack of due process and equal protection, the courts ordered that immigration and customs enforcement cannot detain families for more than 20 days and must reunite families already separated within 30 days. All in all, these rulings forced both sides to the table.

Republican Senate Majority Leader Mitch McConnell promised critics that the Republicans would quickly craft legislation that aims to address family separations, although a comprehensive and broad immigration bill did not pass amid in-party divisions and fighting. The Republicans vowed that if the other immigration bills failed to pass, Republicans would not be willing to vote on a separate bill to end family separations.

The most substantial obstruction toward a solution to stop the human atrocities occurring at our southern border came from Trump himself in his refusal to compromise, and his refusal to work with Congress, including those in his own party.

THE IMPACT ON OUR ECONOMY
(60 Million Dollars Per Week)

The separation of families at our southern border, with many still held without end, not only has a moral impact on our nation but a significant impact on our economy. The cost of caring for these migrant children who were separated from their parents by immigration authorities, and the cost of reuniting them, has ballooned to upwards of sixty million dollars per week. The Health and Human Services Department reported to the New York Times that the official cost on our economy comes to about $30,000 per child per week. In addition to the rising price tag on our economy it is essential also to weigh the cost this has on the United States regarding our foreign policies, our trade policies, and our standings with the world concerning our humanitarian efforts. Jessica Leanaweaver, a professor of anthropology at Brown University studying the impact of this crisis stated,

"I predict that the U.S.'s increasingly authoritarian and inhumane stance (Initiated by Trump) against children will lose its allies, partners, and influence in many years to come".

INTEREST GROUPS

The ACLU, in a lawsuit called for a reversal of the zero-tolerance policy, which resulted in a U.S. Federal Judge ruling for a class action lawsuit by all migrant families separated during the government's border clampdown as far back as 2017. The American Bar Association, (ABA) which vehemently opposes the government's policy of separating families, sent its president Hilarie Bass to the Rio Grande Valley of Texas to assess how American Lawyers can help the anguished families separated by immigration authorities.

The ABA is also investigating the repercussions on due process from the "zero tolerance" policy announced by AG Jeff Sessions last April and championed by President Trump. A coalition of sixteen states filed suit over the policy, claiming it violates the 5th Amendment that guarantees due process and equal protection. There are over four dozen interest and advocacy groups that oppose this policy. Among them are the ACLU, The American Bar Association, Neta, The Texas Civil Rights Movement, Act Blue, Kind, The Florence Project, Asylum Seeker Advocacy Project, Detained Migrant Solidarity Committee, and numerous Catholic compassion groups.

THE PUBLIC

According to a Gallup Poll which surveyed more than 1,500 adults in June of 2018, 75% of Americans say that immigration is good for our country. The poll also indicates a divide along party lines with 85% of Democrats who view immigration positively, compared to 65% of Republicans. Americans' strong opposition to separating families, however, is indicated in recent polls that found that most Americans, two-thirds according to several polls, oppose Trump's policy of forcibly separating children from their parents, no matter the pollster's stance on immigration. Despite this large number, there is still a sizeable partisan divide among voters with Republicans more likely to support separating families, while Democrats overwhelmingly oppose it. The two-thirds number is by far the most crucial though, and this is how public opinion can sway action. Since those polls signaling American's opposition have come to light, Trump has surrendered to the public pressure, and agreed, at least in his rhetoric, to stop separating families even though he continually blames the Democrats for the problem. After the overwhelming public outcry over his "zero tolerance" policy separating families, Trump abruptly promised he would sign an executive order to end the family separations at the southern border.

FAMILY SEPARATIONS CONTINUED

The practice of separating children, including babies from their parents, continued, however, regardless of Trump's rhetoric, and the Trump administration did not seem to be taking any real action soon to stop it. The separation of families is meant to send a clear message of the United States' toughness on immigration, but in turn it weakens the nation socially, morally, and economically. Most important to remember is that the policy of tearing small children from their parents, causing irreversible trauma, is not only cruel; it does not represent America. This famous image of a little girl traumatized in anguish as, whom we assume to be her mother, gets frisked by a faceless armed immigration officer, is not only visceral but unforgettable in the political message it conveys on Trump's zero tolerance policy on immigration. Trump's immigration policy whereby he separated children and babies from their parents when they crossed into our border.

Ripping children and toddlers from their mother's arms, then locking them up in glorified cages indefinitely without mommy or daddy, is a policy established by Trump and championed by Trump.

THE CIRCUS: TRUMP'S WALL HEARINGS
TRUMP SAID IT, SO THERE!

I watched a recording of Trump's Wall hearings because I am a comedy writer, and I knew it would be absurd. It delivered.

On April 27, 2017, The Committee on Oversight and Government Reform in the House of Representatives of the One Hundred and Fifteenth Congress hosted a national security hearing on the fiscal and human toll of illegal immigration in determining the value of building a wall along our southern border. The oversight hearing on the security of the Mexican/U.S. border was titled "The Border Wall: Strengthening our National Security" and was also hosted by the Subcommittee on National Security with Ron DeSantis, Chairman of the Subcommittee presiding. Before I dive into the circus of the border wall hearings, it is vital to understand that:

Study after study performed over the last decade shows that illegal immigration does not lead to increased crime, violence, or drug problems. In fact, the decade long study indicate that undocumented immigrants commit crimes and acts of violence at rates far lower than native-born Americans.

The hearing was a range of emotional to pragmatic, sometimes inflammatory testimonies by witnesses and experts on illegal immigration. DeSantis spoke first, and his introductory remarks made it very clear that he believes a wall is the only and most viable solution to reduce the influx of illegal immigrants crossing our border. Well kind of, maybe. He acknowledges that a wall will not entirely stop illegals from crossing into our country, DeSantis argues that a wall is the only way to reduce them effectively.

DeSantis said a wall would not help solve the problem, but it will maybe, kinda-sort of help, maybe?
Plus, Trump said it, so there!

DeSantis spoke of the victims of violent crimes at the hands of illegal immigrants, including Agnes Gibboney. Gibboney, a key witness in the hearing, later testified on the murder of her son by an illegal immigrant. The immigrant had recently been deported, but because of, as Gibboney states, "our open borders", got back in. DeSantis argued that these types of violent crimes are preventable had the government secured the border. DeSantis fervently argued that the wall is the first step to stopping illegal immigration, citing the success of the security fence along the Israel-Sinai Border. DeSantis, in a show of support for Trump's wall, in his opening comments, stated that the Israeli security fence cut illegals from crossing from 16,500 to just 43, in a 99% decrease.

GO MARK DESAULNIER!

DeSantis eventually yields back, and U.S. representative Mark DeSaulnier gives his opening remarks, which starkly counter DeSantis's view. DeSaulnier, states:

"The wall that the president is proposing simply won't work in my view and in others' and will divert resources away from the areas critical to protecting the health, safety, and security of Americans."- Mark DeSaulnier

DeSaulnier plainly argued that not only will the wall not effectively and indeed advance our security as Trump promises, but that working Americans will be the ones paying for it. The culmination of De-Saulnier's remarks opposing Trump's wall is possibly the most glaring example of just one of Trump's false claims regarding the wall—that Mexico will pay for it. After playing a Trump rally video where the crowd at Trump's directive when asked who will pay for the wall? shout: "Mexico!" DeSaulnier adds, "His request for Congress to appropriate billions of dollars is a shortsighted request for Congress and breaks one of his most fundamental campaign promises that the American people would not pay a dime for the wall on the U.S.-Mexico border".

DeSaulnier succinctly argued that a wall across the length of our southern border would not be effective nor workable, and in no way cost effective. Moreover, DeSaulnier argued that Trump's wall will cost billions, at the sacrifice of cutting vital funds for critical domestic programs—including 20 percent of the funding allocated toward the National Institutes of Health that is necessary to advance cures for diseases, cancers, and saves lives.

Trained personnel on DHS border security tactics, and technical border control at key entry points, all are less costly and far more effective at protecting our borders than a wall that will cost working Americans billions and billions of dollars.

Steven A. Camarota, Ph.D., Director of Research, Center for Immigration Studies, takes the Fiscal argument for stopping the flood of illegal immigrants to America. Camarota cites the National Academy of Sciences, Engineering and Medicine research on the fiscal costs of immigration by education level. Immigrants who illegally cross our border have a low level of education, which in turn means a deficient level of employability. These individuals create higher costs for our government than any taxes they can pay. Camarota testifies that the research shows the likely low education level of illegal immigrants combined with the costs of the services they create is a deep fiscal disparity that the taxpayer must cover, which is $75,000 per illegal crosser per year. Camarota argues that if America can stop even just 10 percent of illegals coming through, this could generate 10-15 billion in savings for the government that can be applied toward the wall. Thus, the wall will eventually pay for itself, as it reduces immigrants from coming through.

<u>Not really, though. Not at all.</u>

Brandon Judd, a Border Control Agent with extensive experience working with and without border barriers and fences, argues for only some wall in conjunction with other means. Judd argues that a border wall in strategic locations, not 2,000 miles of wall, will be most effective. He argues that his years of experience in Border Control give him no doubt of how effective a wall could be but is only needed at strategic entry points. What is most vital is that it be in conjunction with the proper technology, security infrastructure, and heavy human resources. Judd argues that only if all of these are proactively and comprehensively working together can we truly secure the border.

GO SETH!

Seth Stodder, former Assistant Secretary for Border, Immigration, and Trade Policy for the DHS ended the testimonies with a stark opposition to the building of the wall. Stodder testified that a wall would waste billions of taxpayers' dollars and will not help address the most critical immigration challenges our nation is facing. Stodder argues that:

**The wall will not only do nothing to keep us safer.
It will, in turn, make our nation less safe.**

Stodder also testified that a wall will not keep illegal drugs out because they are smuggled through an intricate network of cars and trucks. A wall will do nothing to stop the dangerous cartel from crossing over. Stodder's most acute argument for the inability of a southern wall to effectively address our immigration crisis comes when he not only states how Mexicans are crossing through but that the crisis in Central America is far more significant. Stodder testified to the thousands of Guatemalans, El Salvadorans, and Honduran families fleeing violence, extreme poverty, and environmental crises, crossing our border to seek asylum. A wall along our southern border will not stop this.

A wall will only channel those asylum claims to the other open ports of entry. So then, are the fiscal and human costs of illegal immigration offset by the fiscal costs of a wall that will cost billions to build? No. Additionally, Trump's wall would undermine our national security by redirecting critical funds from programs that have proven to effectively secure our border.

The underlying force behind this "build a wall" circus is the glaring presence of anti-immigration sentiments that propagate false and fear-inducing rhetoric about the dangers posed by illegal immigrants.

CHAPTER ELEVEN

Globalization, Abject Poverty, and The Childcare Crisis

"Together, we can eradicate extreme poverty and erase barriers to opportunity."

- Barack Obama

"If they can stay so poor for so many generations, how smart can they be? They're morons."

- Donald Trump

CORE NATIONS THRIVE OFF ABJECT POVERTY

Just to give a little background on our global system, here is a breakdown of how the world economic system is built. Nations around the world are grouped into three different categories: the Core Nations, the Semi-Periphery Nations, and the Periphery Nations. Each of these categories helps define the connection between capitalism and stratification; and how globalization flourishes in a system that

225

creates populations of people who live in abject poverty. In fact, the success of the wealthier nations and many industries in capitalism can only remain super wealthy if the poorest of the poor remain poor.

This world system of categorizing nations based on development and wealth seem more valid and ever-deepening with booming globalized industries that thrive off the poorest in our world.

Who are the Core Nations? Who are the Semi-Peripheral nations? Who are the peripheral nations? Here are the categories of the three types of nations explained and a few nations that fall under each category to give you a basis for the make-up of our global economic system of abundance v. scarcity. Some may surprise you.

THE CORE NATIONS

The Richest Most Developed Nations

The core nations are the ones that produce products and innovations that require populations of people to have advanced skills or advanced educations; and the core nations have the wealth to make strong financial investments in innovations and the production of products. The core countries are highly developed nations with high income capitalistic societies that dominate global industries; and have an unbalanced economic relationship with the semi-periphery and periphery nations. Core nations have the most political, economic, and military power, which enables them to exploit periphery and semi-periphery nations for cheap labor and cheap goods. Furthermore, the population of the Core nations is by far on average the wealthiest and best educated on the planet…you get it by now.

The list changes every few years, but these are the nations that fall into the Core category in Alphabetical order: Australia, Austria, Belgium, Canada, Denmark, Finland, France, Germany, Iceland, Ireland, Israel, Italy, Japan, Luxembourg, Netherlands, New Zealand, Norway, Portugal, Spain, Sweden, Switzerland, United Kingdom, and the United States.

Semi-Periphery Countries

These countries represent the intermediate state of development. They are often still exploited by core countries but have developed to the extent that they too source cheaper labor, food, and resources from periphery countries. They act as a buffer between the powerful core nations and the underdeveloped periphery nations. Some nations that made the Semi Periphery list in the last five years are: Belize, Brazil, Chile, China, Fiji, Greece, Hungary, India, Iran, Jamaica, Malaysia, Mexico, Nigeria, Panama, Seychelles, South Africa, South Korea, Taiwan, Tunisia, Turkey, Ukraine, Uruguay.

Periphery Countries

These are the least-developed countries around the world and have the highest ratio of extreme poverty per capita than other nations. They produce labor-intensive and/or low-skill products and are typically exploited as a source of cheap labor, raw materials, and agricultural production for core and semi-periphery countries. The list of periphery nations is far too long to put in its entirety, so here are the most well-known underdeveloped nations that make the list (not in alphabetical order): Iraq, Vietnam, Afghanistan, Egypt, all countries in Latin America but for those listed as Core or Semi-Periphery nations, Thailand, Rwanda, Senegal, Pakistan, Poland, Russia, Romania, Philippines, Sudan, United Arab Emirates, Nepal, Indonesia, Kenya.

Industries can employ those around the globe, regardless of nationality or status, and this is a slippery slope. The Core nations have labor laws, labor unions, and regulations restricting labor abuses. The periphery nations where the labor force is unprotected and unregulated are exploited for profits by industries in the Core Nations. My sweater is from the American company The Gap, but the label says it is made in the periphery country of Pakistan where the working people live below the poverty line, with very little labor wage requirements. Core nation industries are increasingly more globalized with the Core nations thriving on the periphery nations remaining in the periphery. The costs to profit margins of having goods manufactured in periphery nations, benefit the Core nations who thus will remain the Core nations.

The system is built upon maintaining the impoverished in perpetual poverty so the elite in the core can amass wealth.

The richest nations and their corporations flourish at the expense of those enduring abject poverty.

Not one nation escapes this system as all are dependent upon the poor being poor for greater profit, for greater gains, and for the periphery nation's (below adequate) survival in a system that remains cyclical. Stratification is a direct result of this capitalism, and industrialization on a global scale. (Just like when Marx observed how the Bourgeoisie owned the factories, and the workers sold the owners their labor for a price, but the profits of the factory benefitted the bourgeoisie that already had the wealth to own the factory to begin with). Our global economic system and social stratification has long been solidified and sharp. It's important to note that in this system women and girls often suffer the most.

Women and girls categorically suffer the most in nations where school is not allowed, and education to help lift females out of the periphery is forbidden.

This world theory and current state of globalization does not seem to be changing or evolving any time soon. The Periphery seems stuck in a global economic system that depends upon it being stuck. This is precisely due to the core nations having standards and wage requirements for workers, whereas the periphery does not. If you can pay people substantially less in the periphery nations to do the same work you could have done here in the USA for triple the cost—what global industry would turn that down? The system is working just fine, for the Core nations, and the semi-periphery ones too.

Profits are what enable an industry's success and if the periphery nations do not protect their workers or require a fair living wage, the global system will remain this way.

I was shocked at how hard it was to find clothes in my closet made in the USA. I do not own designer clothes. I own Gap, J. Crew, Banana Republic, Nike; All giant American companies who are clearly booming off the periphery nations. The only items I found in my closet that were made in the USA were two vintage dresses I have worn to galas or charity events; not currently made items. In periphery nations there could be young children, young girls and boys making the clothes I wear. There is usually slave like conditions for these workers in periphery nations that make the clothes and shoes I wear, just so they can simply survive and stay on the periphery, and the core can remain in the core.

SOCIALISM AND CAPITALISM NEED EACH OTHER

Social Democracy Helps Human Beings
Thrive in a Global System

Socialism and Capitalism need each other and rely upon each other. This might seem surprising because in their basic meanings, Capitalism and Socialism are in stark contrast to one another. But if we look at this deeper, we can see how in fact, it is socialism that greatly influences, and has greatly influenced how Capitalism functions in the best of ways. If in capitalism there are labor abuses upon the workforce, the workforce will cease or revolt. Without a satisfied workforce, there is the risk that production will not continue, therefore capitalism will ultimately fall. This is where capitalism needs elements of socialism to thrive.

The United Auto Workers' Union strike of 2023 is a clear example of how capitalism must utilize aspects of socialism, (and empathy too, remember Kant?). Capitalism must use a socialist approach toward the workforces that help build the very capitalism that makes the rich, so very rich. For Capitalism to thrive, the workforce must be treated as if they are key players. If the workforce is not thriving, then Capitalism is failing and will falter. Even if you don't care that members of the United Auto Workers Union work 40-hour weeks yet still live in poverty, taking care of the workforce only benefits the economy on every tier.

Just like the auto union workers strike, the labor abuses in England in the 19th century is another prime example of how capitalism needs elements of socialism's ideals to flourish. The abuses on the workforce were highly counter-productive to thriving industry and resulted in lesser profits, especially for those at the helm. The labor movement in the 19th century actually helped stabilize industry and capitalism. It is the socialism within this movement, creating an equally flourishing workforce that protects capitalism from its own power and greed that would ultimately destroy it.

**If capitalism is to flourish and succeed for a profit,
then a stable, thriving working class is crucial.**

Capitalism has been influenced and improved throughout history by the ideals of socialism. Only with socialistic ideals and socialism's value of equality among workers can capitalism truly flourish. If production is designed to meet human needs, then if only strict capitalistic ideology is applied to industries and production, they would ultimately falter. Trade unions needed to reconstruct their doctrines to protect the interests of workers. The trade unions provide the workers with the socialistic values inherent to and necessary for their flourishment and protection, thus enabling the success of a capitalistic society. I look at this as seen throughout history as socialism keeps capitalism in check, like a school principal. So, they are compatible in a sense, or at the very least capitalism must have certain elements of socialistic ideals within the workforce for its success. Social Democracy is inherently more stable.

**Social Democracy seeks to provide social safety and
dignity within a capitalistic society. If the workers are happy
and have money in their pockets too, then capitalism will
flourish, and everyone wins.**

Social democrats attempt to contain the abuses of capitalism and provide the public with a safety net necessary to live a full human life with dignity and equality. Social democracy provides stability even within an absence of government intervention on some issues. More freedom of course can lead to instability, but just the same has been seen in revolutions and volatile tumultuous instability brought about by oppression and abuses of power.

WELFARE POLICY IN THE UNITED STATES

Welfare policies aim to solve many social and economic singularities, from individual rights and equality to poverty and unemployment.

The United States is globally regarded as grossly insufficient in welfare policies because its expenditures on social and welfare policies are far lower than those in other industrialized core nations. Social welfare programs in the United States, which now cost almost two trillion annually and make up one-third of all federal spending and 40% of public spending. Welfare programs assist disadvantaged people and deal with a myriad of debated issues, including whether or not the government should finance them. Social welfare policies include healthcare, education, housing, childcare, and other economic programs to alleviate poverty and aid marginalized society. Social and economic inequalities result from a tumultuous capitalistic society, and the politics behind welfare policies illuminate the cultural and moral questions that habitually comprise the welfare policy arena.

One question that poses a constant challenge to welfare policies is how much aid ends up going to those who can work but are not, and therefore freeloading off the system? Another question is how much social and economic inequality is the by-product of a capitalist system that creates marginalized groups of poverty-stricken people? The moral and cultural divide on welfare policies is grounded in the question: What should be the government's responsibility versus the responsibility of each individual? The Center for Budget and Policy Priorities argues the "War on Poverty" policy initiatives introduced in 1964 By Lyndon Johnson have continued to cut poverty by half. This is not exactly the case, as the reality is a bit different. In the decade that followed the 1964 legislation, poverty did drop from 17% to 11% which is considerable, but not half. Furthermore, poverty in the United States has maintained a rate of poverty just below 12%, with over 40 million living below the poverty line. The War on Poverty legislation in 1964 did make considerable shifts and improvements in the poverty rates in America, but much more must be done. Opposition to welfare programs argue that throwing money into ongoing programs does not truly help our country's social ills and poverty.

Welfare policies aim to solve many social and economic singularities, from individual rights to equality, poverty, and unemployment. In addition to the Executive Branch and the often profoundly polarized Congress, other governmental institutional groups play vital roles in social welfare policies in the United States. A few are: The U.S. Department of Health and Human Services, Centers for Medicare, and Medicaid Services, The U.S. Department of Housing and Urban Development and The Department of Labor. The welfare policy process also involves many non-governmental organizations (NGOs), which include nonprofits. These organizations produce research to promote social welfare policy initiatives, and some include: The NAACP, National Welfare Rights Organization, The Heritage Foundation, Children and Elderly advocacy groups, and The National Governors Association.

Many social programs are provided directly by the government, but the private sector also provides many programs with indirect support from the government. Welfare policies require significant federal, state, and local expenditures and are continually met with divided views. The attempt to reduce welfare policy expenditures and social programs remains a constant political battle-ground in our nation. Republicans call for a scaling back of policies with stronger accountability for self-reliance. Democrats argue we must financially reshape our system so the middle class and the poverty-stricken can have a fair chance. Compounded with the Republicans' pressure to reform these welfare expenditures is the growing deficit. Simultaneously, an economic crisis makes millions more people reliant on welfare programs, (as we all experienced during the pandemic). Political, cultural, and moral perspectives have shaped the divided ideas of how to help those dependent on welfare programs. The divides are rooted in class politics with two philosophies. According to the BROOKINGS INSTITUTE in "On Welfare Reform and Poverty", liberals in the United States have suggested the federal government should make reducing childhood poverty its responsibility.

Most conservatives oppose making childhood poverty reduction an official goal of federal policies because they believe that liberals would use the goal to increase government spending on welfare programs that may not reduce poverty. Less government and more individual accountability are called for on one side (the Republicans). In contrast, the other side (Democrats) argues more government welfare aid is necessary for the betterment of our nation. Regardless of politics, no nation should leave children, families, the elderly, the sick, or anyone behind in an imbalanced system that produces populations of severely impoverished. The divided ideologies and economic deficit will continue to obstruct compromise on welfare policies. These dividers make it challenging to implement feasible policy solutions to address the welfare crisis and persistence of poverty in our nation.

No matter the intense political or cultural divides behind welfare policies, the humanity of these programs is essential. No nation should leave children, families, the elderly, the sick, or anyone behind in an imbalanced system that produces populations of severely impoverished.

The different approaches to welfare policies help identify revisions that could bring welfare policies up to date with the current political and economic crises. **The Alleviate Approach** is most prevalent in our current economic crisis. It deals with already poor individuals and provides government assistance to alleviate their condition, i.e., TANF in 1996 and the recent stimulus checks. The curative approach addresses the root causes of poverty, such as lack of education and access to job training. This can be seen in the "Head Start" program, literacy training programs, and access to job training.

The Punitive Approach assumes that individuals are poor because of their character deficiencies, and the government should discourage those groups from being lazy by making it difficult to get government benefits, i.e., The Workfare Program. The incomes approach encourages people to work while they receive government assistance, and as their job income increases, their number of benefits decreases. The idea behind the income approach is individuals are better off working than not working, i.e., negative income tax, Earned Income Tax Credit, Supplementary Security Income.

The disparity in classes in our America, with millions, including children suffering in poverty, cannot be alleviated until the root causes, and the systemic ills of our society are addressed.

Welfare policies result from systemic problems in all sectors, from financial, to education, to childcare, to race. Until federal and local governments address the causes of poverty, the need for welfare programs will continue. Our nation must institute an adequate universal educational system for all, provide access to reproductive care and healthcare with increased funding toward disadvantaged areas.

We must focus on educating our youth equally. The way schools are funded, relying on local taxes from the surrounding neighborhoods, only deepens the chasm of inequality and systemic poverty in our country.

It's heartbreaking to see affluent areas boasting well-funded schools, offering a plethora of enriching extracurricular activities, while poorer neighborhoods struggle to provide even the basic resources, after-school programs, and materials that their children desperately need. It's unjust, plain, and simple. **We need to overhaul this broken system.**

We must establish a universal fund for education, where school funding isn't determined by the wealth of the neighborhood.

Every school, regardless of location, should receive equal funding from a federal source. It's the only way to break the cycle of injustice that has plagued our society for far too long. We owe it to our children to ensure they all have access to quality education, regardless of where they live. It's time to put an end to the decades and decades-old systemic inequality, once and for all.

Until our institutions fully attack the crises in our society, any approach other than the curative will only serve as Band-Aids, and reliance on welfare policies will continue, deepening the political divides.

If I were a member of Congress, I would urge my fellow MCs to address the urgent issues creating the welfare crisis through curative measures and legislation. Suppose the ills and inequalities of our society are not addressed. In that case, the government will never solve our nation's welfare policy crisis. Congress must view welfare policies in terms of attacking the causes of their need. Certainly not without measured complexities and challenges, revising Welfare Policies to address the systemic ills of our society is beneficial for both parties aiming to lessen the government's burden and is the best path.

Recent trends, however, are more encouraging. According to the Brookings Institution in "On Welfare Reform and Poverty", both liberals and conservatives agree that it is necessary to maintain substantial work incentives by ensuring financial rewards for work. Although this is the band-aid approach, it is more necessary now (in the aftermath of the pandemic) than ever. Trends also suggest that the Welfare Policy debate between parties is not going anywhere. Welfare policy's mood trends have been on a steady incline for both parties since 1963, with a sharp increase in interest in 2018 and growing. Furthermore, according to the Pew Research Center, Democrats are twice as likely as Republicans to say that there is too much economic inequality in our country. According to the center, the wealth gap between the rich and the poor has doubled since 1989, with trends indicating the gap will only continue to widen.

Pew Research found that the United States has the highest level of income inequality of all G7 countries (by far).

The most viable approach to Welfare Reform and Policy is rife with political, cultural, and moral divides. However, the need for welfare programs in the U.S. is undeniable and critical, and addressing the root causes of such deep inequality must be a priority.

THE CHILDCARE CRISIS AND BIDEN'S PLAN

In July of 2020, months before being elected, Joe Biden released his plan to address the caregiving and childcare crisis in the United States. Biden's public policy is extensive and far reaching in scope covering wage increases for caregivers to subsidies for low income and middle-class working parents. Biden's all-encompassing plan did not pass mostly due to partisanship, but it MUST BE REVISITED. This plan could be a lifeline for so many working families, with positive reverberations in other sectors of the economy.

The Biden "Plan for Mobilizing American Talent and Heart to Create a 21st Century Caregiving and Education Workforce" is a policy measure that aimed to not only cover the childcare crisis we face in this nation, but also covered everything from helping people who care for elderly family members to crucial early education for toddlers.

This encompassing policy would have leveraged federal funds and influenced regulations to increase pay for healthcare and childcare workers. We entrust our most precious people to childcare workers or healthcare workers, yet we do not pay them enough to even call it a living wage. COVID-19 made things dire for so many, but even before the pandemic, access to affordable, quality childcare was becoming an urgent national matter of public concern and no longer an issue regarded as a personal or family responsibility.

The childcare industry and the families who rely upon it were devastated during the coronavirus pandemic and advocates of Biden's policy expressed hope in Biden's policy passing. There was even new bipartisan momentum for President Biden's promise to provide access to affordable, high-quality childcare. Many Republicans across the aisle put aside partisanship and agreed that Biden's policy contains proposals that are necessary for our nation's citizens to thrive.

THE KEY ELEMENTS OF BIDEN'S CHILDCARE CRISIS PLAN

- Free universal pre-kindergarten for 3 and 4-year-olds
- Improve and increase pay and benefits for childcare workers
- Offer a refundable tax credit of up to $8,000 to help families pay for childcare
- Provide sliding-scale subsidies so that no family earning below 1.5 times the median income in their state would have to pay more than 7% of their income for quality childcare.

According to Brookings, most voters, and the public want our government to spend more money on the care and education of young children. This investment is seen as crucial for the betterment of families and for all the positive outcomes that will stem from providing stable, safe homes and supportive environments for both children and adults.

There is a myriad of network participants on this issue. First Focus on Children which is a bipartisan group that advocates for child and family centered federal policies and The Education Trust, a nonprofit that works to advance educational equity, especially for low-income children and children of color are strong proponents and participants in this policy. The National Association for The Education of Young Children (NAEYC) are behind and back this policy initiative that will help ensure that every low-income family and child in poverty has access to childcare and an early pre-k education that is only available to those in higher income brackets.

The Healthcare industry as well as the Social Services arm of local, state, and federal governments are all network participants in this proposal and its policies. The costs, the burdens, and the logistics of implementation of each of these policies will greatly affect those participants, as they are clearly stakeholders in the passage of this sweeping policy. Healthcare and labor industries, social and human services, and the nation's citizens alike are all participants in Biden's $335 billion policy to create universal preschool and accessible child-care for those in need.

The institutional actors' motivations are to secure a successful policy toward economic recovery and for the advancement of a fair economy for all classes at the most root levels. The multi-policy pro-posal introduced by Biden is met with the fervent backing of Demo-crats in Congress and VP Kamala Harris, as its passage would mean a marker of a successful Biden presidency, not just for the party and President-Elect Joe Biden, but for the bipartisanship this policy has unexpectedly summoned. One Key institutional actor is Senator Patty Murray (Democrat WA). She is the top Democrat on the Senate Health, Education, Labor, and Pensions (HELP) Committee.

Biden's plan, which guarantees universal care for 3- and 4-year-olds, adopts many ideas from the Child Care for Working Fam-ilies Act of 2019, which was sponsored by Murray and Rep. Bobby Scott (Democrat, VA.) another key institutional actor in the call for such policies. Throughout the pandemic, Senator Murray and Repre-sentative Scott have stressed the importance of childcare to help working families get back to work and help build back our economy. In June, Senator Murray introduced the Child Care is Essential Act, to address the child care crisis exacerbated by coronavirus, and Biden's policy measure covers that act and much more.

According to the think tank the Brookings Institute and author Russ Whitehurst, The U.S. Department of Health and Human Services concludes that affordable childcare should not exceed 7 percent of family income, but that the poorer ranking classes of our nation pay over 52% of their family income. The motivations of the institutional actors involved are to end that deep disparity. The key Senate Committee involved in overseeing, and evaluating and Biden's plan is the Health, Education, Labor, and Pension Committee or (HELP). Subcommittees on Children and Families in addition to HELP oversee critical pieces of early childhood education, including Childcare and other issues involving children and families. Another key institutional actor that will be involved in the passage and the final shape of the details of this policy is the Senate Finance Committee. Any and all public policy legislation such as this childcare act that has to do with taxes must go through this Senate Finance Committee. The Senate Finance Committee oversees programs that include the Children's Health Insurance Program (CHIP), and what part of financial assistance is used to finance childcare.

The non-institutional actors' motivations are to lower the crippling cost of childcare on families and to ensure the availability of affordable quality childcare and affordable pre-k early education of children. The non-institutional actors involved are a majority of the voters and the general public who according to the think tank the Brookings Institute, say the cost of childcare is extremely high relative to their income. Accredited childcare for a two-income family with two young children is on average 29 percent of their take-home pay and can be as high as 20,000 dollars per year.

According to Brookings, most voters and the general public want the government to spend more money on the care and education of young children, for the betterment of families and everything that will stem from stable safe homes and supportive environments for both children and adults. One influential non-institutional actor on this policy plan who has been involved with sweeping policy measures that involve human and financial services combined is Averi Pakulis. Pakulis serves as the Vice President for Early Childhood and Public Health Policy at First Focus on Children a bipartisan advocacy organization for children.

Biden's childcare policy plan was to be implemented at the Federal Level, then carried out at the state level per federal guidelines with local implementation per city and county-per the locale of childcare facility of the family applying. The policy would have been implemented at all levels but primarily at the Federal, then with the state and local governments follow through. Under Biden's plan, parents would be able to go to a federal website and search for participating childcare centers in their area and apply to the program. Once approved, the state would notify families of the amount they are going to pay and then reimburse childcare centers on the back end. Successful implementation of this policy plan, if it had passed, would have required all levels and tiers of government to cooperate, as well as the cooperation of the departments of health and human services and education and labor committees.

There was no evidence of any disagreements between the states and the federal government concerning this policy formulation and adoption of it. However, and this comes as no surprise, there were party aligned disagreements with Biden's costly legislation, as well as the fact that its success would be on a state-to-state basis. The effect Biden's childcare policy plan would have on American citizens would have been tremendously positive. There did not have to be full agreement on all values and all points of Biden's plan, but the GOP just could not get out of the way. If Biden's Childcare Plan was to succeed it would have required, the coalition and cooperation of many institutional and non-institutional actors sharing a common goal and working under Federal guidelines.

The Executive Branch's proposal on childcare was likely to have bipartisan backing in Congress, as both Democrats and Republicans acknowledged the pandemic's crushing blow to the childcare system; But as part of the much larger $1.9 trillion economic stimulus package, it did not gain support from the Republicans who felt the price tag was too steep and the policy plan too extreme in scope. An indication of Congress's support for Biden's proposal was with the bipartisan acknowledgment of the urgent need for this type of proposal, with an earlier proposal like it: Congresswoman Rosa DeLauro (Chair of the House Appropriations Subcommittee on Labor, Health and Human Services, and Education), Congressman Bobby Scott (Chair of the House Education and Labor Committee), and Senator Patty Murray (Ranking Member of the Senate Health, Education, Labor, and Pensions Committee), introduced new legislation, the 'Child Care is Essential Act' to create a $50 billion Child Care Stabilization Fund within existing Child Care. So, there is hope…

There are signs of bipartisan recognition of how vital childcare is for our economy, for our families, and for getting people back to work.

Biden's entire caregiving proposal encompassing seniors, military veterans and people with disabilities would have cost $775 billion over 10 years, with $335 billion earmarked for this new childcare funding policy plan. This would have been paid for by rolling back unproductive and unequal tax breaks for real-estate investors with incomes over $400,000 and taking steps to increase taxes for higher-income earners and those in the wealthiest brackets of income. Putting 335 billion dollars of taxpayer money toward childcare seems daunting, but the issue is critical and necessary, especially for the economy. With every public policy a cohesive, coherent coordination is necessary to accomplish and implement it.

The gridlock caused by aggressively staunch partisanship in our policy-making system continually stalls progress, and certainly happened with Biden's childcare policy plan——a plan that would have helped millions of struggling families.

CHAPTER TWELVE

Humanity is All Connected
and
We Must Believe This

SHOULD AMERICA COME FIRST?
THE QUAGMIRE OF FOREIGN ENTANGLEMENTS

There is an increasing sentiment that the United States assumes an excessive burden in terms of military interventions or foreign aid commitments. Over the past year, the United States has provided Ukraine with $113 billion in aid since the onset of the war. Many contend that these nations should shoulder their own defense and that America must cease its role as the universal rescuer and savior of all nations in distress as we have so much that need fixing here. Many argue we must start spending less money and energy on foreign entanglements and more on the pressing domestic issues that demand attention and resolution here in the United States. In places where our military serves, there's often a profound sense of bewilderment and anger as we struggle to grasp the true nature of the commitments that repeatedly place our young men and women in harm's way. These commitments seem fruitless and endless while precious lives are lost. America, why? The answer is simple: All of humanity is connected, and the United States must stand up and support all democratic nations that uphold the sacred ideals of a free society.

America must intervene to aid free and democratic nations and relentlessly combat oppression, tyranny, and genocide. The United States must stand firmly alongside fellow democratic nations ensuring their freedoms endure against all odds.

The critical importance of American aid, both in financial resources and military support to nations enduring oppression and terrorism cannot be overstated. The United States' involvement is not only a humanitarian imperative, but also vital for our nation's moral integrity and global leadership. By aiding countries facing human rights atrocities, we uphold our commitment to human rights justice, and the values of a democracy. In fighting against genocide, terrorism, and oppression The United States is defending not only the dignity and rights of those directly affected, but the principles that underpin our nation's identity and America's purpose on the global stage.

America's involvement in foreign affairs in the battle against terrorism is an indispensable pursuit that consistently presents itself as a convoluted and seemingly perpetual dilemma with no foreseeable resolution. Many argue: Shouldn't the U.S. spend more time and money on affairs here? As we are facing significant problems domestically. Trump was his own story, however, and we saw with his leadership, impulsivity, and lack of desire to fully understand the nuances and sophisticated elements regarding our international agreements. In Syria, Yemen, Afghanistan, Iraq, and Somalia, the United States is trying to influence the course of terror and civil conflicts with no solution in sight. Yet, does that mean we abandon these people?

<u>**Here is my argument against that notion:**</u>

Should the United States just pull out of every one of these conflicts?- No. Doing so would pose a grave threat to those vulnerable people in those regions, thus, the fallout globally with America as a direct target.

When it comes to our nation's entanglements in foreign affairs and how these specifically affect, abate, and often fan the flames of terrorism, the United States faces a continuing battle. Our involvement in world affairs is necessary, especially with our allies, and most critically when regarding the preservation of human rights around the globe. There is no greater importance than protecting human rights and protecting innocent victims of terror. Terrorism and war grossly affect young children, women, and those in profoundly impoverished nations. These groups suffer the resulting starvation, torture, and loss of life groups, with no feasible way to defend themselves. The United States must step in as a world leader.

Terrorism and war grossly impact women, young girls, children, and those in profoundly impoverished nations.

Our military engagement in regions with the aim of eliminating terrorism not only serves to exacerbate the fervor of terrorist groups advocating for the downfall of Americans but, more crucially, lacks a discernible endpoint. Persevering in prolonged warfare within these regions entangles us in a quagmire of catastrophic losses of American lives, accompanied by escalating costs contributing significantly to our burgeoning national debt, which has now reached the trillions.

<u>The Predicament:</u>

If we leave those regions, then chaos and even stronger holds of terrorism can move in. Nothing has been solved, terrorism and terrorist groups feel more emboldened because of our entanglement, and tremendous human life has been lost for zero gains. It's a lose-lose for the United States. However, America must be involved in foreign conflicts, or we risk appearing without a spine, and without strength as a nation.

The Question that Matters:

Can the United States of America stand by and let a humanitarian crisis or genocide continue? Can America stand by and let the perpetration of war crimes continue without stepping in? No. Absolutely, not. <u>NEVER.</u>

Trump cozied up to foreign adversaries and sidled up to dictators who carry out horrific human atrocities and terror in their own nations, (Putin, Kim) yet he offended and abandoned our allies abroad?

Donald Trump during his presidency did not grasp the facts nor the depth of the foreign entanglements our country is engaged in, yet he proclaimed a path that was…well… Here is what he tweeted at one point:

> *"Bringing peace to the mess I inherited in the Middle East. I will get it all done, but what a mistake, in lives and dollars (6 trillion), to be there in the first place!" - Donald Trump*

This tweet starkly demonstrates Trump's profound inability to comprehend the intricate nature of our foreign entanglements in the Middle East. Trump's lack of intellectual acumen and respect for the nuances of this foreign policy arena, alongside his evident lack of fundamental knowledge, exacerbates the perpetuation of this complex situation and is utterly perplexing. I won't even delve into his interactions with Kim Jong Un and Putin; their implications are self-evident.

PART FOUR

WHAT MATTERS NOW

THE CLIMATE AND SCIENCE

CHAPTER THIRTEEN

Climate Change
(Biden Wants to Kick Its Ass)

"You all have a duty right now to our economy,
to our competitiveness in the world, to the young
people in this nation, and to future generations
—and that sounds like hyperbole but it's not;
it's real — to act boldly on climate".

-- President Joe Biden

"The concept of global warming was created by
and for the Chinese in order to make U.S.
manufacturing non-competitive."

-- Donald Trump

BIDEN IS KICKING ASS FOR THE PLANET

President Biden's Executive Order 14008, "Tackling the Climate Crisis at Home and Abroad" aggressively addresses the global climate crisis, overhauling fossil fuel industries in the cessation of drilling leases while requiring significant reductions in emissions to achieve net-zero emissions by mid-century, all without Congressional approval. Biden's EO 14008 circumvents the gridlock brought on by partisanship—he did this to promote his policy agenda and advance its progress.

One thing is certain, Biden's not waiting for approval to kick ass and take names to save our environment and tackle the climate crisis.

Go, Joe!

Without political backing, sound and solvent public policy fails regardless of how well it will solve the urgent crisis or quell the ostensible problem for which it is designed. With a simple signature, Biden executes orders avoiding the sometimes-necessary bargaining, compromise, conflict, and concessions that often bog down policy formulation. Executive orders cannot create laws, they must follow existing statutes as well as the Constitution. Political feasibility has a direct impact on the success of EOs, particularly their longevity, as future presidents can reverse them (Remember Chapter Two?) After Republican backlash, notably after Biden's promises of unity and bipartisanship, the president defended his actions:

> *"There's a lot of talk with good reason about the number of executive orders that I've signed...*
> *I'm not making new law. I'm eliminating bad policy."*

With increasing GOP support of climate policy, shown in the Pew data in the next few pages, EO 14008 may be politically feasible. Executive orders can be the equivalent of very formal written press releases that allow the president to signal to the public that they are delivering on the promises they made when they ran for office; this occurs even if the executive action is only the first step in a long arduous battle toward change.

Biden's "Tackling the Climate Crisis at Home and Abroad," has support from major public and private policy actors from both sides of the bipartisan divide. Opposition to Biden's climate crisis plan comes from those who are against environmental policies because they believe they poses a threat to the United States' current energy industrial complex. Those who oppose and those who support Biden's overarching plan aim to influence the perception of Biden's policy, and ultimately the conversation on our Climate Crisis and how to solve it.

Biden, within EO 14008, states that it is the policy of his administration to "organize and deploy the full capacity of its agencies to combat the climate crisis to implement a government-wide approach that reduces climate pollution in every sector of the economy."

President Biden and his administration used elements of both the Issue-Attention Cycle and the Agenda Setting Model to elevate the policy above the agendas of energy industry giants who would love to block it. The major institutional actors that support Executive Order 14008, or "Tackling the Climate Crisis at Home and Abroad," are President Joseph R. Biden and his administration (of course), but in particular, the Secretary of the Interior, Secretary of Treasury, the Secretary of State, the Secretary of Energy, the Director of National Intelligence, the Secretary of Defense, Chairman of the Joint Chiefs of Staff (JCS), and the Secretary of Homeland Security are highlighted in this sweeping EO.

Biden's Climate Task Force is comprised of Gina McCarthy, former head of the EPA under Obama; Deb Haaland, head of the

Interior and a co-sponsor of the Green New Deal; Jennifer Granholm, energy secretary; Michael Regan, the head of the EPA; Brenda, Mallory, a long-time environmental attorney, and John Kerry as the president's diplomat on climate change.

INDUSTRIES AND INSTITUTIONS ARE BEHIND IT

Current major non-institutional supporters include the auto industry, one of the largest stakeholders in fossil fuels. One day after Biden announced, "Tackling the Climate Crisis at Home and Abroad," General Motors announced it would exclusively offer electric vehicles by 2035. Green Global USA and The Center for Resource Solutions (CRS), wind and solar industries along with the International Council for Local Environmental Initiatives also support the order that tackles the crisis without any appeasements to the fossil fuel industries. Earthjustice, dedicated to litigating environmental issues, and current Democratic institutional actors in Biden's party and The EPA support it as a reversal of Trump's assault on environmental protections. However, Senate Democrats and Republicans from fossil-fuel states could stand in this order's way to phase out coal and oil. Senator Joe Manchin (D-WV) opposes the order in defense of coal in his state.

Biden's order restricts funding for carbon energy industries and instead allocates it to clean energy projects.

The fossil fuel industries that oppose the order are backed by institutional actors satisfying constituencies (no surprise). Western Energy Alliance filed a lawsuit challenging the order the day it was issued, and Republicans introduced bills in the House and Senate to counter the order. Congresswoman Cheney introduced bills to prohibit Biden's coal, oil, and gas leasing cessations. Biden's order restricts funding for carbon energy industries and instead allocates it to clean energy projects. Major non-institutional actors that oppose this policy are the heads of the Fossil Fuel giants, such as the Export-Import Bank (ExIm) and the Development Finance Corporation (DFC).

To have an issue on the agenda policy, there must be an awareness that something is wrong and that the problem can be ameliorated through public action. Biden took precautions to avoid being limited by social construct by hiring multiple policy actors with direct knowledge and experiences with climate change and the problems that derive from it. Biden has even gone so far as to say that all agencies, not just those focused on climate, going forward will have some role in a "government-wide" approach. Notably, EO 14008, "Tackling Climate Change at Home and Abroad," created new cabinets and positions for these experts specifically targeted to mitigate the damage, such as through GHG regulatory policy, as to further our understanding and, thus, change social reality.

JOE CLEARLY DOESN'T LIKE PING PONG

To avoid the dreaded ping pong game his policy would no doubt face in Congress, The Biden Administration consulted with climate professionals and passed Executive Order 14008 to fight the climate crisis avoiding Congress in its formulation. Smart. Completely dodging the game that Congress plays Biden will garner support for the implementation of his sweeping policy by using the Agenda Setting Model (research says ample support is there on mitigating the climate crisis). In addition, the Biden Administration used the momentum provided by the media and public opinion to gain and maintain support for Executive Order 14008, utilizing the Issue-Attention cycle, very effectively. Go Joe.

The reality of the climate change crisis is backed by 99.9% of scientists, yet over two-thirds of U.S. adults believe the government is lacking in its mitigation.

A recent study led by Pew states that: There is strong consensus among Democrats (90%, including independents who lean to the Democratic Party) on the need for more government efforts to reduce the effects of climate change, Republican views are divided along ideological, generational and gender lines. A majority of moderate or liberal Republicans (65%, including GOP-leaning independents) say the federal government is doing too little to reduce the effects of climate change. In contrast, only about one-quarter of conservative Republicans (24%) say the same, while about half (48%) think the government is doing about the right amount and another 26% say it is doing too much.

Pew also found that opinions on climate change differed by age and gender. While the GOP is still divided from within, the Democratic party remains unified on the issue. Thus, Republicans continue to focus on strengthening the U.S. economy through the energy industry, while Democrats view climate change as a health and environmental emergency. As Biden's environmental policy was presented as an Executive Order, the agenda-setting process is not as vulnerable to the public theater that might have influenced legislative actors otherwise. Yet, the decisional stage of the policy cycle can still present challenges as the EO states that "climate considerations shall be an essential element of United States foreign policy and national security".

**EO 14008 also directs the Secretary of the Interior to
cease granting leases on federal lands and for all federal
agencies to terminate fossil fuel subsidies by 2022; while
creating more environmental policy councils to advise
Biden in reaching his goal of conserving at least
30 percent of federal lands and waters by 2030.**

Legislative actors from states that economically prosper from the industries that EO 14008 aims to regulate naturally oppose this policy. In Texas (Oil Country), four Democrats have opposed Biden's EO, calling it far-reaching as it jeopardizes energy production in their state. This may have been wise for these politicians in terms of popularity (in Texas); but at the price of opposing their own party's leader, and the necessary change this EO presents for the betterment of our futures. Executive Order 14008 engages the entire U.S. government and additionally requires international action to address the current climate crisis. Sec. 219 is one of the most important policy factors regarding the livelihoods of Americans. <u>This policy could benefit from more explanation as to how it supports the historically marginalized and overburdened communities. I have no doubt that Joe in on it though.</u>

**Biden's EO must expand on its plan to address environmental
justice in minority and low-income populations. Those
communities would feel more reassured knowing that their
government is acting to better their health in addition to
increasing employment opportunities.**

A LITTLE PING PONG WOULDN'T HURT

Had this EO contained timelines for states and businesses to combat parties in disagreement with this order, the possibility of opposition might be higher—as the door would be open for those who would try to block it. Many fuel companies and manufacturers have already begun to plan for and implement climate change planning into their long-term strategies. Giving these opposing parties and institutions some guidance and support will be key to avoiding further litigation as well as making this policy and future climate change policies more efficient. A little ping pong wouldn't hurt.

With EO 14008 some states have indicated what revisions they would like to see. Seventeen Governors called for Biden to revise his EO and lift the ban on drilling leases in oil reliant states to meet consumer demand and stabilize electric grids. The leaders argued that their states rely on energy sourced from private and public lands to serve their people, to sustain economic growth, and to provide public goods. Critics also suggest revisions be made that separate tasks and establish new positions for each of the order's proposals which might otherwise become watered down inside departmental politics.

Data indicates that interest in mitigating climate change has increased over the last twenty years, doubling since 2000 and quadrupling since 1970. Since 2004 both Republicans and Democrats have increased twofold the use of the environment as a party platform, indicating that revisions to Biden's EO must cross party lines to succeed. Since Executive Order 14008 was passed so recently, the policy's details have not been finalized and it is hard to say which area of the executive order might be removed. Section 205(b)(ii) requiring Federal, State, local, and Tribal government agencies to reach the same goal within the same fourteen-year time frame (by 2035) are a bold call for aggressive and collective action. The Federal Register states that Section 205, Federal Clean Electricity and Vehicle Procurement Strategy, includes:

"(b) The plan shall aim to use, as appropriate and consistent with applicable law, all available procurement authorities to achieve or facilitate:

(ii) clean and zero-emission vehicles for Federal, State, local, and Tribal government fleets, including vehicles of the United States Postal Service."

Since EO 14008 may be costly for future taxpayers, this portion will likely receive less support from the financially stressed communities. Those primarily responsible for implementing this Order put EPA at the helm but not alone. Early into his term, Biden Established the National Climate Task Force to head the implementation of his Climate Policies. VP Harris and White House aides convened cabinet secretaries along with the acting heads of 21 federal agencies to begin implementing President Biden's Order that fulfills his promise to mobilize the entire federal government in confronting our climate crisis.

Early into his term, Biden established The National Climate Task Force to head the implementation of his climate policies.

The EPA's Office of Enforcement and Compliance Assurance (OECA), The Secretary of State, The Department of Treasury, and The Secretary of Energy will work with the Export-Import Bank of the United States to effectively implement Biden's environmental and energy order on all fronts. The order's call to end fossil fuel-based energy financing while simultaneously advancing green ones requires numerous agencies' cooperation and leadership. The Director of the Office of Science and Technology Policy (OSTP) reviews the effectiveness of each agency's scientific-integrity and practices going forward to ensure efficient implementation of the policies under this order. 14008 is a sweeping order with multiple agencies primarily responsible for its implementation, and the states' compliance is necessary for the order to succeed.

TOM VILSACK -
THE HURDLES AND THE OBSTACLES

One potential problem is Tom Vilsack, Biden's pick for Secretary of Agriculture. Agriculture irrigation is the largest usage of freshwater in the United States, annually withdrawing over 42% of our fresh surface and groundwater. The agricultural department is essential in implementing EO 14008, including targets in climate mitigation such as carbon sequestration methods and GHG emission goals. Environmental policy groups have attacked Vilsack for "Being too cozy with 'Big Ag.'" and he earned $1 million a year lobbying for the dairy industry alone - (Remember the chapter on the power of money in our policies?)

EO 14008 is a government-wide order which poses challenges within The National Climate Task Force and departmental agencies. Challenges to implementing this policy are also coming from states that rely on coal, oil, and nuclear industries. During the formulation stage of this order, the fossil fuel industries' challenges were expected, but mitigating them would require weakening the order itself. These challenges can be combated by providing statistical evidence of this EO's longevity, especially espousing claims the economy and employment rates will not be negatively affected by this order, regardless of a shift from fossil fuels to clean energies. (Sec. 217, EO 14008). And this it to be expected. There will always be political interests who support the findings of an evaluation and those who oppose them regardless of how objectively accurate the data may be. Translating the goals of this aggressive environmental policy into enforceable criteria with definable actions will still hinder gaining compliance.

Furthermore, the EPA cannot politically afford to shut down the fossil fuels industries that are a tremendous source of employment in many communities around America. Political opposition is also one of Biden's EO's most significant challenges as it is evaluated for implementation. Like the measurement process, the political debate of climate change will influence the public's view of this aggressive policy. In a divided Congress with this type of New-Deal legislation, climate advocates might be forced to make some concessions if we are going to have any climate legislation pass and succeed in the near future.

An indication of the obstacles 14008 will face was seen when twenty-one attorneys general filed lawsuits against Biden, claiming he overextended his presidential power to halt the Keystone XL's construction when he signed EO 13990. Domestic politics will not be the only likely obstacles for this order. The Canadian company TC Energy, the owner of the Keystone XL, has recently alluded to suing Biden as well. Implementation of President Biden's climate policy will require both foreign and domestic commitments. Domestically, implementing the order will be executed through the White House Office of Domestic Climate Policy while utilizing the Paris Agreement's objectives for its implementation abroad. EO 14008 taps the National Climate Task Force to create the immediate implementation of scientific integrity, foreign policy, national security, and economic policies to help ensure the success of the policies behind the order.

While Biden's EO 14008 builds upon the Paris Agreement's objective to exercise leadership internationally, implementing the policy as an Executive Order allows Biden to forgo the process of partisan Congressional approval.

However, if passed through Congress, it would make implementation challenges less combative, and the order would be less subject to possible revocation by future administrations. Republicans in Congress would likely pass legislation that would impede the order by removing necessary funding. Biden's strategy for bypassing this policy's political and partisan vulnerabilities means other ways of implementing this order must rely on cooperation over adversarial relationships, federally and locally. **Good luck.**

During Obama's presidency, the United States pledged to decrease carbon emissions and joined the Paris Agreement on climate. Then later, President Trump, supported by most Republican legislators in an egregious partisan move, reversed the previous administration's course, and rescinded many of the Obama administration's executive orders. The polarization of climate policies reflects the economic, behavioral, and partisan divides that must be solved for any climate crisis solutions to have a chance.

Republicans used climate change as a campaign platform over a third less than their Democratic counterparts in 2020, indicating that although that divide is lessening, polarization on climate policies is still powerful. Given Biden's Climate Task Force's homogeneous political ideologies, Biden's awesome climate mitigation policy wouldn't stand a chance if a Republican Congress gets a hold of it.

THE COSTS OF GREENHOUSE EMISSIONS

The cost of greenhouse gases, i.e., the social cost of carbon dioxide, methane, and nitrous oxide, are critical variables to understanding how to monetize the costs and benefits from reducing greenhouse gas emissions.

President Biden restarted the "Interagency Working Group" (disbanded by Trump) on the Social Costs of Greenhouse Gas Emissions.

Biden directed the Interagency Working Group to lay out a temporary social cost of carbon to make sure that agencies are accounting for the full cost of pollution greenhouse gases, including "climate risk, environmental justice, and intergenerational equity".

Under the Trump administration, the cost of carbon/ greenhouse emissions was as low as $8 per ton by using only the domestic effects and not on the global scale of climate change: Last I checked, The United States deals internationally with exports and imports, and what affects the globe affects the United States—but way to go fudging the numbers, Trump! Armed with more accurate statistics Biden has proposed an interim SCC value of $52 per ton.

According to the Environmental Defense Fund, total CO2 emissions from fossil fuel combustion in the U.S. are on the order of five billion tons a year, so that would be roughly $250 billion dollars in damages per year just from burning fossil fuels. Currently, environmental activists and economists are urging President Biden to lower the 3% rate set by Obama. Biden addresses the importance of protecting public health, conserving lands, waters, biodiversity, and ensuring environmental justice for the impacted, vulnerable communities.

As part of an unprecedented push to cut the nation's greenhouse gas emissions and to create new jobs, as the United States shifts toward cleaner energy, Biden directed agencies across the federal government to invest in low-income and minority communities that have continually borne the brunt of the pollution.

THE MONETARY AND HUMAN COSTS

Ever committed to Keynesian principles, Biden espouses the belief that the most effective method to bolster aggregate demand, thereby stimulating increased production and prosperity, lies in leveraging the formidable tool of government budgeting and his comprehensive "government-wide" strategy. In sec 102.f, Biden's EO 14008, "Tackling Climate Crisis at Home and Abroad," makes the following comment regarding budget: "The United States will also immediately begin to develop a climate finance plan, making strategic use of multilateral and bilateral channels and institutions." By means of his executive order, Biden, and his administration, particularly the Special Presidential Envoy for Climate, the Secretary of State, the Secretary of the Treasury, and the Secretary of Energy, will use the international climate funding from the fiscal year 2021 spending package passed by Congress in December 2020 as a base for the financial plan to be broken down as follows:

- $811 million - bilateral allocations for environmental programs addressing biodiversity protection, sustainable landscapes, renewable energy, and adaptation.
- $140 million - the Global Environment Facility
- $1.48 billion - multilateral development banks
- $32 million - the Montreal Protocol Multilateral Fund
- $6.4 million - the Intergovernmental Panel on Climate Change (IPCC) and the UN Framework Convention on Climate Change (UNFCCC)

Since the 2020 fiscal year, under Biden, Congress has made renewable energy and adaptations to mitigate the effects if the climate crisis a top priority. These adaptations are alongside existing calls for sustainable landscapes and biodiversity within the spending bill and this EO. In relation to section 102.f, Congress has directed allocations for environmental objectives, drawing funds primarily from the Development Assistance and the Economic Support Fund which received a $5 million increase from the previous fiscal year.

For 29 years, the Global Environment Facility has "financed projects that help developing countries meet commitments under a variety of global environmental agreements... and has enjoyed long-standing bipartisan support in Congress. Despite the Trump administration's repeated efforts to halve U.S. contributions, Congress has maintained Global Environment Facility funding over the past four years."

The United States is also a major shareholder in multilateral development banks, which provide climate finance for developing countries. To help developing countries reduce their use of ozone-depleting chemicals, including several greenhouse gases, the United States has maintained funding for the Montreal Protocol Multilateral Fund at the same level as last year. UN entities have also maintained the same level of funding from the last year; however it is less than the $10 million previously budgeted under Obama. IPCC and UN-FCCC benefit the United States' climate initiative through their "support climate science and international negotiations, respectively. The United States provides around two-fifths of the IPCC's total budget and one-fifth of the UNFCCC's."

Building on the Congressional spending bill, Biden plans on taking the next four steps regarding climate finance:

1. "Fulfill and Double the US Pledge to Green Climate Fund," also known as GCF.— **The Trump administration had previously stopped the $3 billion pledge made by the Obama administration.**
2. "Contribute to Other Multilateral Climate Institutions;"

3. "Integrate Climate Throughout All Development Funding;"
4. "Push Development Banks to Align with the Paris Agreement." (Thwaites, 2021).

There have been debates and concerns raised by Biden's increased expenditures and the ballooning deficit. Biden hopes and argues to be able to fund his ideas by taxing "rich" households, or more specifically households earning more than $400k/year. These tax increases however have led to expressed concern that they would also "dampen and perhaps threaten any economic recovery." Thus, whatever is not financed through new taxes would then be the burden of future taxpayers through increased government borrowing.

To determine the costs and benefits of EO14008, Federal Agencies must quantify the costs of global damages caused by rising temperatures thus the offset of benefits brought by Biden's plan. Biden's policy creates 10 million clean energy jobs in the first phase to offset the losses in fossil fuel industries. Under 14008, the U.S. will spend $1.7 to $2 trillion over the next 10 years, with private, state, and local investments pushing the total sum closer to $5 trillion. The coal industry employs a disproportionate share of workers in two states-Wyoming and West Virginia. In Wyoming, 3% were employed in coal-based power generation last year. In West Virginia, the coal industry accounted for 2% of jobs. To counter the jobs lost in fossil fuels, the majority of the states will see an increase in jobs in the hundreds of thousands. However, the benefits of a new economy based on clean jobs will continue for decades if 14008 is successfully implemented while the benefits of a more habitable planet are undeniable in increasing human well-being.

Biden's policy creates 10 million clean energy jobs in the first phase to offset the losses in fossil fuel industries.

Assigning monetary value to climate change policies when conducting a cost-benefit analysis is a difficult task given that they are non-market issues. Since climate change is an ongoing challenge, it makes the task of assigning a value further complicated. Thus, rather than focusing solely on monetary value, researchers use both quantitative and qualitative analyses to capture the most accurate picture possible of potential policy outcomes. <u>Analyses are presented under the</u> <u>following (**seriously basic**) three scenarios</u>:

1. World with no climate change
2. World with climate change
3. World with climate change and adaptation

Policymakers and the public should be provided with basic scientific data that explains that human health, environmental health, and economic stability that cannot be monetized by just an analysis of "potential" costs. What is certain, however, is had Biden's policy not been enacted as an executive order, a cost benefit analysis that not only considers a budgetary analysis, but also an analysis of ethical issues and would have provided policymakers with information that would likely serve as a partisan call to block it. Additionally, providing a cost analysis of the budgetary demands of not enhancing and selecting environmental policies could change the trend of the continued disregard of environmental issues. Due to this policy being implemented as an executive order, President Biden has had the advantage of declaring and setting the policy's budget through his cabinet members. This grants his administration much more freedom to form this policy's budget and set a projected funding amount.

Biden's bold implementation of " Tackling Climate Change at Home and Abroad" as an Executive Order allows for a much more expedited process. While this was a very strategic move by Biden and his administration to enact environmental policy as swiftly as possible, there might have been enough support to pass this policy as legislation through Congress. As mentioned before, data trends for environmental policy are increasing, showing both Republicans and Democrats swaying toward supporting environmental policies. The coordination between politicians from both the Republican and Democrat parties must occur to achieve any real action on climate mitigation. Due to federal government inefficiencies, Biden's Executive office is taking strong and effective action on climate, economic, and industrial policy by using agenda-setting models that disregard our Congressional branch.

Trump first demonstrated the dangers of the extent of POTUS's power when deregulating the Environmental Protection Agency and exiting the Paris Agreement.

President Biden has undone many of Trump's actions by re-entering the Paris Agreement and reinstating regulations from the Environmental Protection Agency.

At our current rate of destruction and development, earth will be unable to sustain life on the planet sooner than we realize. This threat to the earth must be at forefront of 21st-century politics.

ECOLOGISM AND SCIENCE—IT IS EVERYTHING

Remember the section on ideologies? I neglected to include a new ideology that has emerged in the last few decades; an ideology based on fact and science instead of beliefs, that is at the forefront of 21st century politics. ECOLOGISM. Ecologism is a political ideology that uses science as its backbone. Using science, ecologism argues that our planet is currently under severe and catastrophic threats that include climate change, biodiversity losses, rapid deforestations (that enhance the climate crisis) and our abundance of waste. Ecologism is focused on the relationship people have with nature, the critical partnership between humans and natural world. Ecologism armed with science argues that we must take sweeping action on improving how we treat our planet and our environment. Our current over consumption and economic growth rates in the industrialized world are simply unsustainable.

Our planet is under severe and catastrophic threats that include climate change, biodiversity losses, rapid deforestations that enhance the climate crisis, and our abundance of waste. Protecting the environment must be at the center of human justice.

Science backs up the very ideology behind Ecologism creating a powerful argument for its urgency. It is the science, not just the moral, philosophical, or economic arguments behind Ecologism, that give this ideology its meat and power. The science is where it all starts in backing up every other facet to Ecologism that centers around climate, energy, and our planet. Even the economic arguments in Ecologism are founded on the science that reveals the dangerous and perilous issues that created this new ideology to begin with.

Chances are you have never seen or heard of Rachel Carlson's Silent Spring, which exposes through scientific research and statistics the dangerous impact of pesticides and chemicals used upon our food chain. Carlson dives into, (in Silent Spring) the use of immensely powerful and toxic poisons used in agriculture and on our food supply. She uses Ecologism as the motive behind her investigative work into the chemicals that are put into the food we eat. Carlson also uses science to expose not just the dangers in consuming foods that have been sprayed with DDT or other pesticides, but how the spraying of these chemicals negatively affects our atmosphere in every way. Carlson mixes moral outrage with science for a compelling and powerful expose that grounds Ecologism as a valid ideology necessary in modern society. Carlson uses scientific research and study to strengthen the ideology of Ecologism through just one issue; the powerful pesticides used in agriculture. Ecologism, however, is a very powerful ideology used in politics and campaigns to set in motion actions and endeavors to save our environment and our planet.

The environmental crisis is at a tipping point with horrifying consequences, through each devastating hurricane, flood, or wildfire—with catastrophic loss of life and livelihoods. We are reminded that the science is real.

These concerns are echoed powerfully by activists, politicians, the people, and economists. There is no greater threat to us than climate change and the deterioration of our environment. Many say it's too late at this point to save it, but under the ideals of Ecologism, it is possible. We must reevaluate our system entirely and how we function as a society in relation to our natural world, otherwise it is game over. We need to change how we manufacture our goods and stop our over consumption and waste of everything. We over manufacture and over consume. If we reprioritize all these elements, we can be propelled into a new economic prosperity led by Ecologism's ideals. We can create innovative progressive technology and the U.S. can lead the world into a new frontier. This is possible, and even exciting if we start acting in unity on every level from the top down, and now.

Each day, we find ourselves caught in a whirlwind of responsibilities: paying bills, enduring long workweeks, nurturing our children, grappling with the daunting task of saving for retirement or their increasingly expensive college education, and coping with serious illness or the unexpected loss of a loved one. Sometimes, all we strive for is to make it through the day, allowing ourselves the simple pleasure of streaming something before drifting off to sleep. Ecologism's goal of transcending human habits to a deeper human awareness of our moral responsibility to our natural world seems impossible.

> **To achieve the goals of Ecologism we need to become a society who regards nature, who regards the science behind the arguments for the goals of Ecologism and we MUST value our earth.**

I want my kids and hopefully, my future grandkids to grow up in a safe, clean, livable world. Ecologism's goal is to restructure society in how we live in relation to our natural world.

CHAPTER FOURTEEN

Under Vaccination
and
Hunger in America

America, why?

UNDER VACCINATION: THE CDC and WHO reports the percentage of the population in the United States that must be vaccinated falls far short of what is needed to keep outbreaks of once eradicated diseases at bay. The abject disregard for proven and lifesaving science in America is now at a tipping point.

AMERICA, WHY?

According to UNICEF and the World Health Organization, 'vaccine hesitancy' or under vaccination has been the cause behind the recent measles outbreaks in the United States and other developed nations. Vaccine hesitancy and the emphatic refusal of vaccines despite science proving their efficacy was the primary cause for the measles outbreak in 2019. The outbreaks are not solely attributed to the United States population that does not believe in vaccinations or those without healthcare and access to vaccines—although this is the root cause to blame. The Center for Disease Control and Prevention attributes the increase in measles outbreaks in the United States and other developed nations to an increase in the number of unvaccinated travelers who encounter infected people abroad, contract the disease, and return home while still contagious and spread the disease to (you guessed it) other unvaccinated people.

This ties in with another CDC finding that those under-vaccinated, under-immunized people also tend to live in close-knit communities, further spreading the disease to the other unvaccinated populations among them. Measles is highly contagious, so 95% of the population must be vaccinated. With millions of anti-vaccination believers or those who do not receive medical coverage, this 95% has become more challenging to meet—with the United States population that has been vaccinated with the first dose at only 85%, and the 2nd dose at only 67%.

"The earth is round, the sky is blue, and vaccines work. Let's protect our kids."— Hillary Clinton

The CDC reported in 2019 that there were 22 measles outbreaks in 17 states, and eight of those outbreaks happened in under-immunized, close-knit communities. Those eight outbreaks accounted for 85% of all cases. The increase in unvaccinated people, close-knit under-immunized communities, and travel abroad to regions with measles all combine to cause over 500,000 people in the United States to contract measles in 2019, and why measles cases are on the rise in every developed nation.

HUMAN POTENTIAL LOST TO POOR HEALTH IS IMMENSE

The world population lost 1.65 billion years of potential life due to premature death in 2019, before the COVID-19 Pandemic arrived. Disease and disability meant that an additional 853 million years of healthy life years were lost. At a global level, collective rates across all ages have been in steady decline. Although global health has improved considerably over the course of the last generation, a global crisis of chronic diseases and the failure of public health to stem the rise in highly preventable risk factors have left populations vulnerable to acute health emergencies such as COVID-19, and future pandemics. America is no exception. Urgent action is needed to address future and impending chronic diseases, social inequalities, and pandemics like COVID-19 to ensure more robust health systems, and healthier people that will make America more resilient to future pandemic threats. A focus on the disease burdens per region, with a comparative analysis of disease burdens on different groups using economic stratification, access to affordable healthcare, area of residency, gender, and education levels; would enable decision-makers to compare the effects of different variables on health conditions. Knowing the patterns and trends in causes of death by age and sex in a population is critical to understanding how to target interventions and to maximize population health and control disease.

HUNGER IN AMERICA

Access to nutritious and safe food is a fundamental human right but millions in America a WEALTHY DEVELOPED, CORE NATION, go hungry daily.

This is SHAMEFUL.

More than 44 million people in the U.S. face hunger, including 1 in 5 children. Millions of people in the U.S. don't have enough food to eat or don't have access to healthy food.
--Feeding America

AMERICA, WHY?

Eradicating the systemic ills in our nation that create tremendous and lifelong poverty cycles for so many should be the focus on ending hunger in America. Hunger is a solvable problem, and ending poverty and eradicating food deserts is where we must start.

FOOD DESERTS IN AMERICA

There are over 6,500 Food deserts across America. A Food Desert is an area or neighborhood in America where it is nearly impossible to find affordable nutritious food. In these Food Deserts there is very limited access to fresh and healthy foods, and the food that is available comes from convenience stores or fast-food chains. Eradicating these food deserts must be a priority. Prioritizing the gentrification of impoverished rural and urban areas, where access to nutritious whole foods and well-stocked grocery stores is scarce or nonexistent, is imperative.

The prevalence of comorbidities among individuals residing in these areas stemming from limited access to nutritious food choices, is significant. Fast food and packaged foods are major contributors to conditions such as hypertension, high cholesterol, cancer, high blood pressure, and diabetes, often leading to premature death. These lower-income families lack adequate healthcare, which they need more than ever due to the poor quality of available food options. It's a vicious cycle, leaving the impoverished to suffer from illness and malnutrition in the wealthiest country in the world, compounded by inadequate healthcare to address the health issues exacerbated by the existence of food deserts.

America could also begin turning the tide on lifelong inadequate food sources and lifelong inadequate nutrition in poorer urban and rural areas, with resilient agricultural practices in areas less affected by the increasing climate and weather catastrophes. Agricultural skills and practices in underdeveloped and untapped lands in America can lift people out of poverty while helping to eradicate hunger with sustainable food and livelihoods.

America must increase the income and productivity of small-scale food producers, connecting hunger to poverty in breaking these cycles. Investments in infrastructure and technology to increase agricultural productivity in areas with shortfalls is vital (although there really is no shortage of food in America, just healthy food). Access to nutritious foods in every area, neighborhood and district in America must be made a priority.

There are over 6,500 Food Deserts in America.

Institutions, corporations, and politicians must invest in ending this humanitarian crisis. America is an abundantly wealthy first world nation, so why are millions of people and children here still hungry for nutritious healthy food, or hungry for any food at all to eat?

This is shameful.

AMERICA, WHY?

PART FIVE

EXTRA TIDBITS

THE PRIVACY OF OUR INFORMATION AND A FEW WORDS ON NANCY PELOSI

CHAPTER FIFTEEN

The Privacy of Our Information

(Especially On Social Media Sites)

"Arguing that you don't care about the right to privacy because you have nothing to hide is no different than saying you don't care about free speech because you have nothing to say."

- Edward Snowden
(Whistleblower and Privacy Advocate)

OUR PRIVATE INFORMATION ON SOCIAL NETWORKING SITES

We, the users of all social networking platforms, are literally the currency of those platforms.

With our society's addiction to and dependence upon social media as strong as ever, our usage comes at a great cost to our privacy. The security of our identities and what we do while online is consistently exposed. The irony lies in our concern over the excessive use of social media platforms that exposes our information, considering that the majority of us have never read, nor will ever read, the privacy policy of any social networking platform. Most people have no idea when these sites are legally able to or bound by law to fork over our private information to a requesting entity—as this is less concerning to users than the content on the sites themselves, and how we can contain it.

Our reliance on social networking platforms has ballooned into a critical area of privacy control, and we are more exposed to online predators, online scammers, and identity thieves than ever before.

FACEBOOK AND INSTAGRAM

Facebook and Instagram are perhaps the most scrutinized platforms and have been held under a microscope most recently with employees testifying before Congress about the abuses of these platforms and the effect they have on teenagers. Facebook and Instagram have been sharply criticized for allowing dangerous false news stories to be peddled on their platforms, along with abusive behaviors between teens, hateful speech groups, and dangerous disinformation that incites violence.

The dangers that social media platforms such as Facebook, Instagram, Twitter, and Snapchat pose to the mental health of our society (and our very democracy) has been cause for outrage among the public, with a call for policy and actions to be legislated to protect our youth (as well our democracy). However, the privacy of the users of these platforms has yet to be as scrutinized and is a critical component to these sites' safety as well. (Unless someone like me, who was curious enough to read the privacy policy of each social networking site), most have not, nor will ever be made aware of the circumstances under which these sites will hand over your private information when an entity requests it.

Facebook and Instagram have several circumstances that enable or compel them to hand over users' private information. These circumstances are under legal process requirements with user consent. There are legal circumstances when user consent is not necessary or the law overrides any privacy protection of the user in emergency requests, and when the safety of a child or minor is at stake. Facebook and Instagram state in its privacy policy that their company will only disclose a user's private information "in accordance with their terms of service and as applicable by law".

If a member of a law enforcement agency is seeking information about a Facebook user who has also provided his or consent to the official gaining access to the user's private information, there is a procedure that Facebook follows. The user will be directed to obtain the information on his or her own from his or her account then give access to law enforcement officials.

There are legal processes where consent by the user is not required for the legal official to gain access to user account information. In issues concerning national security and criminal matters Facebook and Instagram will hand over a user's private information without his or her consent if a valid subpoena, court order, or search warrant is presented. The valid subpoena must be in connection with an official criminal investigation that compels the necessary disclosure of a user's information. This information can include name, location, credit card information, email addresses, and a recent login/logout IP address if available. A court order can also compel the release of certain records or other user information attached to the Facebook or Instagram account. Unlike the subpoena, a court order does not compel the release of the user's contents of communications, which may include message headers and IP addresses.

When a search warrant is presented, Facebook and Instagram must release all user information including nonpublic private information. The search warrant must be issued under the federal rules of criminal procedure or with proof of probable cause. Under federal criminal procedures of probable cause, Facebook and Instagram will share a user's information when probable cause is present and will disclose all contents (public and nonpublic) of the user's account, which includes messages, photos, videos, timeline posts, and location information.

The other two circumstances that compel Facebook and Instagram to hand over your private information are in emergency requests and child safety matters, when a child or minor is in danger. Facebook and Instagram must respond when there is harm to a child or there is risk of death or serious injury to any person by releasing all involved users' private account information.

In the case of when a child or minor is in danger, because of activities and communications done via Facebook or Instagram, the social networking platforms must respond swiftly, and consent is not needed. In their privacy policy Facebook and Instagram state that "Users aware of an emergency situation should immediately and directly contact local law enforcement officials, and if a request relates to a child exploitation or safety matter, please specify those circumstances in the request to ensure that we are able to address these matters expeditiously and effectively."

TWITTER 'X'

"X" (formerly Twitter) where rants and online feuds can become quite entertaining fodder, is a place where users are more than just "tweeters". An X account profile contains more than just the person's tweets. An X""/Twitter user's profile consists of a profile photo, header photo, and background image. The account holder has the option to fill out a location and a short "bio" about himself or herself and private user information is also a part of a user's account.

Under what circumstances will "X" fork over that information? "X" in their privacy policy states, "We offer strong privacy controls for everyone" but there are circumstances where "X" will hand over a user's private information when an entity requests it. Like Facebook's and Instagram's procedures when law enforcement requests for users' information, 'X"s is the same.

In its privacy policy, 'X' states: "Twitter responds to valid legal processes issued in compliance with applicable law." Under "X"s privacy policy, private information of any user requires a subpoena or court order by a law enforcement official. Their policy states: all "nonpublic information about 'X' users will not be released to law enforcement except in response to appropriate legal process such as a subpoena, court order, other valid legal process, or in response to a valid emergency request." 'X' also makes it very clear that they "preserve, use, share, or disclose your personal data or other safety data if we believe that it is reasonably necessary to comply with a law, regulation, legal process, or governmental request."

ALGORITHMS AND MONEY: OUR PRIVACY

There is an area less obvious that bleeds into the exposure of an unsuspecting user's private information and that is algorithms and money. The users of all social networking platforms are the currency of that platform, and Twitter seems to be just as dubious as Facebook and Instagram in the exposure of private information of its unsuspecting users. In the fine print of Twitter's privacy policy, it states: "When you watch or otherwise interact with content from these partners (partners on X) they may receive and process your personal data as described in their privacy policies. If you've shared information like Direct Messages or protected Tweets with someone else who accesses X through a third-party service, keep in mind that information may be shared with the third-party service."

SNAPCHAT IS THE WORST

Snapchat is one of the most popular social networking sites and has similar privacy policies, with one significant difference from Twitter, Facebook, and Instagram. The privacy policy of Snapchat (unlike Facebook, Instagram, and X) is broad and vague—ultimately stating that they will share a user's information whenever it can improve the user's experience on Cnapchat or make it easier to connect to other "snap chatters". WOW.

Snapchat itself, not the users or "snap chatters" themselves, shares the information of their "snap chatters" with other users including non-specified, nonpublic information about them. What?

This includes information about how users have interacted with Snapchat services and information about a user's private device, such as the operating system and device type, to help the user receive Chats, Snaps, and other content in the most efficient manner. This seems dubiously vague and gives Snapchat tremendous leeway with user info and behavior; that leeway is masqueraded and sold as promoting a user's optimal experience, but seems more to benefit Snapchat, while hooking in users. Like the legal processes that compel Facebook, Instagram, and Twitter to share a user's private information with or without consent, Snapchat's privacy policy states: "We may share information about you for legal, safety, and security reasons. We may share information about you if we reasonably believe that disclosing the information is needed to comply with any valid legal process, governmental request, or applicable law, rule, or regulation." (And apparently all other times too.)

Snapchat's privacy policy, as well as Facebook, Instagram, and Twitter's privacy policies, all have a system for requesting and sharing user's private information in the event of an emergency, under the legal processes, or when a person or child is in immediate danger. What is most obvious in reading the privacy policy of each of these social networking sites, is that none of them willfully hand over private content to law enforcement as the proper requirements must be met. However, these social networking platforms (without putting this fact in writing) can only guarantee and protect what is actually in their servers.

Our private information is fair game to third-party apps accessing these sites.

HIPPA AND FERPA
The Privacy of Our Health and Medical Information

There is a conjoined relationship between the Family Educational Rights and Privacy Act (FERPA) and the areas of privacy protection covered under the Health Insurance Portability and Accountability Act of 1996 (HIPAA) Privacy Rule. Both HIPAA and FERPA protect how medical and academic records are shared, safeguarding the information of medical patients and students from nonconsensual disclosure of their records and private facts. HIPAA and FERPA protect when and what information can be shared, whether health and medical history records or education and academic records. HIPAA Privacy Rule established a national standard to protect almost any part of a person's medical records and other individual and personal health information. HIPAA protects what is known as "protected health information" or individual medical records under patient (non)consent.

Under this area of privacy in the disclosure of information, HIPAA gives patients control of access to their medical records by requiring Americans to decide what medical information they wish to keep confidential. HIPAA also controls/protects the release of personal medical records to health care providers and ensures that health care transactions electronically are confidential. The HIPAA Rule protects the privacy of "protected health information" and limits the disclosures and uses of medical records that apply to and affect health coverage and costs. Most critical to the area of privacy covered under HIPAA are the patients' rights (not just to privacy) of their medical information, but access to their medical records freely and without limits; including the right to transmit "protected health information" to a third party and request corrections. HIPAA protects against the invasions of privacy in unauthorized disclosures and uses of private facts and information.

FERPA, Family Educational Rights and Privacy Act, like HIPAA, covers the same areas of privacy. FERPA allows parents the right to have access to their children's educational records, the right to have their child's records corrected, and the right to control the disclosure of personally identifiable information in those records. When a student turns 18 years old or enters a postsecondary institution, the rights under FERPA transfer from the parents to the student but are still in effect as they now become self-reliant eligible students. FERPA protects the privacy of education records and the right to control the disclosure of educational information. FERPA, however, allows schools to disclose a student's records without consent in certain circumstances: to school officials with legitimate educational interest, other schools to which a student is transferring, specified officials for evaluation purposes, parties in connection with financial aid to a student, organizations conducting certain studies on behalf of the school, when complying with a judicial order or lawfully issued subpoena, in health and safety emergencies, and to state and local authorities per state law. In addition, FERPA requires schools to notify parents and students annually of their rights under FERPA (HHS.gov-HIPAA and FERPA). To put it plainly, HIPAA and FERPA protect the privacy and disclosure of our personal information and private facts. HIPAA and FERPA protect our rights to control access, uses, and disclosures of medical and education records. FERPA and HIPAA overlap in implementation and conjoin together to protect our information and the right to our privacy of that information.

UP FOR SEXTING ANYONE?

Legal and societal implications reach far beyond the original text of someone's naked genitals, which is where the education of minors and sexting must begin before we start locking teens up.

SEXTING LAWS FOR MINORS ARE HARSH YET CHILD MARRIAGE (FOR GIRLS) IS LEGAL IN 46 STATES.

In most states with the harshest sexting laws against minors, consensual real-life sex between teens is less than sixteen years of age, and yet the marriage of a girl under fifteen is legal.

Even more alarming is that child marriage is legal in forty-six states, with some states allowing the legal marriage of GIRLS at just FOURTEEN.

<u>AMERICA, WHY?</u>

Minors can be charged with manufacturing, disseminating, and possessing child pornography for "sexting" nude photographs of themselves to other minors. "Sexting" or sending nudes, or sexually explicit content via text messaging is not a crime between consenting adults, but it is a federal crime for an adult to "sext" with a minor, with or without the minor's consent. The application of child pornography laws in those cases where an adult is involved is appropriate and necessary for the protection of minors. The application of felony child pornography laws is harsh and extreme when applied to "sexting" between minors. Teenagers in high school are infamously sending pics of themselves to crushes, girlfriends, or sports teammates as a joke. Teens can be dumb, and often do not understand the enormous scope of what it means to text a nude selfie or genitalia selfie.

The notion that teens/kids should consider, while in a moment of stupid hilarity, or rampant hormones, that taking a nude selfie could become a crime of trafficking child porn is incredibly unrealistic and unjust. Teens are wholeheartedly an uneducated group on the future implications of doing something idiotic, especially in the moment of doing it; it is why teenagers are teenagers. The idea that when they are sexting each other willingly, both can be charged with child pornography is not even in the realm of their thought process when sending a nude pic or something sexually explicit to each other. The current application of felony child pornography laws is too harsh against minors.

Separating consensual sexting from nonconsensual sexting and actual child pornography is critical in minor-to-minor sexting cases and for law enforcement policymakers to discern what constitutes a federal crime or something less egregious. Consensual teen-to-teen sexting does not warrant law enforcement involvement but instead should be a health and education issue that is better addressed at home, in schools, and by primary caregivers. However, legal, and societal implications reach far beyond the original text of someone's naked genitals, which is where the education of minors and sexting must begin before we start locking them up, the same way we lock up serious child porn traffickers and pedophiles. State's differing laws help illuminate the implications, and while these laws are harsh, the reasoning is not without merit and importance. Some states realize that minors sexting this "porn" are just children, and education and less harsh punishments would serve as a sufficient means to abate the behavior.

For example, New Mexico and Maine have adapted to less harsh punishments and exempted teen sexting from the scope of child pornography statutes under specific circumstances. In New Mexico, child pornography laws do not apply when a teen is younger than eighteen and when the image of a minor is 14 to 18 years old, and the depicted teen knowingly consented to the possession of the image. In Maine, there is no prohibition on the possession of sexually explicit material if the person is at least 14 or 15 years of age. Perhaps what is most interesting in Maine's laws is that this leniency also considers the age gap between the "sexters" - which is critical to the maturity level of both parties regarding harshness. In Maine, when the possessor is less than five years older than the person depicted, sexting is not criminal. Essentially, these two states have decriminalized sexting between minors altogether, given reasonable circumstances.

New York, Georgia, and Utah have also followed suit and created leniency for minors who "sext". Under a more lenient child pornography state statute, New York created a diversionary program for minors rather than fully prosecuting minors. Such programs in New York require the education of the teenagers who have been charged, on the legal and non-legal consequences of sharing sexually explicit materials: the life and legal lessons that follow when a nude or sexually explicit selfie is sent into the ether. Georgia and Utah allow for reduced misdemeanor penalties of sexting that are not as harsh as child pornography prosecutions. Georgia's less harsh laws apply when the possessor is 18 years or younger, and the minor depicted is at least 14 years, and when consent exists and there has been no distribution. Indiana and Nebraska are less lenient but certainly adapting to a need for less harsh penalties for minors. Both states have added "affirmative defenses" to their child pornography statutes. In Nebraska, a visual depiction that portrays only the possessor constitutes one affirmative defense. The second defense is when only one teen is depicted, and he or she knowingly and voluntarily participated in capturing the image without any coercion and there is no distribution.

So far, all but twenty-three states have addressed the overly harsh application of child pornography laws to minors who consensually sext each other.

The most appropriate name for a provision that addresses a less harsh punishment for teens who "sext" is called the "Romeo and Juliet" provision. Nineteen states separate sexting as misdemeanor offenses and often have this "Romeo and Juliet provision" to address those minors charged with sexting. For example, in Texas, if the minors are within two years of age of each other and are in a dating relationship, there is a viable defense under the Romeo and Juliet provision. So far, all but twenty-three states have addressed the overly harsh application of child pornography laws to minors who consensually sext each other. In the twenty-three other states, teens who engage in "sexting" can still be prosecuted, convicted, and sentenced to up to 20 years in prison and can receive a lifetime sexual offender status for production and possession of child pornography. Interestingly, in these states, a teen "sexter" can be charged as both an offender and a victim. When a young kid creates a "sext" to be shared consensually with another similar-aged minor, he or she is not an exploited or abused child victim but rather a hormone-driven adolescent engaging in teenage sexual behavior in the digital age.

Even if many states' child pornography laws consider consensual minors who "sext" to be guilty of a felony crime equal to that of child pornographers, incarcerating them will not protect them nor stop the dissemination of that image for which they were convicted. The harsh application of child pornography laws to teens who consensually "sext" does not serve to educate them and proves unnecessarily harsh in relation to the act. Are not these laws aimed at protecting children? When the laws lock children up in the name of a child protection law, how does that serve the purpose of the law itself? When harsh child pornography laws are applied to minors who 'sext", they only serve to diminish the quality of life and future possibilities of those minors and teens. Furthermore, what kind of society are we when consensually sexting teens are locked up like child predators and pedophiles?

This bears repeating:

In most states with the harshest sexting laws against minors, the marriage of a girl under fifteen is legal: some states allow the legal marriage of girls at <u>just fourteen.</u> AMERICA, WHY?

Nancy Pelosi

GRACE AND PERSISTENCE

A great way to end this book is to say a little something about Nancy Pelosi, a courageous, tireless, barrier breaking, brilliant, badass. Nancy once said, regarding the first impeachment of Donald Trump (there were two), that he was "Not worth it". She endorsed his impeachment a few months later with the hammer of her gavel, in a historic show of leadership, defiance, and strength; uniting the Democratic Party behind her. Nancy also remarked that Trump was unfit to be president "ethically," "intellectually" and "curiosity-wise". Nancy Pelosi is the first and ever woman to hold the post as Speaker of The House and the first person in over seventy years to be elected twice to the position. Nancy once recalled in a press conference the words of advice given to her by Congresswoman Lindy Boggs: "Darlin', know thy power and use it."

In 2007, Nancy began her term as the first woman second in line to the presidency by holding her gavel aloft to a room full of boisterous applause and cheers. She then invited all the children and grandchildren of members of Congress to join her on the floor as she took her historic oath of office. Nancy's style of melding her roles as a mother and grandmother with her unwavering role as the determined new leader of the Democratic Party was exemplary of her style and how she represented her brand of inclusive government. Her passionate and determined strength was also seen through displays of defiance against assaults to our standards and rules that make our nation so indelibly democratic and just.

An example of her passion for what is intractably right, and her lack of shyness in expressing her disdain for crimes against it, is when she famously ripped up President Trump's State of the Union address. She sat right behind the president as cameras and America watched, and without reserve, ripped up what she knew (and millions of Americans also knew) to be words of dangerous and divisive untruths, by a president who repeatedly committed crimes and violated our constitution. Many on the other side of the aisle called her display of rebellion childish, but Nancy's strong will has certainly left an imprinted impression of what she stands for and what strength means. Nancy's courage, resolve, and dignity were equally matched by her outspokenness as she became the most powerful woman in US History. No matter what aisle you sit on, or to what party you belong, Nancy wielded authority more forcefully, with more grace, and more effectively than many of the male speakers before her. She unabashedly used her voice for what she believed was best for America and was not shy to express what she could not tolerate.

Nancy is the first and only woman to spend more than a decade as the top Democratic leader.

Nancy's leadership exemplified determined strength and unwavering resolve, clearly demonstrated through her passionate defiance against every injustice that undercut the democratic and just standards of America.

Nancy's calm unifying abilities within the Democratic party enabled her steady rise to power. Nancy possesses a skillful command of inside politics and policy, but what made Nancy (other than being a woman) the most historic and powerful leader of the Democratic party, was her adept talent in uniting conflicting factions within her party. Nancy's ability to unite the Democrats to achieve legislative successes make her the most effective party leader, and the only Speaker of the House in Seventy years to be elected twice to the position (I know I already said that, but it bears repeating). Make no mistake with Nancy: The smiling, heel wearing, lipstick-wearing grandmother and mother, was tougher than anyone amid a very divided government and Congress. She calmly made it clear that the Republican's divisive government and their leader, Trump, would not break her determination to accomplish what she knew needed to be done to protect the sanctity of our democracy and its processes.

When sworn into office as the first ever woman speaker of the house, Nancy proclaimed: "I pledge that this Congress will be transparent, bipartisan and unifying, that we will seek to reach across the aisle in this country and across divisions across our nation.". In this time of such deep divisions and animosity, our government could use more leaders like Nancy. Nancy does not want to be known for her defiance, or the impeachments of Donald Trump, but for her unifying abilities within her party and her tremendous legislative accomplishments, such as the Affordable Care Act. Her open display of inexhaustible will against all things Trump and destructive Trump loyalists in the Republican Party, fueled her ability to unite the Democrats with such strength.

Nancy's tirelessly passionate yet calm defiance was a grounding hope for the Democrats when they really needed it most. Nancy, in her showdowns with Trump and his unethical Congress, proved that she could not be frightened away, bullied, or exhausted by her boorish opponents. Leon Panetta, the former CIA director, and Defense Secretary described Nancy's leadership when declaring that

"Donald Trump, really met his match with Nancy". Panetta also expressed his confidence in her when he said: "She is, Thank God, the right person in the right place at the right time." Nancy's style has also impressed even her deepest opponents. Nancy is known to be a master legislator on many fronts, not just during her time in the Obama administration, but she is known for garnering support, exchanging favors, and making deals. Nancy passionately stood up against immorality making her one of the strongest leaders America has seen, possessing a deft ability to unite support for her causes. Lindsey Graham one of Trump's most passionate defenders was even impressed with her, calling Nancy's ability to advance bipartisan legislation on many issues "quite a feat."

Nancy's was proud to be part of the establishment, but she was never afraid to challenge the establishment and stand up against it with passion. Her ability to be both a leader and a rebel are great feats in her leadership style, that proved a uniting factor within her party (and even at times across strong party lines). Nancy Pelosi's decision-making skills among the Democrats under her leadership, were not always centralized, but backed with undying support, especially against the Republican-led Senate. Under the Trump Administration there was no way for decisions to ever be "centralized." Under Nancy's leadership, her outspoken disdain for the immorality of so many in the opposing party, centralization in decisions and actions was impossible. One thing is certain, Nancy might have been treated like a piñata, but she was not easily rattled. Congresswoman Anna Eschoo said of Pelosi: "Her steady hand has helped to bring members to be deeply reflective about how serious this is."

Sexism and GOP attacks were her biggest obstacles, but as a veteran of politics, Nancy was unshaken by her attackers. The ceaseless sexism she encountered and the onslaught of attacks against her became sources of strength, reigniting the fervor among her supporters. Nancy Pelosi was a veteran politician and a fighter and was not one to give up or be bullied. She did not just survive her attacks, she flourished under them. Trump childishly undermined her by calling her "Nervous Nancy", while also having then White House Spokeswoman Mercedes Schlapp proclaim that the "Democratic Party is obsessed with investigating Trump."

These classless bully tactics didn't shake her but became resources to her in unifying her supporters and her party against the very type of politics she stands against. Nancy's attackers and Trump's bully tactics were a powerful part of the solidifying glue which she used masterfully to her advantage.

Nancy's influence as the legislative leader of the Democratic party was a constant battle for her under the Trump Administration and against a Senate led by the Republicans (it was more like a war). However, because of her savvy, strong fight, and determination, legislation was continually accomplished. Nancy led the successful negotiations over a new trade deal, known as the United States-Mexico-Canada Agreement. Nancy quickly and with indelible focus shot down questions about the impeachment to discuss this achievement in legislation and bipartisanship under her leadership in a direct contradiction to Trump's attack on the Democrats as "Do Nothing Democrats".

Nancy Pelosi used her obstacles as resources and fuel for her fight, and she was committed to not just protecting the constitution and our democracy, but also the more centralized forces in legislation. Nancy made it clear that she was not just about the ideologies of the left or of her party, and intended to protect and back more moderate representatives, especially the ones who flipped Republican seats. This approach was not only a unifying tactic that helped more centralized members of Congress feel loyal to the Democratic party and their legislation but proved that Nancy was no newcomer to what was needed to gain support for the betterment of our union. Again, she was, and will always be a badass.

Nancy Pelosi's tenure in the White House was a remarkable fusion of effectiveness and respect.

Serving as the first and only woman Speaker of the House during a fervently Republican administration, Nancy defied countless barriers. Nancy emerged as a beacon of leadership, courage, accountability, ethics, and dignity.

Conclusion

Throughout history, we have witnessed the ebb and flow of political ideologies, the rise and fall of movements, and the clash of differing worldviews. I believe it is critical to engage in thoughtful and respectful discourse, to bridge divides, and to find common ground whenever possible. The strength of a democratic society exists in its ability to accommodate diverse perspectives, fostering an environment where the best ideas can rise to the surface while disinformation and confounding ignorance lose out. This book is a testament to that pursuit—a yearning to understand and illuminate the rationale shaping the lives of most Americans. In concluding this book of our history, our Supreme Court, our Constitution, our ideologies, the corrupt power of money in our legislature and in our courts, the heinous crimes and destructive dangers of Trump, and everything in between, I am left with a profound sense of determination.

Throughout this journey, I have come to understand that at the core of a great America lies an unwavering commitment to ethical accountability, individual rights, social justice, and the relentless pursuit of progress. As I reflect on the arguments and history presented in these pages, I am reminded of the enduring power of human collaboration and empathy, and the "Categorical Imperative" that Kant espoused—to create a world that is fair, inclusive, and just for everyone. The journey within these page traverses not only the moments and people that shape our baffling American experience, but also the dichotomy of ideals in this country. These pages scrutinize Trump's brand of politics, selling fascism under the guise of patriotism, while then dispelling the detailed policymaking of the Biden administration tackling the urgent crises of childcare and climate change.

There is much that is broken here in America, from the power of money in our legislature, to The Electoral College's destructive existence, to the die-hard partisanship in our policy-making arena that strangles progress and is killing America (and Americans, literally). We must hold to account the ethical fabric of the Supreme Court (specifically a few of our Justices) and Supreme Court rulings that evoke both fury and heartbreak. What moved me the most were the cases of the unwavering courage of everyday citizens to take on the labyrinth of our Supreme Court to fight for what is right and just. In another way, I was also very disheartened. In trying to ascertain what in the hell has been transpiring in the esteemed halls of our Supreme Court lately, it is undeniable that there is a shroud of darkness hanging over the integrity of our highest court and a few of its justices. What is also now very clear is that amidst the triumphs of everyday people in our courts, there also lies the haunting notion that justice, the pillar of a democratic society, seems to be much more attainable for those wielding power, money, and influence, and it goes all the way up to our highest court.

In composing this book, I sought to bridge the chasm between comprehension and confusion—the relentless pursuit of understanding the intricate 'whys' that underpin the baffling actions of Americans, our politicians, our judges and why people vote the way they do. I researched and studied political science out of a burning need to understand our nation and its people; a nation shaped by moments both laudable and lamentable, ideologies both inspiring and utterly confounding.

Embedded within our nation is a disheartening reality; the pervasive menace of ignorance and misinformation that permeates the very fabric of American society. The devastating perils and destructive power of rampant disinformation campaigns in the erosion of truth and the manipulation of beliefs is currently the most dangerous threat to our democracy. I embarked on my years-long study of political science because I find this so very confounding and alarming. So, I extend an invitation to all of you readers to traverse a journey of enlightenment, empathy, and introspection. How did we get here as a nation? America, why?

Diversity and empathy are not merely sources of strength but fundamental pillars upon which our societies should be built; from economic systems that prioritize a social safety net to ensure every citizen can pursue their dreams without fear of destitution or discrimination, to policies that promote environmental protections, equal rights, and representation for all marginalized communities. I embarked on my research for this book because I needed to make sense of some of the reasons we have landed where we are today. America, why? is an endeavor born from the desperate need to understand the ignorance and ugliness that seems to be increasing daily in our nation. I deeply value and live by the ideals of creating a safe, gun-controlled, highly educated, nurturing environment for every single child and person, no matter their race, religion, gender, neighborhood, level of wealth, or political affiliation. This book hopes to educate, inspire (and shock) you, but mostly drive you to go march in the streets calling for the abolishment of The Electoral College, for stringent environmental protections, to get money out of politics and out of our courts, and for sound gun control once and for all—I mean really, assault rifles? How many children must die?

As I bid adieu, I extend an impassioned plea to you, dear reader, to carry forth the torch of inquiry, empathy, and activism. Let our collective voices echo through the halls of power, demanding a more just, accountable, equitable, and enlightened America. Let us educate, inspire, and challenge the status quo. And, above all, let us strive together to forge a future where justice, truth, and compassion reign supreme. When the power of human ingenuity and adaptability aligns with compassion and determination; nothing is impossible. So, here's to a much safer, kinder, more intelligent, more compassionate, and more mentally sound America than the one we have been experiencing. So, stop watching Fox News (if you do), and think about what you hear and read, and ask if it sounds right and just. Then go make a friend who doesn't look like you or live like you, and for God's sake, put down your guns.

Zombies are NOT coming.

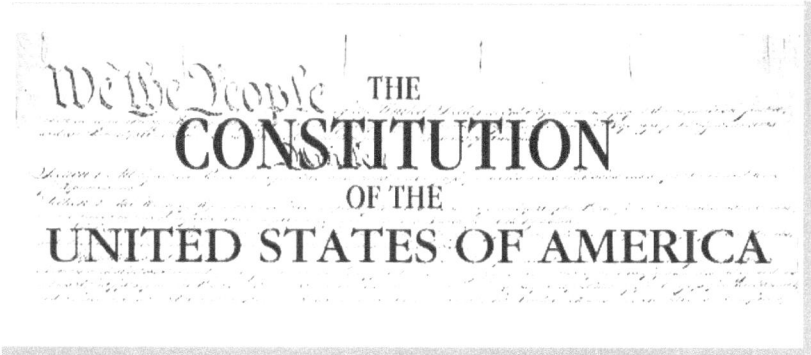

NOTE: This version of the US Constitution contains the original <u>syntax</u> and spelling.

Preamble: We the People of the United States, in Order to form a more perfect Union, establish Justice, insure domestic <u>tranquility</u>, provide for the common defence, promote the general Welfare, and secure the Blessings of Liberty to ourselves and our <u>posterity</u>, do ordain and establish this Constitution for the United States of America.

Article. I.

Section 1.

All legislative Powers herein granted shall be vested in a Congress of the United States, which shall consist of a Senate and House of Representatives.

Section. 2.

Clause 1: The House of Representatives shall be composed of Members chosen every second Year by the People of the several States, and the

Electors in each State shall have the Qualifications requisite for Electors of the most numerous Branch of the State Legislature.

Clause 2: No Person shall be a Representative who shall not have attained to the Age of twenty-five Years, and been seven Years a Citizen of the United States, and who shall not, when elected, be an Inhabitant of that State in which he shall be chosen.

Clause 3: Representatives and direct Taxes shall be apportioned among the several States which may be included within this Union, according to their respective Numbers, which shall be determined by adding to the whole Number of free Persons, including those bound to Service for a Term of Years, and excluding Indians not taxed, three fifths of all other Persons. *(See Note 2)* The actual <u>enumeration</u> shall be made within three Years after the first Meeting of the Congress of the United States, and within every subsequent Term of ten Years, in such Manner as they shall by Law direct. The Number of Representatives shall not exceed one for every thirty Thousand, but each State shall have at Least one Representative; and until such enumeration shall be made, the State of New Hampshire shall be entitled to chuse three, Massachusetts eight, Rhode-Island and Providence Plantations one, Connecticut five, New-York six, New Jersey four, Pennsylvania eight, Delaware one, Maryland six, Virginia ten, North Carolina five, South Carolina five, and Georgia three.

Clause 4: When vacancies happen in the Representation from any State, the Executive Authority thereof shall issue Writs of Election to fill such Vacancies.

Clause 5: The House of Representatives shall chuse their Speaker and other Officers; and shall have the sole Power of <u>impeachment.</u>

Section. 3.

Clause 1: The Senate of the United States shall be composed of two Senators from each State, chosen by the Legislature thereof, *(See Note 3)* for six Years; and each Senator shall have one Vote.

Clause 2: Immediately after they shall be assembled in Consequence of the first Election, they shall be divided as equally as may be into three Classes. The Seats of the Senators of the first Class shall be vacated at the Expiration of the second Year, of the second Class at the Expiration of the fourth Year, and of the third Class at the Expiration of the sixth Year, so that one third may be chosen every second Year; and if Vacancies happen by Resignation, or otherwise, during the Recess of the Legislature of any State, the Executive thereof may make temporary Appointments until the next Meeting of the Legislature, which shall then fill such Vacancies. *(See Note 4)*

Clause 3: No Person shall be a Senator who shall not have attained to the Age of thirty Years and been nine Years a Citizen of the United States, and who shall not, when elected, be an Inhabitant of that State for which he shall be chosen.

Clause 4: The Vice President of the United States shall be President of the Senate, but shall have no Vote, unless they be equally divided.

Clause 5: The Senate shall chuse their other Officers, and also a President pro tempore, in the Absence of the Vice President, or when he shall exercise the Office of President of the United States.

Clause 6: The Senate shall have the sole Power to try all Impeachments. When sitting for that Purpose, they shall be on Oath or affirmation. When the President of the United States is tried, the Chief Justice shall preside: And no Person shall be convicted without the Concurrence of two thirds of the Members present.

Clause 7: Judgment in Cases of Impeachment shall not extend further than to removal from Office, and disqualification to hold and enjoy any Office of honor, Trust or Profit under the United States: but the Party convicted shall nevertheless be liable and subject to Indictment, Trial, Judgment and Punishment, according to Law.

Section. 4.

Clause 1: The Times, Places and Manner of holding Elections for Senators and Representatives, shall be prescribed in each State by the Legislature thereof; but the Congress may at any time by Law make or alter such Regulations, except as to the Places of chusing Senators.

Clause 2: The Congress shall assemble at least once in every Year, and such Meeting shall be on the first Monday in December, *(See Note 5)* unless they shall by Law appoint a different Day.

Section. 5.

Clause 1: Each House shall be the Judge of the Elections, Returns and Qualifications of its own Members, and a Majority of each shall constitute a quorum to do Business; but a smaller Number may adjourn from day to day, and may be authorized to compel the Attendance of absent Members, in such Manner, and under such Penalties as each House may provide.

Clause 2: Each House may determine the Rules of its Proceedings, punish its Members for disorderly Behaviour, and, with the Concurrence of two thirds, expel a Member.

Clause 3: Each House shall keep a Journal of its Proceedings, and from time to time publish the same, excepting such Parts as may in their Judgment require Secrecy; and the Yeas and Nays of the Members of either House on any question shall, at the Desire of one fifth of those Present, be entered on the Journal.

Clause 4: Neither House, during the Session of Congress, shall, without the Consent of the other, adjourn for more than three days, nor to any other Place than that in which the two Houses shall be sitting.

Section. 6.

Clause 1: The Senators and Representatives shall receive a Compensation for their Services, to be ascertained by Law, and paid out of the Treasury of the United States. *(See Note 6)* They shall in all Cases, except treason, felony and Breach of the Peace, beprivileged from Arrest during their Attendance at the Session of their respective Houses, and in going to and returning from the same; and for any Speech or Debate in either House, they shall not be questioned in any other Place.

Clause 2: No Senator or Representative shall, during the Time for which he was elected, be appointed to any civil Office under the Authority of the United States, which shall have been created, or the Emoluments whereof shall have been encreased during such time; and no Person holding any Office under the United States, shall be a Member of either House during his Continuance in Office.

Section. 7.

Clause 1: All Bills for raising Revenue shall originate in the House of Representatives; but the Senate may propose or concur with Amendments as on other Bills.

Clause 2: Every Bill which shall have passed the House of Representatives and the Senate, shall, before it become a Law, be presented to the President of the United States; If he approve he shall sign it, but if not he shall return it, with his Objections to that House in which it shall have originated, who shall enter the Objections at large on their Journal, and proceed to reconsider it. If after such Reconsideration two thirds of that House shall agree to pass the Bill, it shall be sent, together with the Objections, to the other House, by which it shall likewise be reconsidered, and if approved by two thirds of that House, it shall become a Law. But in all such Cases the Votes of both Houses shall be determined by yeas and Nays, and the Names of the Persons voting for and against the Bill shall be entered on the Journal of each House respectively. If any Bill shall not be returned by the President within ten Days (Sundays excepted) after it shall have been presented to him, the Same shall be a Law, in like Manner as if he had signed it, unless the Congress by their Adjournment prevent its Return, in which Case it shall not be a Law.

Clause 3: Every Order, Resolution, or Vote to which the Concurrence of the Senate and House of Representatives may be necessary (except on a question of adjournment) shall be presented to the President of the United States; and before the Same shall take Effect, shall be approved by him, or being disapproved by him, shall be repassed by two thirds of the Senate and House of Representatives, according to the Rules and Limitations prescribed in the Case of a Bill.

Section. 8.

Clause 1: The Congress shall have Power To lay and collect Taxes, Duties, imposts and excises, to pay the Debts and provide for the common Defence and general Welfare of the United States; but all Duties, Imposts and Excises shall be uniform throughout the United States;

Clause 2: To borrow Money on the credit of the United States;

Clause 3: To regulate Commerce with foreign Nations, and among the several States, and with the Indian Tribes;

Clause 4: To establish an uniform Rule of Naturalization, and uniform Laws on the subject of Bankruptcies throughout the United States;

Clause 5: To coin Money, regulate the Value thereof, and of foreign Coin, and fix the Standard of Weights and Measures;

Clause 6: To provide for the Punishment of counterfeiting the Securities and current Coin of the United States;

Clause 7: To establish Post Offices and post Roads;

Clause 8: To promote the Progress of Science and useful Arts, by securing for limited Times to Authors and Inventors the exclusive Right to their respective Writings and Discoveries;

Clause 9: To constitute tribunals inferior to the supreme Court;

Clause 10: To define and punish Piracies and Felonies committed on the high Seas, and Offences against the Law of Nations;

Clause 11: To declare War, grant Letters of Marque and Reprisal, and make Rules concerning Captures on Land and Water;

Clause 12: To raise and support Armies, but no Appropriation of Money to that Use shall be for a longer Term than two Years;

Clause 13: To provide and maintain a Navy;

Clause 14: To make Rules for the Government and Regulation of the land and naval Forces;

Clause 15: To provide for calling forth the Militia to execute the Laws of the Union, suppress Insurrections and repel Invasions;

Clause 16: To provide for organizing, arming, and disciplining, the Militia, and for governing such Part of them as may be employed in the Service of the United States, reserving to the States respectively, the Appointment of the Officers, and the Authority of training the Militia according to the discipline prescribed by Congress;

Clause 17: To exercise exclusive Legislation in all Cases whatsoever, over such District (not exceeding ten Miles square) as may, byCession of particular States, and the Acceptance of Congress, become the Seat of the Government of the United States, and to exercise like Authority over all Places purchased by the Consent of the Legislature of the State in which the Same shall be, for the Erection of Forts, Magazines, Arsenals, dock-Yards, and other needful Buildings;--And

Clause 18: To make all Laws which shall be necessary and proper for carrying into Execution the foregoing Powers, and all other Powers vested by this Constitution in the Government of the United States, or in any Department or Officer thereof.

Section. 9.

Clause 1: The Migration or Importation of such Persons as any of the States now existing shall think proper to admit, shall not be prohibited by the Congress prior to the Year one thousand eight hundred and eight, but a Tax or duty may be imposed on such Importation, not exceeding ten dollars for each Person.

Clause 2: The Privilege of the Writ of Habeas Corpus shall not be suspended, unless when in Cases of Rebellion or Invasion the public Safety may require it.

Clause 3: No Bill of attainder or ex post facto Law shall be passed.

Clause 4: No Capitation, or other direct, Tax shall be laid, unless in Proportion to the Census or Enumeration herein before directed to be taken. *(See Note 7)*

Clause 5: No Tax or Duty shall be laid on Articles exported from any State.

Clause 6: No Preference shall be given by any Regulation of Commerce or Revenue to the Ports of one State over those of another: nor shall Vessels bound to, or from, one State, be obliged to enter, clear, or pay Duties in another.

Clause 7: No Money shall be drawn from the Treasury, but in Consequence of Appropriations made by Law; and a regular Statement and Account of the Receipts and Expenditures of all public Money shall be published from time to time.

Clause 8: No Title of Nobility shall be granted by the United States: And no Person holding any Office of Profit or Trust under them, shall, without the Consent of the Congress, accept of any present, Emolument, Office, or Title, of any kind whatever, from any King, Prince, or foreign State.

Section. 10.

Clause 1: No State shall enter into any Treaty, Alliance, or Confederation; grant Letters of Marque and Reprisal; coin Money; emit Bills of Credit; make any Thing but gold and silver Coin a Tender in Payment of Debts; pass any Bill of Attainder, ex post facto Law, or Law impairing the Obligation of Contracts, or grant any Title of Nobility.

Clause 2: No State shall, without the Consent of the Congress, lay any Imposts or Duties on Imports or Exports, except what may be absolutely necessary for executing it's inspection Laws: and the net Produce of all Duties and Imposts, laid by any State on Imports or Exports, shall be for the Use of the Treasury of the United States; and all such Laws shall be subject to the Revision and Control of the Congress.

Clause 3: No State shall, without the Consent of Congress, lay any Duty of Tonnage, keep Troops, or Ships of War in time of Peace, enter into any Agreement or compact with another State, or with a foreign Power, or engage in War, unless actually invaded, or in such imminent Danger as will not admit of delay.

Article. II.

Section. 1.

Clause 1: The executive Power shall be vested in a President of the United States of America. He shall hold his Office during the Term of four Years, and, together with the Vice President, chosen for the same Term, be elected, as follows

Clause 2: Each State shall appoint, in such Manner as the Legislature thereof may direct, a Number of Electors, equal to the whole Number of Senators and Representatives to which the State may be entitled in the Congress: but no Senator or Representative, or Person holding an Office of Trust or Profit under the United States, shall be appointed an Elector.

Clause 3: The Electors shall meet in their respective States, and vote by Ballot for two Persons, of whom one at least shall not be an Inhabitant of the same State with themselves. And they shall make a List of all the Persons voted for, and of the Number of Votes for each; which List they shall sign and certify, and transmit sealed to the Seat of the Government of the United States, directed to the President of the Senate. The President of the Senate shall, in the Presence of the Senate and House of Representatives, open all the Certificates, and the Votes shall then be counted. The Person having the greatest Number of Votes shall be the President, if such Number be a Majority of the whole Number of Electors appointed; and if there be more than one who have such Majority, and have an equal Number of Votes, then the House of Representatives shall immediately chuse by Ballot one of them for President; and if no Person have a Majority, then from the five highest on the List the said House shall in like Manner chuse the President. But in chusing the President, the Votes shall be taken by States, the Representation from each State having one Vote; A quorum for this Purpose shall consist of a Member or Members from two thirds of the States, and a Majority of all the States shall be necessary to a Choice. In every Case, after the Choice of the President, the Person having the greatest Number of Votes of the Electors shall be the Vice President. But if there should remain two or more who have equal Votes, the Senate shall chuse from them by Ballot the Vice President. *(See Note 8)*

Clause 4: The Congress may determine the Time of chusing the Electors, and the Day on which they shall give their Votes; which Day shall be the same throughout the United States.

Clause 5: No Person except a natural born Citizen, or a Citizen of the United States, at the time of the Adoption of this Constitution, shall be eligible to the Office of President; neither shall any Person be eligible to that Office who shall not have attained to the Age of thirty-five Years, and been fourteen Years a Resident within the United States.

Clause 6: In Case of the Removal of the President from Office, or of his Death, Resignation, or Inability to discharge the Powers and Duties of the said Office, *(See Note 9)* the Same shall devolve on the VicePresident, and the Congress may by Law provide for the Case of Removal, Death, Resignation or Inability, both of the President and Vice President, declaring what Officer shall then act as President, and such Officer shall act accordingly, until the Disability be removed, or a President shall be elected.

Clause 7: The President shall, at stated Times, receive for his Services, a Compensation, which shall neither be encreased nor diminished during the Period for which he shall have been elected, and he shall not receive within that Period any other emolument from the United States, or any of them.

Clause 8: Before he enter on the Execution of his Office, he shall take the following Oath or Affirmation:--"I do solemnly swear (or affirm) that I will faithfully execute the Office of President of the United States, and will to the best of my Ability, preserve, protect and defend the Constitution of the United States."

Section. 2.

Clause 1: The President shall be Commander in Chief of the Army and Navy of the United States, and of the Militia of the several States, when called into the actual Service of the United States; he may require the Opinion, in writing, of the principal Officer in each of the executive Departments, upon any Subject relating to the Duties of their respective Offices, and he shall have Power to grant Reprieves and Pardons for Offences against the United States, except in Cases of Impeachment.

Clause 2: He shall have Power, by and with the Advice and Consent of the Senate, to make Treaties, provided two thirds of the Senators present concur; and he shall nominate, and by and with the Advice and Consent of the Senate, shall appoint Ambassadors, other public Ministers and Consuls, Judges of the supreme Court, and all other Officers of the United States, whose Appointments are not herein otherwise provided for, and which shall be established by Law: but the Congress may by Law vest the Appointment of such inferior Officers, as they think proper, in the President alone, in the Courts of Law, or in the Heads of Departments.

Clause 3: The President shall have Power to fill up all Vacancies that may happen during the Recess of the Senate, by granting Commissions which shall expire at the End of their next Session.

Section. 3.

He shall from time to time give to the Congress Information of the State of the Union, and recommend to their Consideration such Measures as he shall judge necessary and expedient; he may, on extraordinary Occasions, <u>convene</u> both Houses, or either of them, and in Case of Disagreement between them, with Respect to the Time of Adjournment, he may adjourn them to such Time as he shall think proper; he shall receive Ambassadors and other public Ministers; he shall take Care that the Laws be faithfully executed, and shall Commission all the Officers of the United States.

Section. 4.

The President, Vice President and all civil Officers of the United States, shall be removed from Office on Impeachment for, and Conviction of, Treason, Bribery, or other high Crimes and Misdemeanors.

Article. III.

Section. 1.

The judicial Power of the United States, shall be vested in one supreme Court, and in such inferior Courts as the Congress may from time to time ordain and establish. The Judges, both of the supreme and inferior Courts, shall hold their Offices during good Behaviour, and shall, at stated Times, receive for their Services, a Compensation, which shall not be diminished during their Continuance in Office.

Section. 2.

Clause 1: The judicial Power shall extend to all Cases, in Law and Equity, arising under this Constitution, the Laws of the United States, and Treaties made, or which shall be made, under their Authority;--to all Cases affecting Ambassadors, other public Ministers and Consuls;--to all Cases of admiralty and maritime Jurisdiction;--to Controversies to which the United States shall be a Party;--to Controversies between two or more States;--between a State and Citizens of another State; *(See Note 10)*--between Citizens of different States,—between Citizens of the same State claiming Lands under Grants of different States, and between a State, or the Citizens thereof, and foreign States, Citizens or Subjects.

Clause 2: In all Cases affecting Ambassadors, other public Ministers and Consuls, and those in which a State shall be Party, the supreme Court shall have original Jurisdiction. In all the other Cases before mentioned, the supreme Court shall have <u>appellate</u> Jurisdiction, both as to Law and Fact, with such Exceptions, and under such Regulations as the Congress shall make.

Clause 3: The Trial of all Crimes, except in Cases of Impeachment, shall be by Jury; and such Trial shall be held in the State where the said Crimes shall have been committed; but when not committed within any State, the Trial shall be at such Place or Places as the Congress may by Law have directed.

Section. 3.

Clause 1: Treason against the United States, shall consist only in levying War against them, or in adhering to their Enemies, giving them Aid and Comfort. No Person shall be convicted of Treason unless on the Testimony of two Witnesses to the same overt Act, or on Confession in open Court.

Clause 2: The Congress shall have Power to declare the Punishment of Treason, but no Attainder of Treason shall work Corruption of Blood, or Forfeiture except during the Life of the Person attainted.

Article. IV.

Section. 1.

Full Faith and Credit shall be given in each State to the public Acts, Records, and judicial Proceedings of every other State. And the Congress may by general Laws prescribe the Manner in which such Acts, Records and Proceedings shall be proved, and the Effect thereof.

Section. 2.

Clause 1: The Citizens of each State shall be entitled to all Privileges and Immunities of Citizens in the several States.

Clause 2: A Person charged in any State with Treason, Felony, or other Crime, who shall flee from Justice, and be found in another State, shall on Demand of the executive Authority of the State from which he fled, be delivered up, to be removed to the State having Jurisdiction of the Crime.

Clause 3: No Person held to Service or Labour in one State, under the Laws thereof, escaping into another, shall, in Consequence of any Law or Regulation therein, be discharged from such Service or Labour, but shall be delivered up on Claim of the Party to whom such Service or Labour may be due. *(See Note 11)*

Section. 3.

Clause 1: New States may be admitted by the Congress into this Union; but no new State shall be formed or erected within the Jurisdiction of any other State; nor any State be formed by the Junction of two or more States, or Parts of States, without the Consent of the Legislatures of the States concerned as well as of the Congress.

Clause 2: The Congress shall have Power to dispose of and make all needful Rules and Regulations respecting the Territory or other Property belonging to the United States; and nothing in this Constitution shall be so construed as to Prejudice any Claims of the United States, or of any particular State.

Section. 4.

The United States shall guarantee to every State in this Union a Republican Form of Government, and shall protect each of them against Invasion; and on Application of the Legislature, or of the Executive (when the Legislature cannot be convened) against domestic Violence.

Article. V.

The Congress, whenever two thirds of both Houses shall deem it necessary, shall propose amendments to this Constitution, or, on the Application of the Legislatures of two thirds of the several States, shall call a Convention for proposing Amendments, which, in either Case, shall be valid to all Intents and Purposes, as Part of this Constitution, when ratified by the Legislatures of three fourths of the several States, or by Conventions in three fourths thereof, as the one or the other Mode of Ratification may be proposed by the Congress; Provided that no Amendment which may be made prior to the Year One thousand eight hundred and eight shall in any Manner affect the first and fourth Clauses in the Ninth Section of the first Article; and that no State, without its Consent, shall be deprived of its equal <u>suffrage</u> in the Senate.

Article. VI.

Clause 1: All Debts contracted and Engagements entered into, before the Adoption of this Constitution, shall be as valid against the United States under this Constitution, as under the Confederation.

Clause 2: This Constitution, and the Laws of the United States which shall be made in Pursuance thereof; and all Treaties made, or which shall be made, under the Authority of the United States, shall be the supreme Law of the Land; and the Judges in every State shall be bound thereby, any Thing in the Constitution or Laws of any State to the Contrary notwithstanding.

Clause 3: The Senators and Representatives before mentioned, and the Members of the several State Legislatures, and all executive and judicial Officers, both of the United States and of the several States, shall be bound by Oath or Affirmation, to support this Constitution; but no religious Test shall ever be required as a Qualification to any Office or public Trust under the United States.

Article. VII.

The Ratification of the Conventions of nine States, shall be sufficient for the Establishment of this Constitution between the States so ratifying the Same. done in Convention by the Unanimous Consent of the States present the Seventeenth Day of September in the Year of our Lord one thousand seven hundred and Eighty seven and of the Independence of the United States of America the Twelfth In witness whereof We have hereunto subscribed our Names,

GO WASHINGTON--President and deputy from Virginia

[Signed also by the deputies of twelve States.]

NOTES

Note 1: This text of the Constitution follows the copy signed by Gen. Washington and the deputies from 12 States. The small superior figures preceding the paragraphs designate Clauses, and were not in the original and have no reference to footnotes.

The Constitution was adopted by a convention of the States on September 17, 1787, and was subsequently ratified by the several States, on the following dates: Delaware, December 7, 1787; Pennsylvania, December 12, 1787; New Jersey, December 18, 1787; Georgia, January 2, 1788; Connecticut, January 9, 1788; Massachusetts, February 6, 1788; Maryland, April 28, 1788; South Carolina, May 23, 1788; New Hampshire, June 21, 1788.

Ratification was completed on June 21, 1788.

The Constitution was subsequently ratified by Virginia, June 25, 1788; New York, July 26, 1788; North Carolina, November 21, 1789; Rhode Island, May 29, 1790; and Vermont, January 10, 1791.

In May 1785, a committee of Congress made a report recommending an alteration in the Articles of Confederation, but no action was taken on it, and it was left to the State Legislatures to proceed in the matter. In January 1786, the Legislature of Virginia passed a resolution providing for the appointment of five commissioners, who, or any three of them, should meet such commissioners as might be appointed in the other States of the Union, at a time and place to be agreed upon, to take into consideration the trade of the United States; to consider how far a uniform system in their commercial regulations may be necessary to their common interest and their permanent harmony; and to report to the several States such an act, relative to this great object, as, when ratified by them, will enable the United States in Congress effectually to provide for the same. The Virginia commissioners, after some correspondence, fixed the first Monday in September as the time, and the city of Annapolis as the place for the meeting, but only four other States were represented, viz: Delaware, New York, New Jersey, and Pennsylvania; the commissioners appointed by Massachusetts, New Hampshire, North Carolina, and Rhode Island failed to attend. Under the circumstances of so partial a representation, the commissioners present agreed upon a report, (drawn by Mr. Hamilton, of New York,) expressing their unanimous conviction that it might essentially tend to advance the interests of the Union if the States by which they were respectively delegated would concur, and use their endeavors to procure the concurrence of the other States, in the appointment of commissioners to meet at Philadelphia on the Second Monday of May following, to take into consideration the situation of the United States; to devise such further provisions as should appear to them necessary to render the Constitution of the Federal Government adequate to the exigencies of the Union; and to report such an act for that purpose to the United States in Congress assembled as, when agreed to by them and afterwards confirmed by the Legislatures of every State, would effectually provide for the same.

Congress, on the 21st of February, 1787, adopted a resolution in favor of a convention, and the Legislatures of those States which had not already done so (with the exception of Rhode Island) promptly appointed delegates. On the 25th of May, seven States having convened, George Washington, of Virginia, was unanimously elected President, and the consideration of the proposed constitution was commenced. On the 17th of September, 1787, the Constitution as engrossed and agreed upon was signed by all the members present, except Mr. Gerry of Massachusetts, and Messrs. Mason and Randolph, of Virginia. The president of the convention transmitted it to Congress, with a resolution stating how the proposed Federal Government should be put in operation, and an explanatory letter. Congress, on the 28th of September, 1787, directed the Constitution so framed, with the resolutions and letter concerning the same, to "be transmitted to the several Legislatures in order to be submitted to a convention of delegates chosen in each State by the people thereof, in conformity to the resolves of the convention."

On the 4th of March, 1789, the day which had been fixed for commencing the operations of Government under the new Constitution, it had been ratified by the conventions chosen in each State to consider it, as follows: Delaware, December 7, 1787; Pennsylvania, December 12, 1787; New Jersey, December 18, 1787; Georgia, January 2, 1788; Connecticut, January 9, 1788; Massachusetts, February 6, 1788; Maryland, April 28, 1788; South Carolina, May 23, 1788; New Hampshire, June 21, 1788; Virginia, June 25, 1788; and New York, July 26, 1788.

The President informed Congress, on the 28th of January, 1790, that North Carolina had ratified the Constitution November 21, 1789; and he informed Congress on the 1st of June, 1790, that Rhode Island had ratified the Constitution May 29, 1790. Vermont, in convention, ratified the Constitution January 10, 1791, and was, by an act of Congress approved February 18, 1791, "received and admitted into this Union as a new and entire member of the United States."

Note 2: The part of this Clause relating to the mode of apportionment of representatives among the several States has been affected by Section 2 of amendment XIV, and as to taxes on incomes without apportionment by amendment XVI.

Note 3: This Clause has been affected by Clause 1 of amendment XVII.

Note 4: This Clause has been affected by Clause 2 of amendment XVIII.

Note 5: This Clause has been affected by amendment XX.

Note 6: This Clause has been affected by amendment XXVII.

Note 7: This Clause has been affected by amendment XVI.

Note 8: This Clause has been superseded by amendment XII.

Note 9: This Clause has been affected by amendment XXV.

Note 10: This Clause has been affected by amendment XI.

Note 11: This Clause has been affected by amendment XIII.

Note 12: The first ten amendments to the Constitution of the United States (and two others, one of which failed of ratification and the other which later became the 27th amendment) were proposed to the legislatures of the several States by the First Congress on September 25, 1789. The first ten amendments were ratified by the following States, and the notifications of ratification by the Governors thereof were successively communicated by the President to Congress: New Jersey, November 20, 1789; Maryland, December 19, 1789; North Carolina, December 22, 1789; South Carolina, January 19, 1790; New Hampshire, January 25, 1790; Delaware, January 28, 1790; New York, February 24, 1790; Pennsylvania, March 10, 1790; Rhode Island, June 7, 1790; Vermont, November 3, 1791; and Virginia, December 15, 1791.

Ratification was completed on December 15, 1791.

The amendments were subsequently ratified by the legislatures of Massachusetts, March 2, 1939; Georgia, March 18, 1939; and Connecticut, April 19, 1939.

Note 13: Only the 13th, 14th, 15th, and 16th articles of amendment had numbers assigned to them at the time of ratification.

Note 14: This sentence has been superseded by section 3 of amendment XX.

Note 15: See amendment XIX and section 1 of amendment XXVI.

Note 16: Repealed by section 1 of amendment XXI.

Interesting Constitutional Facts

- The U.S. Constitution has 4,400 words. It is the oldest and the shortest written constitution of any government in the world.
- Of the typographical errors in the Constitution, the misspelling of the word "Pensylvania" above the signers' names is probably the most glaring.
- Thomas Jefferson did not sign the Constitution. He was in France during the convention, where he served as the U.S. minister.
- Jacob Shallus, a Pennsylvania General Assembly clerk, "penned" the Constitution for a fee of $30 ($261.45 today).
- Governor Morris was responsible for the wording of the Constitution.
- It was stored in various cities until 1952, when it was placed in the National Archives Building in Washington, D.C. During the daytime, pages one and four of the document, are displayed in a bullet-proof case. The case contains helium and water vapor to preserve the paper's quality. At night, the pages are lowered into a vault, behind five-ton doors that are designed to withstand a nuclear explosion.
- The entire Constitution is displayed only one day a year, September 17, the anniversary of the day the framers signed the document.
- Thirty-nine men signed the Constitution. James Madison, "the father of the Constitution," was the first to arrive in Philadelphia for the Constitutional Convention. He arrived in February,

three months before the convention began, bearing the blue-print for the new Constitution.

- At least seven constitutional amendments were passed in order to reverse a Supreme Court decision. Some of the notable ones: The Thirteenth Amendment (1865), barring slavery, and the Fifteenth Amendment (1868), protecting the citizenship of African Americans, effectively overturned the Dred Scott v. Sandford decision of 1857. The Sixteenth Amendment (1913) gave Congress the power to levy an income tax, thereby overturning Pollock v. Farmers' Loan and Trust Co. (1895). And the Twenty-Sixth Amendment (1971) overturned Oregon v. Mitchell (1970) which, among other things, held that Congress could not regulate the voting age in state elections. The amendment set the voting age at 18 years.
- When it came time for the states to ratify the Constitution, the lack of any bill of rights was the primary sticking point.
- The Constitution does not set forth requirements for the right to vote. As a result, at the outset of the Union, only male property-owners could vote. African Americans were not considered citizens, and women were excluded from the electoral process.
- The Great Compromise saved the Constitutional Convention, and, probably, the Union. Authored by Connecticut delegate Roger Sherman, it called for proportional representation in the House, and one representative per state in the Senate (this was later changed to two.) The compromise passed 5-to-4, with one state, Massachusetts, "divided."
- Patrick Henry was elected as a delegate to the Constitutional Convention, but declined, because he "smelt a rat."
- Because of his poor health, Benjamin Franklin needed help to sign the Constitution. As he did so, tears streamed down his face.
- The oldest person to sign the Constitution was Benjamin Franklin (81). The youngest was Jonathan Dayton of New Jersey (26).
- When the Constitution was signed, the United States population was 4 million. It is now more than 250 million.
- Philadelphia was the nation's largest city, with 40,000 inhabitants.

- The first state to ratify the Constitution was Delaware, in December, 1787, three months after the framers had adjourned the convention in Philadelphia.
- When New Hampshire ratified on June 21, 1788, it was the ninth state to do so. By the ratification requirements set forth in Article VII, the Constitution was now officially established.
- Until the Seventeenth Amendment was ratified in 1913, Senators were chosen by a state's legislators. As a result, the Senate brimmed with men who obtained their positions through political patronage. Finally, under threat of a Constitutional Convention on the matter, Congress proposed this amendment.
- The 14th and 15th Amendments were passed in 1868 and 1870, respectively. Initially meant to preserve personal freedoms of African Americans, they now stand, in large part, for the idea that the Constitution implies, but does not enumerate, certain fundamental rights for all citizens.
- To amend the Constitution, a proposal must gain the support of two-thirds of the House and Senate, and three-fourths of the states. As a result, of the thousands of proposed amendments, only 27 have passed.
- Amendments must be proposed either by a two-thirds vote in Congress, or by a Constitutional Convention. Such a convention can only be held if two-thirds of the states' legislatures support it.

Bibliography

A Historic Commitment to Protecting the Environment and Addressing the Impacts of Climate Change. The White House: President Joseph Biden.

A. The Roots of Access Rights Archives. The Reporters Committee for Freedom of the Press, www.rcfp.org/open-court-sections/a-the-roots-of-access-rights/.

ACLU (2019). Family Separation by the Numbers, https://www.aclu.org/issues/immigrants-rights-detention/family-spearation

Albrecht, & U.S. Senate Committee 2020.

Albrecht, Leslie. "Joe Biden has a $335 billion child-care plan — and Republican lawmakers could be on board with parts of it", Market Watch, 7 December 2020.

Allison, G. T. (1971). Essence of decision. Longman.

American Bar Association (2019) Link: https://www.americanbar.org/advocacy/governmental_legislative_work/priorities_policy/immigration/familyseparation.

American Bar. What Is an Executive Order? 25 Jan. 2021, https://www.americanbar.org/groups/public_education/publications/teaching-legal-docs/what-is-an-executive-order-/.

Amira, Karyn, et al. "Adversaries or Allies? Donald Trump's republican Support in Congress" Perspectives on Politics, vol. 17, no 3, 2019, pp. 756-771.

Ascher, William, and Steelman, Toddi."Valuation in the Environmental Pol cy Process." POLICY SCIENCES, vol. 39, May 2006, p. 73–90, SPRINGER.

Bade, R. & Wagner, J. "Pelosi Tells Colleagues She Wants to see Trump in Prison, not Impeached." Washington Post, 6, June 2019.

Barber, Michael and Jeremy C. Pope. "Does Party Trump Ideology? Disentangling Party and Ideology in America." American Political Science Review, vol. 113, no. 1, 2019, pp. 38-54.

Biden Administration Rapidly Advances Climate Change Agenda. The National Law Review.

Biden's Week One: Mapping Ambitious Climate Action - Environmental & Energy Law Program." Harvard Law School, http://eelp.law.harvard.edu/bidens-week-one-mapping ambitious-climate-action/.

Bill of Rights Institute: "The Lessons of District of Columbia v. Heller", 2008.

Binder, Seth, and Stephen Polasky. "Valuing the Environment for Decisionmaking." ISSUES IN SCIENCE AND TECHNOLOGY, Summer 2012.

Bleiweis, Robin. "The Equal Rights Amendment. What you Need to Know", Center for American Progress, 29, July, 2020.

Border security and immigration policy. Department of Homeland Security. (2020, September 3). https://www.dhs.gov/border-immigration-and-trade-policy.

Bowman, Karlyn. "Democrats And Republicans Divided On Climate Change." Forbes, 2019/04/19.

California Law Review - Jstor.org. www.jstor.org/stable/3481080.

Carp et al., Evers v. Jackson Municipal Separate School District, 1964. Judicial Process in America.

Carp, Robert A., et al. Judicial Process in America., 11th Ed., CQ Press, an Imprint of SAGE Publications, Inc., 2020.

Carson, J. L., Engstrom, E. J., & Roberts, J. M. (2007). Candidate quality, the personal vote, and the incumbency advantage in congress. American Political Science Review, 101(2), 289-301. doi:10.1017/S0003055407070311

Chokshi, N. (2018, June 24). 75 Percent of Americans Say Immigration Is Good for Country, Poll Finds. New York Times, p. NA(L).

Colman, Zach; Pager, Tyler. "Biden to tap former Michigan Gov. Granholm to lead Energy Department", Politico, Dec 15 2020.

Comparative Agendas Project, URL: https://www.comparativeagendas.net/

Congressional Research Service. (2013, February 21). Border security: Understanding threats at U.S. Borders. EveryCRSReport.com. https://www.everycrsreport.com/reports/R42969.html.

Consumer Attorneys of CA, 1994; Lopez, 2016; NY Times(YouTube), 2013.

Davenport, Carol, Lisa Friedman. "The Battle Lines are Forming in Biden's Climate Push." New York Times, 2021.

Davidson, et al. 2018, Congress and Its Members, 16th Edition, Thousand Oaks, CQ Press.

Davie & Caristi, 2022; Nonnecke, 2022; Pitt News v. Pappert, 2004; Educational Media Co. at Virginia Tech v. Swecker, 2010).

Davie, William R., and Dom Caristi. Communication Law: Practical Applications in the Digital Age. Routledge, 2022.

Davies, Alex. "A Liberal Anti-Porn Feminism?" Social Theory & Practice, vol. 44, no. 1, Jan. 2018, pp. 21–48. EBS Cohost, https://doi org.ezaccess.libraries.psu.edu/10.5840/soctheorpract2017112027.

Davis, J.H., "Nancy Pelosi Elected Speaker as Democrats Take Control of the House." The New York Times, 3, January 2019.

DeLauro Media Press Release, 2020.

Dennis, Brady. "Trump Makes It Official: U.S. Will Withdraw from the Paris Climate Accord." Washington Post.

Detterman, Brook, Alan Sachs, Allyn Stern, Zachary Pilchen, and Jack Zietman. "Growing Climate Solutions Act Introduced with Broad Bipartisan Support." Beveridge & Diamond Law. 8 June 2020.

Detterman, Brook, et al. "Biden Administration Rapidly Advances in Climate Change Agenda." National Law Review: Vol. XI, Num. 51. 17 Feb. 2021.

Dickerson, C. (2018, Nov 21). The price tag of immigrant family separations: $80 million and rising. New York Times.

Din, S. (2019, August 27). Fresh Talk: The true cost of partisan politics is national security. courant.com. https://www.courant.com/opinion/op-ed/hc-op-sheroz-din-national-security-0828-20190828-mbocdgtb3zac-ban6zxa42kfspe-story.html.

DISTRICT of Columbia v. heller. (2008, June 26). Retrieved April 21, 2021, from https://www.law.cornell.edu/supct/html/07-290.ZS.html

Dworkin, Andrea. "Against the Male Flood: Censorship, Pornography, and Equality." Harvard Women's Law Journal, 8, 1985, pp. 1-30. Hein Online.

EDF Experts Weigh in: President Biden's Executive Actions on Climate. Climate 411, 27 Jan. 2021.

Editors, T. (2020). U.S. Security Policy in the Trump Era. World Politics Review. https://www.worldpoliticsreview.com/insights/27878/u-s-security-policy-in-the-trump-era-has-been-marked-by-change-and-continuity.

Educational Media Co. at Va. Tech v. Swecker, 602 F.3d 583 (4th Cir. 2010)

Edwards, George C. ""Closer" Or Context? Explaining Donald Trump's Relations with Congress." Presidential Studies Quarterly, vol. 48, no. 3, 2018, pp. 456-479.

Eilperin, Juliet, et al. "Biden to Place Environmental Justice at Center of Sweeping Climate Plan." Washington Post. www.washingtonpost.com.

Ellis, R. (2015). The Development of the American Presidency. New York: Routledge, https://doi- org.ezaccess.librar-ies.psu.edu/10.4324/9781315731766

Epstein, Lee, and Thomas G. Walker. Constitutional Law for a Changing America. 10th ed, Thousand Oaks, CA: CQ Press, an imprint of SAGE Publications, Inc., 2019.

Executive Office of the President. "Tackling the Climate Crisis at Home and Abroad." Federal Register, 27 Jan. 2021.

Executive Order on Ensuring the Future Is Made in All of America by All of America's Workers." The White House, 25 Jan. 2021.

Executive Order on Protecting Public Health and the Environment and Restoring Science to Tackle the Climate Crisis." The White House, 21 Jan. 2021.

Executive Order on Tackling the Climate Crisis at Home and Abroad. The White House, 27 Jan. 2021.

Facebook Privacy Policy. Facebook, Nov. 2009, www.facebook.com/about/privacy/previous.

Fandos, N. & Shear, M.D. 2018. "Trump Impeached for Abuse of Power and Obstruction of Congress", New York Times, December 18.

FAQs HIPAA and FERPA. HHS.gov, www.hhs.gov/hipaa/for-professionals/faq/ferpa-and-hipaa/index.html.

Festenstein, M., Kenny, M. (2005). Political ideologies. New York, NY: Oxford University Press.

Flynn, M. (2018). An 'invasion of illegal aliens': The oldest immigration fear-mongering metaphor in america. The Washington Post.

Foe." Associated Press. 11 Mar. 2021. Accessed 19 March 2021.

Follesdal, Andreas, and Simon Hix. "Why There Is a Democratic Deficit in the EU: A Response to Majone and Moravcsik." Journal of Common Market Studies, vol. 44, no. 3, Sept. 2006, pp. 533–562. EBSCOhost, doi:10.1111/j.1468-5965.2006.00650.x.

Foran, C. & Byrd, H. (2020, March 11). House passes Iran War Powers resolution opposed by Trump, CNN.

Freeden, M. (2003), Ideology, A Very Short Introduction, Oxford: Oxford University Press.

Friedman, Lisa, et al. "Biden, Emphasizing Job Creation, Signs Sweeping Climate Actions." The New York Times, 27 Jan. 2021, https://www.nytimes.com/2021/01/27/climate/biden-climate-executive-orders.html.

Friedman, Lisa. "Biden Introduces His Climate Team." The New York Times 22 Dec. 2020.

Frye, Reilly. "family Separation Under the Trump Administration: Applying an International Criminal Law Framework." Journal of Criminal Law & Criminology, vol. 110, no. 2, 2020, pp. 349-377.

Gallagher, Michael et al. 2011. Representative Government in Modern Europe. Berkshire: McGraw-Hill.

Gambino, L. "Nancy Pelosi: The Woman Who Stood up to Trump.", The Guardian, 23, December 2019.

Glueck, Katie & Friedman, Lisa. "Biden Announces $2 Trillion Climate Plan, New York Times, 1, February, 2021. URL: https://www.nytimes.com/2020/07/14/us/politics/biden-climate- plan.html.

Goldstein, A. (2019, Feb 19). 16 states sue over trump's wall plan. The WashingtonPost.

Golshan, T. & Nilsen, E. (2018, June 20). Congress's chaotic scramble to address Trump's family separation border policy, explained.

GovTrack Insider. (2018, June 18). The Help the Children Act Would Reverse Trumps Policy of Splitting Families Up at the Border.

Gruver, Mead, and Matthew Brown. "As Climate Fight Shifts to Oil, Biden Faces a Formidable Foe." Associated Press. 11 Mar. 2021.

Heinzerling, Lisa. Cost-Nothing Analysis: Environmental Economics in the Age of Trump.

Hon. John M. Walker, Jr., Senior Circuit Judge, United States Court of Appeals for the Second Circuit. "The Role of Precedent in the United States: How Do Precedents Lose Their Binding Effect?" Traditional Commentary No. 15, Stanford law school/ China Guiding Cases Project, 29 Feb. 2016.

Hughes, S., & Radnofsky, L. (2018, Jun 19). Trump sidesteps family separations in talks with GOP; president calls for broad immigration bill amid bipartisan uproar over administration's policy at the border. Wall Street Journal (Online).

Immigration policy directives: Border enforcement and family separation. (2018). Congressional Digest, 97(7), 9.

In the Ghettos. The Economist, Nov 30, 2019, 61-62, http://ezaccess.libraries.psu.edu/login?url=https://search-proquest-com.ezaccess.libraries.psu.edu/docview/2319662964?accountid=13158.

Jordan, M. (2018, June 7). Family Separation at Border May Be Subject to Constitutional Challenge.

Jordan, M. (2019). Family separation may have hit thousands more migrant children than reported. New York: New York Times Company.

Judge Rules. New York Times, p. NA(L). Retrieved from http://link.galegroup.com.ezaccess.libraries.psu.edu/apps/doc/A54 1612706/GIC?u=psucic&sid=GIC&xid=6edfd997

Kahn, Brian. "How Biden Can Ensure Every Federal Agency Is Fighting Climate Change." Ecosystems Marketplace, a Forest Trends Initiative, 8 Mar. 2021. URL: https://www.ecosystemmarketplace.com/articles/how-biden-can-ensure-every-federal-agency-is-fighting-climate-change/

Kahn, Brian. "How Biden Can Ensure Every Federal Agency Is Fighting Climate Change." Ecosystems Marketplace, a Forest Trends Initiative, 8 Mar. 2021.

Keith, Tamara. "With 28 Executive Orders signed, President Biden is off to a Record Start." NPR; Morning Edition. 3 Feb. 2021.

Ketz, Ashley. "Child Marriage Is Currently Legal in 46 States." NewsNation, NewsNation, 21 May 2021, www.newsnationnow.com/us-news/child-marriage-is-currently-legal-in-46-states/.

Kramer, Daniel C. Red Lion Broadcasting Co. v. Federal Communications Commission, mtsu.edu/first-amendment/article/117/red-lion-broadcasting-co-v-federal-communications-commission.

Kyzar, E. J., Nichols, C. D., Nichols, D. E., Gainetdinov, R. R., & Kalueff, A. V. (2017). Psychedelic drugs in biomedicine. Trends in Pharmacological Sciences, 38(11), 992-1005.

Ladewig, Jeffrey W. "Conditional Party Government and the Homogeneity of Constituent Interests." The Journal of Politics, vol. 67, no. 4, 2005, pp. 1006-1029.

Leinaweaver, J. (2017, March 21). Breaking families apart: the moral and economic costs. Hill, p. 20.

Lemieux, Pierre. "Joe Biden's Economic Agenda: An Early Appraisal." CATO INSTITUTE; Spring, 2021: Regulation.

Leonhardt, M. (2018, June 20). "Where to Donate to Help Migrant Children and Families at the Border".

Leonhardt, Megan. "Joe Biden wants to give working families a break on childcare costs, plus paid time off and access to universal pre-K" CNBC Make it, 7 July 2020.

Low, T., Ginsberg, B., Shepsle, A., Ansolabehere, S. (2017), American Government, Power and Purpose, (14th ed.). Harvard University, New York: Norton and Company.

MacKinnon, Catharine A. "Sexuality, Pornography, and Method: "Pleasure under Patriarchy." Ethics, vol. 99, no. 2, University of Chicago Press, 1989, pp. 314–46, http://www.jstor.org/stable/2381437.

Marshall, Bryan W. (2009). Going Alone: The Presidential Power of Unilateral Action. In the Oxford Handbook and the American Presidency, eds. George C. Edwards III and William G. Howell. New York, NY: Oxford University Press.

Mayer, K. R. (2014). Executive power in the obama administration and the decision to seek congressional authorization for a military attack against syria: Implications for theories of unilateral action. Utah Law Review, 2014(4), 821.

McGoldrick, James M. "Katzenbach v. McClung: The Abandonment of Federalism in the Name of Rational Basis." The BYU Journal of Public Law, vol. 14, no. 1, 1999, pp. 1.

McGrath, Matt. "Biden signs 'existential' executive orders on climate and environment" BBC News, Jan 27 2021.

Media Press Release: "DeLauro, Scott, Murray, Members Introduce $50 Billion Child Care Stabilization Fund Legislation" 27 May 2020, URL: https://delauro.house.gov/media- center/press-releases/delauro-scott-murray-members-introduce-50-billion-child-care

Mexperience, says, J., says, G. D., says, G. O., says, J., says, S., says, L., says, S., says, A., says, K., says, S., says, J. M. A. C., says, S., Says, A., Says, M., says, P., says, M., says, L., says, C.…. says, C. K. (2021, July 21). Mexico-US land border Restrictions continue. Mexperience. https://www.mexperience.com/mexico-land-border-restrictions.

Moe, Terry M., and William G. Howell. "Unilateral Action and Presidential Power: A Theory." Presidential Studies Quarterly, vol. 29, no. 4, 1999, pp. 850–872. JSTOR, www.jstor.org/stable/27552053.

National Association for The Education of Young Children (NAEYC), 2020. URL: www.naeyc.org/our-work/public-policy-advocacy/federal-advocacy-key-congressional-committees-caucuses-and-agencies.

Nelson, R. (1993). Political philosophy vs. political ideology. Proceedings of the American Catholic Philosophical Association, 67, 55.

Newburger, Emma. "Biden's climate change agenda will face big obstacles with evenly divided Senate", CNBC, Jan 30 2021.

NLRB v. Jones and Laughlin Steel Corp. Northwestern University Law Review, vol. 52, 1957, pp. 271.

Nye, J. S. (2004). Soft Power and American Foreign Policy. Political Science Quarterly, 119(2), 255–270. https://doi.org/10.2307/20202345.

OECD Better Policies for Better Lives: "Cost-Benefit Analysis and the Environment -Further Developments and Policy Use", 2018. OECD Publishing. Paris.

Organisation for Economic Co-operation and Development. "Executive Summary. 'COST-BENEFIT ANALYSIS AND THE ENVIRONMENT RECENT DEVELOPMENTS'" p. 15–27, ORGANISATION FOR ECONOMIC CO-OPERATION AND DEVELOPMENT.

Oyez/Justia. "District of Columbia v. Heller", 2008, URL: https://www.oyez.org/cases/2007/07-290.

Palmer, Kenneth T., and Edward B. Laverty. "The Impact of United States v. Lopez on Intergovernmental Relations: A Preliminary Assessment." Publius, vol. 26, no. 3, 1996, pp. 109-126.

Perry, Audrey. "Scarcity Rationale." Scarcity Rationale, mtsu.edu/first-amendment/article/1016/scarcity-rationale.

Peters, B. Guy. American Public Policy: Promise and Performance., 11th ed., CQ Press, 2019.

Pew Research Center. "Economy and COVID-19 Top the Public's Policy Agenda for 2021." Pew Research Center, 8 Feb. 2021, https://www.pewresearch.org/politics/2021/01/28/economy-and-covid-19-top-the-publics-policy-agenda-for-2021/.

Phillips, Amber. "A Reader's Guide to all of Trump's Fights with Congress." Washingtonpost.com, 2019.

Pitt News v. Pappert, 379 F.3d 96 (3d Cir. 2004)

Policies. The Policy Agendas Project at the University of Texas at Austin, CAP, 2020. www.comparativeagendas.net. Accessed 11 March 2021.

Porter, D., & Craig, D. (2004). The third way and the third world: Poverty reduction and social inclusion in the rise of 'inclusive' liberalism. Review of International Political Economy, 11(2), 387-423. doi:10.1080/09692290420001672881.

Protecting Public Health and the Environment and Restoring Science to Tackle the Climate Crisis. Federal Register, 25 Jan. 2021.

Psychedelic drugs in biomedicine. Trends in Pharmacological Sciences, 38(11), 992-1005.

Public's 2019 Priorities: Economy, Health Care, Education and Security All Near Top of List." Pew Research Center - U.S. Politics & Policy, 24 Jan. 2019.

Rachidi, Angela. "Biden's childcare plan will unnecessarily expand the government's role in caregiving" American Enterprise Institute, 30 July 2020.

Railroads. Regulation of Rates. Power of Interstate Commerce Commission Over Intrastate Rates. "Shreveport Rate Cases"." Harvard Law Review, vol. 28, no. 1, 1914, pp. 113-113.

Rappeport, Alan, and Michael Corkery. "Biden's Choice of Vilsack for U.S.D.A. Raises Fears for Small Farmers." The New York Times. 21 Dec. 2020.

Raworth, Kate. A Healthy Economy Should Be Designed to Thrive, Not Grow | Kate Raworth. www.youtube.com.

Reeves, A., & Rogowski, J. C. (2016). Unilateral powers, public opinion, and the presidency. The Journal of Politics, 78(1), 137-151. doi:10.1086/683433

Republicans governors send letter to Biden opposing leasing ban—Seventeen governors implore President to withdraw Executive Order 14008." Offshore. 23 Feb. 2021.

Robertson, Stephen. Catharine MacKinnon, www.mtsu.edu/first-amendment/article/1300/catharine-mackinnon%3E.

Rogin, A. (2018, June 19) "Congress Agrees on need to end family separation practice but still divided on how" Link: http://abcnews.go.com/Politics/congress-agrees-end-family separation-practice-divided/story.

Rothenberg, Stuart. OPINION: "Nancy Pelosi: The Democratic Party's Undisputed Leader", Congress: Roll Call, 26, March 2019.

Rothman, Dale S., et al. ESTIMATING NON-MARKET IMPACTS OF CLIMATE CHANGE AND CLIMATE POLICY. Organization for Economic Co-operation and Development, 2003.

Rottinghaus, Brandon (2015) Assessing the Unilateral Presidency: Constraints and Contingencies, Congress & the Presidency, 42:3, 287-292.

Rottinghaus, Brandon (2019). Exercising Unilateral Discretion: Presidential Justifications of Unilateral Powers in a Shared Powers System. American Politics Research 47:1, pages 3-28.

Ryan, Halford Ross."Roosevelt's First Inaugural: A Study of Technique." Quarterly Journal of Speech 65.2 (April 1979): 137.

Sacchetti, M. (2019, Mar 09). Judge rules in favor of ACLU in family separations case. The Washington Post.

Sachs, Alan, Brook Detterman. "Agriculture in Focus Under Biden Climate Policy." The National Law Review: Vol. XI, Num. 40. 9 Feb. 2021.

Sarkesian, Sam C., Williams, John Allen, and Cimbala, Stephen J. (2012). US National Security. Fifth Edition, Rienner Publishers, Inc., pp. 91 - 105.

Savage, C. (2018, June 21). Here Is What the Executive Order Does, and Doesn't Do. New York Times, p. A10(L).

Schenberg, E. E. (2018). Psychedelic-assisted psychotherapy: A paradigm shift in psychiatric research and development. Frontiers in Pharmacology, 9, 733. doi:10.3389/fphar.2018.00733.

Separation of Powers - Foreign Affairs - President Trump Objects to Act Imposing Sanctions on Russia and Congressional Review of Presidential Waivers." Harvard Law Review 131, no. 2 (2017): 674.

Sexting Laws across America. Cyberbullying Research Center, 5 Feb. 2020, cyberbullying.org/sexting-laws.

Shrage, Laurie. "Exposing the Fallacies of Anti-Porn Feminism." Feminist Theory, vol. 6, no. 1, 2012, pp. 45-65.

Shreveport Rate Case." The Yale Law Journal, vol. 60, no. 2, 1951, pp. 356.

Skibba, Ramin. "The Biden Administration Weighs the Social Costs of Carbon", Wired 6, March 2021.

Smith, Abbey. "Biden Orders Social Cost overhaul in bid to Reduce Climate Pollution, Washington Examiner. 22, January, 2021.

Smith, S. (1980). Allison and the Cuban Missile Crisis: A Review of the Bureaucratic Politics Model of Foreign Policy Decision-Making. Millennium: Journal of International Studies, 9(1), 21–40.

Snapchat Privacy Policy. Snap Inc., 17 Nov. 2021, www.snap.com/en-US/privacy/privacy-policy.

Spagat, E. (2021, April 8). EXPLAINER: Is the US border with Mexico in crisis? AP NEWS. https://apnews.com/article/is-us-mexico-border-in-crisis-explained-6a412f3edf07715509e3181b8bc63ca7.

Spitzer, R. J. (2018). The politics of gun control (7th ed.). New York, NY: Routledge.

St. John, Jeff. "Biden Executive Orders Set Broad Federal Role in Clean Energy and Climate Change Mitigation", Green Tech Media, Jan 27 2021.University of Minnesota. "How Presidents Get Things Done." University of Minnesota Libraries, https://open.lib.umn.edu/americangovernment/chapter/13-2-how-presidents-get-things-done/. Accessed Feb. 22, 2021.

State-by-State Differences in Sexting Laws. Bark, 3 Mar. 2022, www.bark.us/blog/state-by-state-differences-in-sexting laws/#:~:text=For%20instance%2C%20federal%20law%20considers,of%20a%20minor%20is%20illegal.

States Sue Biden in Bid to Revive Keystone XL Pipeline. Associated Press. 17 Mar. 2021.

Strasburger, Victor C., et al. "Teenagers, Sexting, and the Law." American Academy of Pediatrics, Oxford University Press, 1 May 2019, publications.aap.org/pediatrics/article/143/5/e20183183/37112/Teenagers-Sexting-and-the-Law.

Tackling the Climate Crisis at Home and Abroad. Federal Register, 1 Feb. 2021.

The Editorial Board. "Biden's Keystone Pipeline Kill." The Wall Street Journal. 20 Jan. 2021.

The happy gambler; france's presidential election. (2017, Apr 29). The Economist, 423, 29.

The Heritage Foundation. "Heritage Explains: Executive Orders." The Heritage Foundation, https://www.heritage.org/political-process/heritage-explains/executive-orders Accessed Feb. 22, 2021.

The impeachment Congress. (2019). Wall Street Journal.

The New York Times. "President Obama's State of the Union Address." The New York Times 24 Jan. 2012.

The White House. "Executive Order on Tackling the Climate Crisis at Home and Abroad." The White House, 27 Jan. 2021.

Theodoulou, Stella, Chris Kofinia. The Art of the Game: Understanding American Public Policy Making. Wadsworth/Thomson Learning; 2004. p. 129.

Thompson, G. (2018). Families still being separated at border — months after Trump's 'zero tolerance' policy reversed. USA Today (Online).

Thwaites, Joe. "4 Climate Priorities for the Biden Administration." WORLD RESEARCH INSTITUTE. 28 Jan. 2021.

Trenta, Luca. "Clinton and Bosnia: A Candidate's Freebie, a President's Nightmare." Journal of Transatlantic Studies (Springer Nature), vol. 12, no. 1, Mar. 2014, pp. 62–89. EBSCOhost, doi:10.1080/14794012.2014.871434.

Twitter Privacy Policy. Twitter, 18 Apr. 2018, www.twitter.com/en/privacy.

U.S. Public Views on Climate and Energy." Pew Research Center Science & Society, 25 Nov. 2019.

U.S. Senate Committee on Health, Education, Labor & Pensions, 14 January 2021. URL: https://www.help.senate.gov/ranking/newsroom/press/senator-murray-praises-biden-on- plan-to-include-significant-child-care-relief-in-covid-package

Ullen, Magnus. ""A Tangled Web of Mindfuck": Andrea Dworkin and the Truth of Pornography." Tulsa Studies in Women's Literature, vol. 35, no. 1, 2016, pp. 145-171.

Utah Governor, 16 Others Sign Letter to Pres. Biden Opposing Oil and Gas Leasing Ban." ABC4 Utah, 22 Feb. 2021, https://www.abc4.com/news/politics/utah-governor-16-others-sign-letter-to-pres-biden- opposing-oil-and-gas-leasing-ban/. Accessed 13 March 2021.

Uzonwanne, Francis. (2016). Rational Model of Decision Making. 10.1007/978-3-319-31816-5_2474-1.

Van Boven, Leaf, Phillip Ehret, and David Sherman. "Psychological Barriers to Bipartisan Public Support for Climate Policy." Sage Journals. 2 July 2018..

Wagner, J., Miroff, N., & DeBonis, M. (2018, June 20). Trump reverses course, says he will put an end to family separations on border. Washington Post.

White House. Executive Order on Tackling the Climate Crisis at Home and Abroad. 27 Jan. 2021.

White House. FACT Sheet: President BIDEN Takes Executive Actions to Tackle the Climate Crisis at Home and ABROAD, Create Jobs, and Restore Scientific Integrity across Federal Government. 27 Jan. 2021.

Whitehurst, "Russ". "Why the federal government should subsidize childcare and how to pay for it", the Brookings Institution, 9 March 2017. UR: https://www.brookings.edu/research/why-the-federal- government-should-subsidize-childcare-and-how-to-pay-for-it/

Whittaker, Alan G., Brown, Shannon A., Smith, Frederick C., & McKune, Elizabeth (2011). The National Security Policy Process: The National Security Council and Interagency System. (Research Report, August 15, 2011 Annual Update). Washington, D.C.: Industrial College of the Armed Forces, National Defense University, U.S. Department of Defense. pp. 19-31.

Whittle, Patrick, and Cathy Bussewitz. "Biden Faces Steep Challenges to Reach Renewable Energy Goals." Associated Press. 2 Mar. 2021.

About the Author

Jill Shea is a writer, mother, and avid political advocate. Her career encompasses a prolific portfolio of screenplays and television pilots. Her journey began at USC in a renowned program of only thirty young minds from around the globe, followed by stints at NBC and MSNBC in New York. Returning to Los Angeles, she worked on various successful series and in film for Michael Douglas in script development. Jill subsequently joined James Cameron's private enterprise, dedicated to creating groundbreaking content that pushed the boundaries of exploration. In response to the political climate after the 2016 election, rather than move to Canada, Jill committed three years to Political Science research and studies earning membership in Pi Sigma Alpha, The National Political Science Honor Society. Living in Los Angeles with her family, Jill continues to champion a more unified and enlightened society, channeling her passion into creating a better understanding of the complexities shaping our nation's societal fabric and promoting a more informed America.

For more on Jill Shea and her other books visit jillsheawriter.com

www.ingramcontent.com/pod-product-compliance
Lightning Source LLC
Chambersburg PA
CBHW030356130626
46549CB00004B/1518